THE
LIBERAL
DILEMMA

THE
LIBERAL
DILEMMA

Harvey C. Bunke

PRENTICE-HALL, INC.
Englewood Cliffs, New Jersey

to Peg

CONTENTS

Preface

THIS IS A BOOK ABOUT VALUES—values that are rooted in the materialism of a restless science and an irreverent commerce; values that draw strength and energy from the doctrine of natural law and the theory of the market place; values that cluster under the somewhat ambiguous but useful concept of liberalism.

Out of these values came beliefs, creeds, and purposes which in fusing formed a social theory upon which was erected a brilliant society. Recently, however, certain distressing signs have provoked the indictment that this once vital philosophy is fading, causing the liberal society to fall victim to a critical, yet not fully understood, crisis. In this context, the liberal tradition has been the prime subject of examination and reassessment. Yet despite the materialistic origins of liberalism, there exists an almost inviolable tendency to treat economic thought and social values as if they, like Kipling's East and West, were two distinct realms destined never to meet.

Perhaps this is because the typical contemporary economist, unlike a Mill or a Keynes, is beset with an incurable mania to become a "pure" scientist; or perhaps the blame rests with the present-day social philosophers who, in ignoring the lead of a Locke or a Bentham, refuse to venture into the formidable and demanding world of economics. Whatever the cause of the division, one objective of this book is to bridge this arti-

ix

ficial gap which, with some notable exceptions, separates economic thought from social values.

To pursue this objective it has been necessary to make a number of brief, conventional excursions into history for the purpose of illustrating how simple, private materialism became the great driving force which, through fostering the spirit of individualism, changed the direction and position of the Western world and placed America in a position of supreme eminence, to be envied and emulated by peoples of all nations. Then suddenly, after pursuing a steady course for centuries, history dramatically turned a corner. Just as the flame of private materialism burned with new brilliance, this self-generating beacon of natural law flickered and burned low, never again to regain its old brightness.

Men, however, still continued and continue to cling to old beliefs and to talk of the glories of material progress, even as a conspiracy of an indifferent science, a world depression, and a concentration of economic power fashioned profane forces destined to threaten the very existence of the liberal society. Slow to admit the presence of these hostile forces, men were even slower to abandon traditional creeds. Without a new social philosophy for instilling purpose and organizing society, there was no alternative.

But as time passed, an unruly world compelled new action violating sacred ideals. It could not be avoided—not if progress was to be served, not if the worth and dignity of the individual were to remain the heart of Western philosophy. And in striving to combat these hostile forces and to preserve the liberal society, man discovered that with his own power he could accomplish great things: through science he pushed back disease; through education he spread knowledge and dispelled superstition; through social legislation he elevated the poor and fought unemployment. But the more he learned, the less certain he was of what he knew; and when he took things into his own hands, apparently simple problems grew in magnitude and complexity as he often aided the very forces he was committed to destroy. Less and less sure of his purpose, he suffered a sense of guilt, as his actions belied his faith, as his behavior enlarged the gulf separating the world of the real from the realm of the ideal. Consigned to live in a mundane world which forever compelled action hostile to their vision of perfection, men of the liberal society divided themselves into two warlike camps. The old 19th-century liberals clung desperately to an ideal never to be realized, while the modern 20th-century liberals struggled uncompromisingly to realize simple achievements not yet idealized.

Such is the state of the liberal society. Although any inquiry into the forces leading up to the present dilemma should necessarily cut across many disciplines, I must address a few private remarks to my fellow economists. Regrettably, for the conscientious economist this work must be incomplete. He will note the absence of many great economic names; he will see Hansen relegated to a footnote and Mill and Marshall mentioned only in passing, while men of lesser contribution to the profession as a profession are here given an emphasis which may seem excessive, in view of their perhaps minor influence on the economic mind.

To these honest objections I can only say that as the work took shape, it seemed to develop an inner momentum and a Machiavellian will, causing means to be subordinated to ends. Moreover, the ends are unconventional. Customarily economists underscore the impact of Western thought on economic doctrines. Here the process is deliberately reversed. The emphasis is placed on the influence of economic doctrines on the mainstream of Western thought, and more particularly upon the shaping of contemporary social values. Although the judgment underlying the selection and interpretation of the materials presented may provoke dissent, the spirit and importance of their intended use should, I hope, invite general agreement.

One other word: In this highly-specialized and organized 20th century, even a small effort is difficult without assistance. I cannot acknowledge all of my many debts; a few, however, I must mention. For expressions of confidence and encouragement, I owe thanks to Professors Albert S. Norris, William W. Kaelber and George S. Peck, all of the University of Iowa. To Professors John S. Harlow, Walter Krause, Robert Michaelson, and Mrs. George Peck, all of whom read all or parts of the manuscript, I am indebted for constructive suggestions, many of which are reflected in the finished work. To Professor Richard Lloyd-Jones, who painstakingly read the entire manuscript, I am most grateful. An accomplished rhetorician who unsnarled some of my tangled prose, he displayed a rare quality of literary compassion toward my sometimes 18th-, sometimes 20th-century writing style. Finally, to Mrs. Mark Pabst, guardian of the syntax and typist par excellence, I am deeply appreciative for her interest, help, and patience. Although the responsibility is mine, I could not have done without the assistance and encouragement of these and others.

I

An Uneasy Brilliance

AMERICA IS A PROUD NATION. YOUTHFUL, OPTIMISTIC, AND "the hope of mankind," it is robust and vibrant. Unmatched in comfort and convenience, it knows a level of health, prosperity, and literacy unequaled by all of history. Rebellious by nature, it, like any young and aspiring idealist, has been guilty of certain excesses; sometimes because of and other times despite a disregard for tradition and distrust of culture, it has been a land of opportunity populated by dynamic institutions which have made for a record of economic and political freedoms unchallenged by any nation, race, or civilization.

Nor are our achievements purely provincial. Long a world leader in medicine, technology, and science, our recent contributions have been given a place of respect and stature in the realm of art, literature, and music—once the "private" domain of the Old World. Nor has our entry into world affairs been wholly selfish. With unprecedented generosity we have opened our treasury in the hope that some small measure of relief may be granted countless millions who are condemned to live in ignorance and poverty.

Because of our advances in science, our military strength and above all our immense wealth, world attention centers on us. Some resent, some deprecate, some despise, but all copy. All this, of course, is confirmation of what the average

1

American has always fervently believed: that our customs, our values, and our institutions are uniquely tailored by a divine force.

Yet, despite this fascination and pride in a brilliance which all but blinds us, we seem to be tormented by a kind of national hypochondria which reveals our profound sense of inadequacy. Indeed I have been told by men of my father's generation that—despite new-found creature comforts and national glory—we who missed living in pre-World War I America have been badly cheated by the prime mover of the universe. When the 20th century was in its infancy, there was, so they say, peace, security, and, through faith in a benevolent God, hope for mankind. Two world wars, a tragic depression, a growing lack of self-reliance, and above all the awesome shadow cast by a profane and unpredictable science have, they say, forever shattered the simplicity of this kinder world. Their words are ignored.

We might have listened if things had been different. But if these men continue to cherish thoughts of returning to a gentler life, few of us would choose the simpler life which is prerequisite to it. We may be less than wholly satisfied with life in this mid-20th century, but there is little evidence that many of us would be willing to turn the calendar back to any earlier age. How many of us, for all our fussing, would sacrifice the comforts and advantages that only a highly complex and interdependent society can bestow? We complain of a loss of independence, but would we forego electric power, gas heat, or a car in return for the opportunity to be unobligated to the public utility company and the sellers of automotive supplies and services? How many Americans would do without their comfortable homes, their well-stocked larders, their appliances and gadgets for the spontaneity and self-sufficiency that is offered by life in a stark cabin on the Alaskan frontier?

Indeed the prospect of self-sufficiency holds no attraction for us. In truth, we seem to fear it almost as much as death itself. Horrified by the threat of nuclear explosion or fallout, we seem equally terrified by the thought of life on this planet following a nuclear holocaust. Too highly trained and specialized to satisfy our most elementary needs, many of us apparently feel that a quick death would be preferable to the suffering that would accompany the fight necessary to preserve life against starvation and the elements. However exaggerated, such expressions reflect the extent to which we as individuals have abandoned self-sufficiency and economic independence as a goal of life.

The truth of the matter is that we are pleased and proud of our complex society. To be sure, a number of people in the South, in their desperation to preserve the myth of white supremacy, look back to the antebellum days as the high point of human achievement. And the rest of us have our bad moments. Statistics on alcoholism and mental illness are distressing, as are suicide and homicide rates. Loose morality, incorrigible juvenile vandals, young men and women searching for purpose, the crushing impersonality imposed by technology and the population explosion, and that brute unconscionable thing more terrifying than death itself, the Bomb, are only a few of the problems that cause many Americans to have sober second thoughts about the destiny of man; but on the whole we are disposed to ignore or dismiss these disturbing matters by simply explaining that every age has its problems and ours has less than its share.

Besides, because there is little, if anything, that the individual can do to alleviate these problems, we are prone to find comfort in the thought that nothing is to be gained by brooding over them. Still enchanted with the idea of progress, we confidently look forward to a better tomorrow, while firmly maintaining that America is history's most favored nation. Perhaps it is just as well, for our passion for science, our fascination with technology, and our worship of the modern organization and the material comforts it can provide, have irrevocably committed us to proceed at an ever increasing rate along the road of industrialization and interdependence.

But for all our brave words, serious and obvious social tensions have created an atmosphere of uneasiness, a haunting sense of anxiety, a growing feeling of inadequacy. Some indeed say that our society is sick, that, to put it in Freudian terms, it suffers from an acute case of "social neurosis"— a state reached when a society is incapable of adjusting to or satisfying the needs of man. Such judgment implies, of course, that man has certain unchanging needs and that any society which fails to gratify fundamental human nature is perforce pathological.

One need hardly venture into the uncharted waters of "universal" and "eternal" human nature to point out that a large and expanding cleavage between principle and practice is conducive neither to peace of mind nor mental health. For an individual to practice one thing and preach another requires only a modicum of rationalization, but for an entire society to indulge in such perverse maiming and self-deception, a most elaborate and sophisticated social philosophy is required. The integrity and consistency of our social philosophy we will examine later; for the moment it is our purpose to look only at some of its broader implications.

For one born into and nurtured by 20th-century America, it is difficult to question traditional American values without experiencing a sense of guilt. Individual initiative, endurance, courage, self-reliance, willingness to assume risk in intellectual endeavor as well as economic enterprise seem to be as attractive as they are uncomplicated. Today, however, these basic values are being called into question.

The decline of the individual and the rise of the organization is by now a familiar theme in which present-day society is invidiously compared with some earlier period. Some of the social tensions depicted are apparent even to the untrained eye. Espousing one philosophy and practicing another, we are confused dualists. By faith and conviction we are pious individualists; by action and association we are dedicated conformists. As individualists we place great store on diligence, frugality, self-reliance, and self-discipline. As individualists we consecrate work through which each man is to make his own way and through which life is to be made meaningful. In pratice we flagrantly violate every tenet of our faith. Because work often has no meaning—especially to the blue-collar worker who repeats endlessly a rigidly prescribed task in performing some specialized and isolated operation in the making of a minor part, the purpose of which escapes his interest and his understanding—many of us are bored with our jobs which, at best, we see as unavoidable drudgery. Indeed, instead of worshiping work as did our frontier ancestors, we listen to the voices of the experts who tell us to relax, to take it easy, to remember that the joy of life is in the living. So in practice our emphasis shifts from work to leisure, only to find that aimless inactivity can be even more boring, more unbearable, and more denigrating than the most undemanding kind of work.

Not only are we surrounded with voices telling us not to overtax ourselves, but we are incessantly exhorted to indulge ourselves. Live for today, we are told, for tomorrow we may die. Frugality, saving, self-discipline, these are fine things; everyone should respect such high ideals, but don't put off till tomorrow what you can enjoy today. Buy now and pay later has become so much a part of our way of life that the loyal 100-per-cent American is expected to be in debt for a home, a car, a freezer, and last year's vacation. As for independence and self-reliance, at one end of the scales our older citizens demand and look to government and privately sponsored pension plans while, at the other end of the scale, our youth, realizing that they have no alternative but to work for some established organization, search for those jobs with the least risk and the greatest security. At the same time the bulk of the working population finds some comfort in the fact that they have unemployment benefits—inadequate though they may be—to fall back on should they suffer temporary loss of work.

Few deny the growing cleavage separating faith and reality; many proclaim that a return to faith is our only salvation. Our lack of interest in work, our installment buying, our search for security, and our ever increasing demands that someone provide for us when we are unable to work, are to them sure manifestations of the serious malignancy which is destroying the very foundations upon which this nation is built. If we are not to become soft and decadent, we are warned, we must cleanse ourselves by returning to the true virtues of hard work, self-discipline, and above all individual independence.

Would that it were so easy. Would that modern society and economic independence were so easily reconciled. But they are not. And since we are committed technologically and psychologically to industrialization, the individual, dependent upon the system and other men for his most urgent needs, often suffers a gnawing sense of powerlessness.

Such then is the dilemma of the modern American. A pious economic individualist by faith, he lives in an existential world that with each passing day grants him less independence and more and more compels him to violate the creed by which he professes to live.

In some ways, of course, there is nothing unique about the dilemma of modern man and the world he symbolizes. Man has always inhabited two distinct worlds. Indeed the dualism of flesh and faith is as old as the West itself and was no less present in ancient Greece than it is in our contemporary society. Condemned by his finiteness to an unpredictable and inhospitable universe, man employs his contemplative powers to fashion an ideal world from which he can draw inspiration and to which he can dedicate himself. And by their very nature, these two worlds can never coincide. Ideals are something to be aspired to; once realized, they lose their inspirational qualities, only to be replaced by new ones from which men can draw energy and toward which they can direct their talents and bend their capacities.

The purpose of this book is to examine the dualism of our age. To accomplish this in any meaningful sense, it is not sufficient to restrict our vision to the contemporary "worlds" in which men dwell. To appreciate these "realms" and their impact on liberalism and the open society, we must first know something of their origin. It is with this purpose that we turn to history.

II

Conspiring Forces

With the single exception of christianity, economics, more than any single faith or creed, was to capture the head and heart of Western man. As such it must be ranked among the great inspirational forces which were to shape the Western world. The lust for land and the lure of the purse, of course, have always influenced the behavior of civilized man; but as long as Europe was divided into countless autonomous and essentially self-sufficient political units, economic motives were perforce subordinated to the forces of law, tradition, and other-worldly considerations. Slowly, however, all this was to change. Ancient trade routes were reopened, rudimentary roads were constructed, towns became linked one with another by traveling merchants, and the just price of Aquinas was challenged. Imperceptibly, the impersonal pressures engendered by urbanization undermined the stability of an old order.

Custom and command can do their jobs well in a small, stable, intimate society; but when strangers meet to barter goods produced in the four corners of the earth, the old ways and the traditional codes of justice lose their meaning and are discarded as man's proclivities for personal riches and temporal power gain the upper hand. And once the motors of commerce are started, there is no stopping them. Not that the merchants and the money lenders transformed

Western society immediately or even rapidly, for this they could not do. The change was to come slowly and painfully over centuries, as prince and priest alike called upon their temporal and spiritual powers to preserve the orderly world of their fathers.

But for all their efforts, history was turning a corner. Towns and cities grew more numerous and flourished, labor became more specialized, and more and more men, by choice or necessity, looked to the market for solving the problems of daily existence. Piece by piece the medieval world was being dismantled by the same forces of commerce and technology that were to father a surging commercial revolution.

But if the market-oriented society was a long time in the building, the economic doctrines necessary to justify this new social order were even slower to unfold. Not until many events had transpired and not until man was able to conceive his world in the context of a wholly new cosmology could this vital new culture be explained and finally rationalized. Indeed it was this social transformation, which at once tormented and liberated medieval man, that was to provide the very bricks and stuff necessary to the creation of the new philosophy.

First, there was the skeptical humanism of the Renaissance which, in revolting against established values, preached the merits of individual expression and mundane achievements. Then there was the Protestant movement which, in addition to shattering Christian unity, taught that work was a virtue and wealth a reward; thereby was unleashed a burst of human energy which—while generated for the purpose of gaining salvation and eternal life—caused men to direct their attention to the immediate affairs of this world as more and more of them equated piety with riches. Finally, there was the monumental contribution of the Enlightenment, which in its deistic pronouncements proclaimed that man, through his own reason and knowledge of God's immutable laws, could perfect himself and, through day-by-day progress, build for himself an earthly paradise. Only after the West had known the trauma and the intellectual creativity of these periods could a new, full-blown philosophy emerge.

The history of the United States is a chronicle of the rise and triumph of this new philosophy. It began when 55 men gathered in 1787 to draft a masterpiece of statecraft: the United States Constitution. A product of their times, these men were not, as we sometimes seem to believe, without their fears, their hopes, their weaknesses. And when we study closely their brilliant creation, we find that it was conceived and formulated not in the sterile atmosphere of a vacuum, but under the living pressure produced by a climate of opinion. As such, it bears the stamp of vitality, of high ideals, of dark suspicions, of unfounded prejudices. If we ask whence came the fears, the faith, the climate of opinion, we find a forked trail leading back into the past; one path leading to the intellectually rich soil of the Old World, the other running through the rough, untamed pragmatic terrain of the New World. From the Old World we see the unmistakably steadying influence of the Christian tradition—particularly in its newer Protestant form—and the engulfing tide, with its limitless faith in reason and man, of the Enlightenment. Added to Protestantism and the Enlightenment, both liberating forces, is a third factor; the harsh, demanding yet bountiful, wide-flung New World frontier, offering opportunity and richly rewarding industry and diligence. These, then, were the prime forces which elevated the American individual to the simple, spectacular state of political freedom and economic independence. It is to these forces and the role they were to play in producing the vital liberalism of the American experience that we now turn our attention.

Our fixation upon the factors leading up to the discovery of the New World sometimes blinds us to the profound change that the West experienced during the latter part of the 15th and the first part of the 16th century. We know the story of geographical explorations and discoveries; of how the new and rising national powers, Portugal, Spain, and England, chafing under the Italian domination of East-West trade, sought to break this monopoly in the markets of Constantinople, Antioch, and Alexandria, by conducting courageous and imaginative explorations in search of a new route to the Orient. But Columbus' world was a turbulent one, and the resentment against the Italian trade monopoly that inspired geographical discoveries by Portugal and Spain was only one of many factors that made for turmoil and instability. For Columbus' day was an age of change.

The last stronghold of the old order crumbled when Columbus was not yet ten years of age. In 1453, Constantinople, the eastern bastion of Christianity and the most radiant of all medieval cities, fell before the power of Islam and the might of 160,000 Turkish troops. Only a year later, an event transpired that was to have greater force in directing the course of mankind than had the combined influence of all the prior kings and military campaigns in history. In 1454, John Gutenberg produced the first printed Bible. Important in itself, the event was overshadowed by the process. Using movable type and the linen paper that the Moslems had introduced into Spain, Gutenberg could produce books at a fraction of the cost of hand-copied volumes. From 1454 onward, learning would not longer be—as it had been for 1,000 years—the private domain of the clergy and the wealthy few who could and would pay the high price of hand-produced works. From movable type to an educated populace is still a giant step; without Gutenberg's process, however, Jefferson's dream of a free public school system would never have been fulfilled.

Four months before Columbus sailed to the West, Lorenzo the Magnificent lay dying in his villa outside the city of Florence. Wanting the last rites, he called to his deathbed Savonarola, a zealous reformer of the Dominican order, who had long been sharply critical of the decadence of both Church and State. Corruption, greed, and lust, Savonarola eloquently warned, must be replaced with simple living dedicated to glorification of the Almighty. Otherwise, God would surely scourge and regenerate the Church just as he would send an agent to chastise the State and the people. Lorenzo died refusing to free Florence from Medicean rule, and Savonarola's prediction seemed to come true as the Italian States became the pawns in the struggle between the Hapsburgs and French kings. But more important than Savonarola's forecasts of political instability was the revolt which his cries for a cleansed and reformed Church helped to inspire. To understand this, we must take a brief look at the forces unleashed by the breaking up of the Universal Church and the rise of Protestantism.

In 1517, Martin Luther a professor of theology at Germany's Wittenberg University, following the common practice of those wishing to engage in scholarly debate, nailed 95 propositions on the door of Castle Church. The impact of this single act upon Western civilization eventually led to the pitting of Christian against Christian and ultimately to the bloody religious wars—the blackest chapter in Christian history. Never again would the claim that the Roman Church was the one true Church go unquestioned. Other churches, erected on differing creeds, flourished and extended their influence.

Not only did Luther question the validity of Church doctrine on the sale of indulgences and Church teaching prescribing good works as a route to salvation, but later he committed the most heinous of all heresies. He argued that man could communicate directly with God and that priestly intercession between the sinner and God was superfluous—a position that one hundred years earlier had led the Council of Constance to condemn Jan Hus to be burned. Of all Luther's heresies, his concept of the personal God could least be tolerated by the Church. For, as Tawney observed, "Since salvation is bestowed by the operation of grace in the heart and by that alone, the whole fabric of organized religion, which had mediated between the individual soul and its Maker—divinely commissioned hierarchy, systematized activities, corporate institutions—drops away as the blasphemous trivialities of a religion of work."

But we must be careful not to credit Luther with too much. Certainly he was no champion of liberalism. If anything, he was more authoritarian, more intolerant, and more distrustful of the common man than was the Church which he so vigorously attacked. Fanatic to the point of seeking to restore a spiritual purity which never existed, he railed against authority not because it was rigorous but because it was lax and corrupt. "A man should not say," he commanded, " 'I will sell my wares as dear as I can or please,' but, 'I will sell my wares as is right and proper.' " Dismissing the commercial development of the previous two centuries as a relapse into paganism, he held the most orthodox economic theories. On the expediency of the usury laws, he was equally adamant, proclaiming, "The greatest misfortune

of the German nation is easily the traffic in interest. . . .
The devil invented it and the Pope, by giving his sanction to
it, has done untold evil throughout the world."

And, when Luther saw the peasants extend his teaching
of individual freedom to the secular life and, in 1546, revolt
against the tyranny of feudalism by demanding the abolition
of serfdom, he turned savagely on them and exalted the absolutism of lay lords. He branded rebellion "poisonous,"
"harmful," and "devilish," crying, "No one need think that
the world can be ruled without blood. The civil sword shall
and must be red and bloody."

Whatever Luther's inconsistency, his place in history is
secure. For men in all parts of Christendom were to learn of
and be influenced by Luther's teaching. One such man was
John Calvin, who with his logical, systematic, and definitive
Institutes of the Christian Religion, was to provide the
philosophical core of Protestantism. Drawing heavily on St.
Augustine, Calvin's theological system can be summarized
in one word: predestination.

Completely omnipotent, omniscient, omnipresent, Calvin's
God, in creating the universe in all of its dimensions, foreordained all things: all physical phenomena, as well as every
thought, word, or deed ever known or to be known by man.
So all-pervasive is this Divine Will or Plan that no mortal
creature has any volition whatsoever in determining the outcome of even the smallest, most minute detail of daily living.
Within this heavenly plan—a plan no petty, human, rationalistic mind could comprehend—is transcribed the destiny of
every man. A few, a very few, chosen by God through Jesus,
are given grace and salvation. Who these chosen few are is
known only to God, but surely they are Calvinists. Yet whatever his piety and devotion, the Calvinist must always be
tortured by the thought that long before he was born he was
predestined either to salvation or eternal damnation. Since

there can be no concrete proof, no certainty, there is always lurking in the background a lingering, nagging doubt.

It was to silence or at least drive this doubt into the subconscious, that the Calvinist turned to secular matters to demonstrate objectively through daily living that he was one of the chosen few. And what better way to identify himself than by conducting a life which brings glory to God? Thus, although good works were considered powerless to alter the grand scheme of things, the life methodically dedicated to and systematically planned for doing God's work was to provide the Calvinist with one of the primary requisites for eternal life—certainty of salvation. Suffering from the fear that he might not be one of the elect, the Calvinist was always driven by a feverish irrational need to be busy, to be active, to accomplish. "The irrationality of such a compulsive effort is," observed Fromm, "that the effort is not made to create a desired end but serves to indicate whether or not something will occur which had been determined beforehand, independent of one's own activity or control."

The urban Calvin, unlike the peasant Luther, was not— as long as enterprise was conducted in a Christian fashion— repelled by business profit or usury, and he welcomed the opportunity to bring a new province, economic activity, under the auspices of God. Indeed, business success more and more became the standard of grace; failure the mark of damnation. What better measure could be devised? If a man were honest, frugal, and labored diligently in the vineyards of the Lord, he prospered; if he lacked these heavenly virtues, he failed, and he deserved no better fate than eternal damnation. Thus evolved an ethic wherein each man became his own slave driver, driven by an inner compulsion, relentlessly dedicated to one purpose—work, and more specifically work which produced wealth and profits. "In practice," Crane Brinton wrote, "these firm believers in the inability of human effort to *change* anything were among the most ardent workers toward getting men to change their behavior."

Out of this burst of human energy, certainly no less important to secular development than the later harnessing of steam and electricity, was to emerge a new scale of social values, a new set of ideals for social conduct. The consecration of labor, the sanctification of asceticism, and the deification of business success—these bourgeois values—were all favorable to the rise of liberalism, especially capitalism. Dedication to hard work, coupled with the vow of unostentatious living, brought the Calvinist profits which were reinvested in the agency of the Lord and, however unintentional, furthered the prosperity of an already growing world. This, then, was the Protestant's monumental contribution to life in *this* world. Although his philosophy was overwhelmingly other-worldly, his immediate efforts were directed toward worldly accomplishments. This focusing of attention on achievements by the flesh must go down as one of the great forces in the making of the open society and the liberalism upon which it rests.

When Mary Tudor, bride-to-be of Spain's King Philip II, died young and without lineal descendant, Elizabeth, a Protestant, assumed the scepter and crown of England. Tensions between Elizabeth and Philip flared and grew apace, and the stage was set for the most famous of all sea engagements. Philip attacked, but when the last shot had been fired and the smoke of battle had cleared away, not only had Philip's "Invincible Armada" and Spain's trade monopoly been destroyed, but England had established herself as ruler of the seas and once and for all had assured herself religious and national independence. And so it was that Protestant England rather than Catholic Spain came to shape the destiny of North America.

Catholic Spain enjoyed the spiritual comforts and security of medieval unity. In the New World the Spaniard found adventure, fortune, and religious converts. But for all of this, the Spaniard's heart and loyalty remained with the Old World. No matter how great his New World success, achievement, or status, it was to his homeland that he looked for recognition; and, in the last analysis, it was in the land of youth that he expected to enjoy the fruits of his labors.

Such an attitude provides a philosophy for conquering, exacting tribute, and transplanting the feudal system to a new land. It is not, however, the stuff from which pioneering is made. The ingredients essential to successful pioneering are resolute dedication and inspired participation. If the Spaniard was dedicated, it was to secure gold and spread the Gospel; if he participated, it was to assume the role of the ruling caste supervising the peons as they produced the wealth destined for the Old World. In the end it was his reluctance to participate actively in the making of a New World that retarded growth of Spanish settlements and at the same time precluded both the degree of permanency and the sense of purpose that was later to characterize the English colonization.

Unlike Spain, England knew the agonies of disunity. For the small band of settlers who landed in 1620 on the coast of what is now Massachusetts, religion was a driving force that dwarfed all others. Being reformers, the Puritans, like most idealists throughout the ages, were noted more for their implacable dedication than for their merciful tolerance. No sooner had the Puritans docked than the mighty spirit of John Calvin began to stalk the land, constantly reminding men of their wretched, sinful impotency and demanding uncompromising piety and inhuman moral standards.

The regenerate Puritans, like Calvin's elect, were men of virtue who demonstrated self-discipline in the form of industry, frugality, sobriety, honesty, temperance, moderation, and simplicity. It was almost as though the gospel of ascetism had been divinely fashioned to steel these men for the challenge of those cruel and unforgiving early years in the wilderness. Self-discipline, self-reliance, and eagerness to labor long and arduously in making the land habitable and productive, and a determination to forswear the luxury that is the badge of worldly success, all were attributes which inspired the Puritan in his dramatic efforts to conquer and organize for the Lord a raw and savage world. Contemptuous of less vigorous and resourceful men, the great legacy of the Puritan to American civilization was a determination to live his own life and admit the superiority of no man.

But we must not be too generous to the Puritans, for although their legacy was independence and individualism of a sort, it carried scarcely any hint of the open society which we think of when we speak of modern democracy. Indeed, in their righteous reform, their severity and harshness surpassed that of their persecutors, and their leader, Governor John Winthrop, denounced democracy as the "meanest and worst of all forms of government," while the able and articulate early American theologian, John Cotton, praised theocracy as the "best form of government in the commonwealth as well as the church."

For the regenerate Puritan, the State could be nothing more than an instrument of the Church and to disobey or resist either Church or State was to defy the sovereignty of God. Church and State therefore blended into one, and the magistrate was to exercise all his power to discourage and punish idolatry, blasphemy, corruption, and to discipline anyone who would, through word or deed, foment dissension and discontent within the Church or the Holy Commonwealth.

In this rigid ideal, frightened men searching for security and order in a strange and hostile land found comfort. But soon all this was to change. Just as the initial trials of the New World were uniquely suited to reinforce Puritan doctrines, so the gradual alleviation of hardship and the rise of prosperity were destined to erode them. The change in perspective was as dramatic as it was rapid. Out of a growing number of triumphs over nature came an increasing sense of security, dispelling the anxiety and uncertainties which had nurtured a desperate dependence on God. The miracle of God which had guided the first settlers through perilous seas to the promised land inspired little awe in the hearts of second- and third-generation New Englanders, and at the end of a hard voyage new arrivals found comfort and friendly embraces rather than strange men and formidable privation. To these new immigrants and to the New England-born Puritans, the glowing fireplaces and the abundantly stocked storehouses seemed more the product of men than of God—or Satan.

Through work, thought, and experience the blanket of mystery that originally covered the new land was to be rolled back as life became more predictable, more the product of human effort. The fearsome winters were expected and prepared for; the beasts of the forest lost their strangeness; the Indians, once the agents of the devil, were exterminated. Gradually the compelling sense of mystery was dissolved in everyday experience until the glittering generalities of a grand plan began to lose their meaning. In newly found confidence and security, the individual turned ever more to his own resources for the comprehension and mastery of his environment. In so doing he had begun the process which would soon cause men to value freedom more highly than any theocratic ideal.

At the same time another overpowering force was destined to strike at the foundations of Puritan idealism. The theocratic spirit, which welded intellectual and political into one, was incapable of withstanding the assault of the most formidable of all adversaries: the inquiring mind. For inherent in the Puritan faith, as in all Protestant doctrine, which proclaims that each man should read his own Bible, communicate directly with his Maker, and find his own salvation through faith, lay the seeds of dissension and criticism of the established order and church. And once orthodoxy that inhibits the spirit of inquiry has been successfully questioned, the combination of man's critical powers and originality remorselessly conspires to destroy the old and to construct a boundless number of new "orthodoxies." The history of Protestantism, at least until the very recent ecumenical movements, is the story of an ever expanding number of denominations and sects.

In some ways the Puritan experience was unique. Forged under the stress of vanishing Old World conditions, it was corrupted first by man's success in the New World and corroded further as new intellectual winds, spreading the idea of freedom, enchanted the inquiring mind. It is this rising body of thought that we must now consider, for it, above all else, was to provide the philosophical basis for what one day would become known as liberalism.

When unity prevails in secular practices and religious beliefs, free inquiry is necessarily more narrowly circumscribed than when there is conflict over religious and moral issues. In addition to removing some of the fetters limiting the mind, philosophical disputes—the very existence of which makes for a social uneasiness—instill a sense of urgency in the quest for certitude. At once freed and tortured by the destruction and ravages of the religious wars, the 17th-century mind looked more and more to science in its search for truth. In what Whitehead called the "century of genius" appeared the published works of Francis Bacon, Harvey, Galileo, Hobbes, Descartes, Pascal, Huygens, Newton, Locke, and Leibniz. Perhaps it is too much of an oversimplification to say that the greatest contribution of the brilliant men of this brilliant century was to shift the emphasis from theorizing about the teleological—*why* things happen—to the mechanistic—*how* things happen.

Yet this is precisely what they did. Flying in the face of church authority, they figuratively said, "We care not for your irrelevant *a priori* theories; we will determine to our own satisfaction the makeup and operation of the universe. And where your theories are at odds with our discoveries, we will modify or replace them with new ones, compatible with the observed facts." Looking for regularity in an irregular world, they found patterns of persistency from which they adduced the "laws of nature."

Deistic in their outlook, they believed God had prescribed exact and precise laws from which the universe never deviated. "You can substitute," Descartes wrote, "the mathematical 'order of nature' for 'God' whenever I use the latter term." The greatest single achievement during this century of genius was Newton's formulation of the law of gravitation, or as it is often called, the law of inverse squares. Having learned from his fellow scientists to question conventional teachings, he was struck with the thought: "What if the same laws which apply to sizable pieces of matter were applicable to every piece of matter, irrespective of size, shape, or dimensions?" In answering this question Newton concluded that motion between masses, whether they take the form of apple, sun, moon, or earth, was produced by gravitational forces which attract one to another. Using his newly developed mathematics, he demonstrated that these forces, by keeping the planets spinning like clockwork, held the universe together. To prove the correctness of his theories, he predicted the orbits of planets, calculated the time and level of tides, and plotted the paths of comets. In so doing, the willful world of Aristotle was once and for all replaced by the mechanistic world of Newton, the mainspring of which was gravitation.

If Newton's model could not explain why there is attraction between masses, it did cause the world of astronomers and mariners to take on divine orderliness—an orderliness which for more than two hundred years dominated the thinking of natural science, and even today casts a spell over social sciences such as economics, sociology, political science, and psychology, all of which to a greater or lesser extent employ the Newtonian concept of equilibrium. To know this is to understand that Newton, more than any of his brilliant contemporaries, was the true father of the Age of Enlightenment —an age of boundless faith in reason, an age of heroic optimism, an age which was to provide liberalism with its basic beliefs.

Newton's *Principia* quickly conferred fame upon its author. First employed by scholars to demonstrate the simplicity of God's design, it was soon used to illustrate what reason could accomplish if extended to human affairs— politics, ethics, metaphysics. "Very few read Newton," Voltaire observed, "because it is necessary to be learned to understand him. But everybody talks about him." And if Voltaire was the Enlightenment's ablest spokesman, and Paris was its capital, it soon took on some of the aspects of an international movement as Locke, Hume, and Adam Smith in England, and Franklin, Payne and Jefferson joined Diderot and Condorcet in expounding a new philosophy which made nature and reason for the 18th century what grace, salvation, sin, and heaven were to the 13th.

God, these men proclaimed, having put the universe into

motion, withdrew from the affairs of man, leaving man to discover for himself the divine purpose of His will. Through reason—a creation of God—man could gain understanding of the beautiful, orderly workings of the great nature machine. Armed with this knowledge, he could alter his ideas, amend his conduct, change his institutions, and thereby dispel ignorance and superstition, poverty and suffering, privilege and tyranny. Having learned from nature what was natural, man, by eliminating unnatural behavior, could become wiser, and wealthier, and happier. He is, in short, "perfectible" and, as such, instead of looking to another world for an ideal, can, through his enlightened experiences, achieve the ideal life right here on earth.

The implications of such optimistic doctrines should be clear. If man is "perfectible," then ecstasy can be realized here on earth. And, if heaven is to be found in this world rather than in another life, then the mind and energies of man, instead of being other-worldly oriented, should be directed toward converting this world into a state of heavenly bliss. From this, the modern doctrine of progress—a doctrine that above all continues to enchant and hold the American mind—follows inevitably. For as man learns of human affairs what Newton had uncovered in physics, conditions of human life are bound to get better every day in every way. Never before had the great mass of men dreamed of such a thing. In previous ages men had always idealized the past. Now this heritage of pessimism was repudiated as the enlightened individual enthusiastically looked forward to tomorrow—a tomorrow which, if the faith were to be preserved, would never come.

In a world of religious conflict this new faith offered comfort and security. Once again there was fresh hope for the universal ideal Western man had so desperately sought, ever since he cut himself adrift from the secure moorings of an authoritarian Church and a medieval social structure. Once again he could understand and explain the workings of the cosmic processes. That the world was wicked he well knew, but, more importantly, he knew that it was wicked because it had been corrupted by the evil embodied in custom and law. Now, through new-found knowledge, all this could be corrected. Each law, each custom and each institution could be subjected to the test of the new faith. The good could be found and preserved; the evil detected and driven out. Natural law, discoverable by reason, in revealing the objective universal truth, would distinguish right from wrong, good from evil, the sublime from the wretched. The truth would make men free—of bondage, poverty, insecurity. Doubt would disappear, certainty would replace uncertainty. The fear, the guilt, and the anxiety that haunted man would be no more. The right way would become known to all. Peace, happiness, and the good life would be found. Such was the legacy of the Enlightenment!

Never so pure, never so naïve, never so vulgar as depicted here, the gospel of the Enlightenment demonstrated an enormous capacity to withstand the most demanding of all examiners—time.

Who in America could question the teachings of the Enlightenment? Its fruits were everywhere, to be seen by everyone. Food was abundant, and the factory system produced many and wondrous goods. The railroads opened up a new world of adventure and enterprise. In the name of human dignity and the love of personal freedom America abolished slavery and removed a blot that marred our culture and gave us an uneasy conscience. These were all products of the Enlightenment, of the expanding knowledge of God's natural law. Indeed it was Adam Smith, the 18th-century philosopher, who discovered and explained so all could understand the single, unifying, natural law that irrevocably governed human affairs.

Smith did for the social universe what Newton had done for the celestial system. He showed that society was made up of countless interacting human particles, each of which was strongly attracted by profits and violently repelled by economic loss. He demonstrated that, as mysteriously as gravitational forces determine the paths of the planets, so the interaction of forces in the market place caused human behavior to take on persistent, predictable patterns. He proved beyond all doubt that the laws of nature will operate where there is freedom for the individual to pursue his own self-interest; that under perfect liberty, "advantage and disadvantage will tend to equality," "market price" will correspond to "natural price"; and that society will grow ever more prosperous as the unhampered economic mechanism moves inexorably forward and upward, forever providing a better life for all men irrespective of race, color, or creed.

To all of these ideas America responded with thundering affirmations. This validation of natural law and individual freedom found expression in many forms in the maxims of Poor Richard and the eloquent humanism of Thomas Jefferson, in the death of "King Caucus" and the enshrinement of "King Numbers," in the cries of Down with the Privileged and the demise of the Second United States Bank, in the American's buoyant optimism and his contempt for shiftlessness, in his admiration for solid material achievements and his dislike of ostentation, in his carelessness in speech and dress and his impatience with tradition and culture, and in his profound commitment to the practical and his conviction that philosophy was for those who were unhappy or lost, of which he was neither.

Given the American's resentment to authority and his commitment to the virtues of independence and self-reliance, it is not surprising that men like Jefferson were attracted to competitive *laissez faire* economics. Believing that equality of men under law would preclude the government from playing favorites, the good American thought that wealth and position would be the reward of industry and skill. What could be more appropriate than an economic philosophy of perfect liberty for a society composed overwhelmingly of free farmers and independent artisans, each of whom was essentially an entrepreneur; and each of whom, in his independence and self-reliance, had been living in a land that had been practicing classical economics long before Adam Smith was born?

Having been taught, even as a child, that work was the will of divine providence, and having seen with his own eyes the bountiful fruits of hard work, the American was blessed with an eternal optimism, believing that through strength, courage, and morality he could harness the forces of nature. Not only was he generously rewarded for his labors, but through work he best expressed his ability and his individuality. Removed from the world where a man's worth was measured by his success in scaling the hierarchical ladder of some order or institution, the frontiersman had little opportunity and, if his lack of interest in public office was any indication, little desire to prove himself except through the fruits of his labor. In part, success was measured by profit, but only in part; because over and above this a man's worth was in the very best sense gauged by competition which, while enhancing the efforts of all, did a disservice to none.

There was plenty of rivalry, but it was friendly. Instead of doing injury to one's neighbor, it made the game of life more exciting and challenging. To excel in raising hogs, to harvest a superior stand of corn, to win a turkey shoot, to outwork a friend in clearing land or busting sod were accomplishments that gratified the soul. Rivalry of this kind added spice to life, yet it in no way deprived one's neighbor or friend of opportunity or income. If I raise more livestock, chop more wood, or reap more grain per acre than does my neighbor, I am likely only to spur him to greater efforts next year. I don't steal his customers, or narrow his market, or do I either directly or, as is done through present day advertising, by implication, tell people that he and the products he sells are inferior. For in a world of abundance and opportunity, where each man supplies only a minute fraction of the needs of the market, competition, rather than engendering cruel and savage jealousy, induces a spirit of friendliness and respect not unlike that which prevails when two evenly matched opponents engage in dramatic combat over a chessboard.

Thus it was that the American became a living testimonial to the doctrine of *laissez faire*. Few of these men had heard of Adam Smith, much less of his complex and esoteric theories, but each by insisting that he be let alone to employ his own means, to fulfill his own ambitions, in short to become a self-made man, was in principle and practice firmly committed to the doctrine of economic individualism.

What was true for economics was no less true for politics. Having traveled literally to the ends of the earth in order that he might work as he pleased, the American was intolerant, to the point of violence, of any suggestion that he should submit to a government other than that of his own choice or making. Believing that he was master of both himself and his life, he took for granted his right to assert his will, to act for himself, and to deny that any man was his better. Hostile to the slightest hint of superiority, he turned to the average, to the mediocre, for his representation in government. His views were straightforward: any man so presumptuous as to rank himself above the sincere, honest, but essentially ignorant, tillers of the soil should be barred from elective office. Should any one of aristocratic leanings—either through deception or some other miscarriage of the democratic process —gain office, to throw the rascal out was to perform a just and worthy public service which had the effect of announcing to all the world that the common people truly ruled.

Nor could the doctrines of economic liberty and political equality be confined to the back country. The influence of those who espoused these doctrines was soon apparent on a national scale as Eastern states followed the lead set by the Western states, which, upon entering the Union, provided for universal white, manhood suffrage. In the election of Andrew Jackson, the seventh President of the United States and the first one not of the Virginia or Massachusetts aristocracy, the hand of the West could also be seen. Jackson's election may not in fact have been a triumph of the West over East, a victory of common people over aristocrats; but the mobs which in riotous merry-making and unrestrained exhilaration overwhelmed Washington, spilled presidential punch, muddied the presidential rugs and generally left the White House in a state of dishevelment, were ecstatic in the belief that they had placed the control of the government in the hand of a man who understood and appreciated the hopes, the fears, and the dreams of the common people.

As a product of the frontier reared on Jeffersonian ideals, Jackson shared the general distrust of large government, the Westerner's resentment of the entrenched East, and the hatred of the small, independent entrepreneur of the restrictions imposed and the privileges granted by government. In that age of individualism, monopoly was the blackest of evils; and the practice of granting corporation charters only through legislative action was considered a part of a wicked plot perpetrated on the public to enhance the position of the power-seeking monopolists.

With the fall of the Second United States Bank, the election of Van Buren in 1836, and the granting of corporation charters—first by Connecticut in 1837 and then by all the states—to anyone who could meet certain nominal requirements, the opponents of monopoly and power had won the battle—or so it seemed. That theirs was a waning cause; that a dark cloud was gathering even as Jackson was pressing the cause for equality, they could not know. That the days of abundant land, scarce labor, and small entrepreneurship were slowly drawing to a close, they did not comprehend. They could not foresee that just as England was to know the horror of a bewildered people uprooted and impoverished by the enclosures, so the United States was to be staggered by masses of unskilled, poorly educated, propertyless immigrants. Nor could they know that just as the British population was to enjoy the prosperity and suffer the misery and trauma cast by the spell of a Kay, a Hargreaves, an Arkwright, a Compton, and a Cartwright, so the United States was soon to suffer the agonies of social disruption, as the machine process of the rising factory system took away the livelihood and destroyed the status of the self-sufficient mechanic and the artisan.

Beginning in 1840, thousands upon thousands of European immigrants sought the safety and opportunity promised by American shores. So great was the number—almost half a million in 1854 alone—of these poorly trained and poverty-stricken strangers to democracy that only a fraction of them traveled West into agriculture. Compelled to huddle together in squalid slums in mill towns and cities, and to earn their living as day laborers, they made an insecure and dependent urban population which lived in fear and despair rather than freedom and opportunity. Within this flood of poor immigrants were unnoticed warnings of the gradual decline of individualism.

At first imperceptibly, and then unmistakably, America abandoned the characteristics of the simple, unstructured,

rural society. Despite its actual decline, individualism as a
moral philosophy continued to be elaborated and gain
strength until it reached its peak in 1929. It is to this social
philosophy of economic individuals that we now turn our
attention.

III

A Magnificent Abstraction

Man has demanded much from philosophy. at one time he orders it to make his society understandable, at another he asks it to tell him what he can and cannot know, and at still another he expects it to provide him with some lofty ideal for which he may labor and sacrifice. But more than any of these things, man, in his self-conscious struggle, commands his philosophy to prove decisively that the society or system to which he is committed—in fact or faith—is beyond all doubt uniquely suited to provide the highest energy and achievement ever effected by mankind. No doubt philosophy has had other assignments, but if these be the primary ones, as surely they must be, then the philosophy of capitalism must be rated as a brilliant tour de force. As such it was to become a powerful ideology which, in ruling men's minds, determined their actions. To appreciate this, however, one must know in some detail the pure theory of capitalism which in economics has come to be known as the competitive model.

For most of history man's view of the economy might be compared to that of a ship at sea, the course, speed, and general condition of which were set by some central authority. On any good sailing ship there were, of course, many tasks to be performed. Sails had to be trimmed, lines spliced, decks swabbed, sights taken, courses plotted, guns aimed and fired.

31

Essential to the successful performance of these and many other tasks was a full complement of seasoned able-bodied seamen led by competent officers and a firm but fair captain, ever mindful of the advantages of a taut ship. To ease his command, the captain and his officers were assisted by men of lesser rank, such as the boatswain's mate and the quartermaster. But they were a handful among many. Overwhelmingly, the ship's complement was composed of ordinary seamen who, not specialists skilled in the performance of one job, were expected to perform equally well in a great variety of tasks.

As with the ship, so historically with the economy. Traditionally the direction, the level of development, and general character of the economy were determined by the king, the prince, the ecclesiastic, or whoever else held in his hands the power of the state. Like the captain of a ship, the head of state was not without his assistants who specialized in such things as making the king's armor, in presiding over the people in daily worship, or in protecting the kingdom from internal treachery and outside aggression. But the economy, like the ship, was primarily populated by disciplined common men who, while knowing their place, possessed neither unique skills nor valuable talents. During most of history, these ordinary men, because of custom and lack of opportunity, lived narrowly prescribed and closely regulated lives working the soil and raising the food necessary for the survival of the economy.

Unlike most sailing vessels, the economy was inhabited by another breed of men. Originally few in number, they were a venturesome lot who were willing to risk both their possessions and their lives for the opportunity to supply the rulers and the ruled with the precious materials that were not to be found in the confines of the domestic economy. In return for gold or other commodities, these men traveled to the four corners of the earth, bringing back incense, jewels, metals, spices, and fine clothes. Although these men were free spirits who escaped the chains which bound the common man, their destiny was nevertheless closely tied to the general course of the economy. It was, so to speak, as if they fought and roamed the seas in a small rowboat secured only by a sturdy line, firmly attached to the great economic ship. As such the extent of their travels and their hope for achievement were determined by both the length of their lines and the position and course of the economy. In the beginning, the number of men who possessed sufficient will and courage to brave the unforgiving sea in such a small, unseaworthy craft was indeed limited. Stiffen their backs and strain their muscles as they might in an effort to extend the scope of their freedom, the impact of these few men on the course of the ship was so negligible as to be imperceptible. But as time passed, despite persecution and persuasion by prince and priest alike, this class of adventurers rose both in quantity and quality. As their numbers grew and their bravado swelled, so hard did they pull on their oars, so taut became the lines securing them, that slowly they began to exert first a slight and then a pronounced influence on the movement of the economic ship.

Suddenly it seemed as if the whole crew deserted, as men set out in all kinds of rigs, ready to pit themselves against the sea, intent on escaping the tyranny of their captain, and buoyed by the hope of enhancing their own private welfare. Some men, incompetent to cope with the demands of nature, were lost by the wayside and perished, and many were maimed or fell victim to sharks. But most did not. Of those who survived, some fished for cod, oysters, or shrimp; others made and distributed nets, provided ropes, or fashioned new,

seaworthier boats; still others sailed to mysterious lands, only
to return with exotic bits and pieces that charmed and ex-
cited the imagination.

To the once powerful ruler and captain, all this seemed
quite unnatural and wicked. Finding some comfort and
solace in the fact that all these rebellious men must always
return to the main ship for trade and the reprovisioning of
their larders, deep in his heart he nevertheless knew that his
command was irretrievably lost, his mastery forever dissipated. With his rudder gone and his sail a tattered rag idly
flapping in the breeze, it was blatantly obvious that the condition and progression of the economic ship was once and for
all a product of the incessant tugging and pulling exerted
by the small boats filled with arrogant and independent men.

To capitalist theory befell the task of providing a coherent
and logically consistent system of thought which demonstrated that the driving force eminating from the seemingly
uncoordinated small craft was superior to the power generated by any ship manned by a full complement of centrally
organized and directed seamen. This was no mean assignment. To succeed, capitalist theory had to convince a world
accustomed to placing its trust in authority that the diverse
and contending forces generated by the many small, independent forces guaranteed not only higher speed and enhanced comfort, but a truer course as well. This capitalist
theory was to do, and do well.

Riches and commerce did not, of course, escape the attention of earlier philosophers. The Church had frequently and
vigorously denounced profits and usury as barren and contrary to God and nature. But then a new breed of men,
instead of condemning trade and the drive for worldly gain,
exalted the merchant by praising him for his contributions to
economic progress. Still, although opulence and worldly comforts beguiled with charms few men could resist, they were

to cast a spell of confusion and discord. To be sure, on one point there was unanimity and harmony. The poor, lest their heads be turned and their energies squandered, must, if they were to give an honest day's toil, be kept poor and wretched. But beyond this there was only contradiction as the various schools, speaking with authority and conviction, fought over how the goddess of wealth and prosperity must be courted and won.

The Bullionist declared gold the mainspring of human achievement, the Mercantilist proclaimed an excess of sales over purchases as the mother of economic health and national prosperity, and the Physiocrats pronounced agriculture the source of all human wealth and power. From this welter of bickering was to arise a new philosophy that not only would make understandable the seemingly chaotic workings of the market, but indeed would prove to all who would see that it was the market itself which promised the fulfillment of man's dreams for material and moral progress. The author of this monumental social innovation was the brilliant and amusingly absent-minded 18th-century philosopher, Adam Smith.

Smith's great contribution was his system, a system which with an elaboration here and a modification there came to be known as classical economics. As the 19th-century passed and the 20th-century slowly unfolded, the system was extended and refined until the avant-garde began to speak of neoclassical economics. Still, it was the doctrines of Smith that remained the heart of what was to become the separate discipline of economics. And although the academic disciples of this rising orthodoxy were to proclaim economics the science of resource allocation, it was the philosophical rather than the scientific contributions of this new system that were destined to shape the course of history. Commenting on the severe scientific limitations of conventional economic theory, Kenneth Boulding declared, "It does lead to some useful elementary proposition at about the level of household wisdom: if we touch a hot stove, we will burn our fingers; if we fix prices 'too high,' we shall have surpluses; if we cannot absorb the capacity output, we shall have unemployment, and so on."

If economics fell far short of the physics which it so passionately admired and sought to copy, as a metaphysical system which explained and justified the operations of the market-oriented economy, it was to become a thing of sheer beauty, bearing eloquent testimony to the creative powers of human intellect. As a strictly logical system it is virtually flawless. Having no Bible it is, unlike Christianity, spared the tensions of somehow reconciling seemingly contradictory passages. Making no specific statements about the precise operations or state of the economy—much less the universe—it need not fear the devastating kind of assault that Christian cosmology suffered at the hands of Copernicus and Galileo. Free from any readily identifiable concepts such as the "withering of the state" and the "classless society," it is not plagued by the general trends which, by any standard of experience, appear to be in direct conflict with the eschatology of communism. As such it has much to offer to both the logician and the layman.

To the purist, the true logician, it must always be a thing of abstract splendor. Fascinated by its elegance and enchanted by its sophistication, he knows a sense of aloof pity because most of the relationships, nuances, and other niceties of this tribute to human creativeness can be mastered and fully appreciated by only a handful of his most dedicated colleagues. Although the mechanics of economics are bewilderingly esoteric, the foundations upon which the system must stand or fall are neither the private property of economists nor unknown to the layman. Just as Scholasticism has its divine revelation and communism its dilectical materialism, so traditional economics postulates certain canons of truth which can be neither proved nor disproved. As such, like all great creeds which enlist and inspire, it does not submit to empirical testing.

Traditional economics does make predictions very well, but the forecasts are in such broad abstractions that no set of empirical scales, however elaborate or ingenious, can ever be devised for weighing them. By those who refuse to accept what cannot be counted, weighed, or measured, the forecasts arising from conventional economics are often viewed with a certain amount of suspicion, almost as if such projections were tinged with mysticism. Not so the true believer, who knows that his logic is impeccable, his system always superior to the crude and frequently erroneous findings provided by the clumsy tools of empiricism. Knowing that the system is infallible, he is certain that if there be any error, it can be traced to human frailties that produce a misapplication of analysis rather than to any weakness within the system itself.

In the final analysis, capitalist theory is philosophical by nature and societies which are moved by it inevitably have at their foundations a system of ethics and a set of institutions which have become the prime shapers of cultural tones and patterns. Such a thought opens up a whole new world of investigation. Before we enter it we must, in some detail, learn the true wonders of the capitalist theory. And this can be accomplished only if we first speak of the nature of man.

Alfred Marshall, the founder of neoclassical economics, defined economics as a "study of mankind in the ordinary business of life." Later economists, particularly some of those sparked by an interest in epistemology and an urge to make economics more scientific, objected to Marshall's definition, claiming that it was unworkably broad. Lionel Robbins, a leader of this dissenting movement, limited economics to the consideration of "the forms assumed by human behavior in disposing of scarce means." But despite the disparity evident in these two definitions, they possess a common element: a reference to human behavior. Indeed both Marshall and Robbins saw man as John Stuart Mill depicted him when he wrote, "Just as geometry presupposes an arbitrary definition of a line—that which has length, but not breadth—so does political economy presuppose an arbitrary definition of man as a being who does that by which he may obtain the greatest amount of necessities, conveniences, and luxuries, with the smallest quantity of labor and physical self-denial with which they can be obtained in the existing state of knowledge."

Thus Mill portrays man as a creature relentlessly driven by self-interest at the same time that he is governed by a high order of rationality. As such his conduct is calculated, his behavior unfailingly mechanistic. Contemporary economics, no less than the classical economics of Mill or the neoclassical economics of a Marshall or a Robbins, is rooted in the supposition that man is a maximizing animal. This view of human nature long antedates economics. To understand this, it is necessary to look briefly at the nature of man as depicted by the mainstream of Western thought.

In A.D. 411, the Council of Carthage officially condemned the teachings of Pelagius. Denying the validity of original sin, Pelagius, by teaching that man could perfect himself, had rendered both the Church and the doctrine of atonement largely superfluous. In A.D. 413, St. Augustine finished his monumental *City of God*. Reflecting Greek thought, he declared, "For in each individual there is first of all that which is reprobate. . . . Not indeed that every wicked man shall be good, but that no one will be good who was not first of all wicked." With these words and the decision of the Council of Carthage, Christian man was forever branded with original sin. Having fallen from grace, man bears the curse of self-love, which is the root of all evil. Unable to transcend his sinful nature, Christian dogma today, as in the time of St. Augustine, depicts man as an egotistic, self-seeking, vain, rebellious creature.

Following the pattern set by St. Augustine, some eleven centuries later the Renaissance philosopher Thomas Hobbes was to write, "If any two men desire the same thing, which nevertheless they cannot both enjoy, they become enemies. . . ." In the state of nature, therefore, men are in a condition of war, of every man against man and, Hobbes adds, the nature of war consists not in actual fighting, "but in the known disposition thereto." Inherent in man Hobbes finds three principal causes for quarreling: "The first makes men invade for gain; the second for safety; and the third for reputation. The first use violence, to make themselves masters of other men's persons, wives, children, and cattle; the second, to defend them; the third, for trifles, as a word, a smile, a different opinion. . . ."

Jean Jacques Rousseau, the 18th-century philosopher, vigorously disagreed with the Hobbesian interpretation of man. It is not uncivilized man, declared Rousseau, but civilized man who is the "depraved animal." The noble savage, Rousseau said, is guided by both self-interest and compassion, but civilized man, using reason and thought, stills the voice of compassion and isolates himself from his fellow man. Primitive man is always "foolishly ready to obey the first promptings of humanity," whereas the refinements of civilization are, as Rousseau saw them, nothing but a "perfidious veil," which hides "jealousy," "suspicion," "fear," "coldness," "reserve," "hate" and "fraud." Thus Rousseau, unlike Hobbes, viewed civilization as a corrupting rather than a purifying force.

Each of these writers was to leave his mark on Western thought. History considers St. Augustine one of the leading Christian theologians, and Hobbes and Rousseau are ranked among the great political philosophers. Adam Smith, a professor of moral philosophy, was aware of these views of human nature. Indeed he gained immediate reputation and prestige from his work on *The Theory of Moral Sentiments* in which he addressed himself to the reconciliation of self-love and individual morality. But it would be another 17 years before Smith was to discover the "invisible hand," which was to give full expression to the Christian interpretation of human nature.

Building on the Christian view of man, Adam Smith observed in his *Wealth of Nations,* "It is not from the benevolence of the butcher, the brewer, or the baker that we expect our dinner, but from their regard to their own interest. We address ourselves, not to their humanity, but to their self-love, and never talk to them of our own necessities, but of their advantage." Thus did Smith, in one broad sweep, convert the Christian man of original sin into the economic man of the market place and, in so doing, provide a new Western focus out of which would arise the splendid edifice of capitalist thought. With this worldly philosophy came a new picture of man, as the vice of self-love became the virtue of self-reliance, as rebellion against God was transformed into the high ideal of independence.

Instead of the corrupt, predatory, and depraved animal of which Hobbes and Rousseau spoke, man became a separate and unique personality who, as Jeremy Bentham phrased it, "lived under the governance of two sovereign masters, *pain* and *pleasure*." And since each person has a different pain threshold and each a distinct pleasure pattern, so that one man's meat is another's poison, the best of all possible ways to gratify man's innate self-interest was to give to each the freedom of charting his own course in life. With the rediscovery of this ancient idea, modern man found a whole new world— a world in which society was nothing more than the individual "writ large."

Thus it came about that man was expected, encouraged, and finally, if he was to satisfy his existential requirements, compelled to heed his self-seeking nature. This new philosophy taught that man was to behave in whatever manner necessary for the realization of maximum pleasure and minimal pain. For some this meant striving for power, for others a search for peace of mind, for still others a struggle to achieve position and prestige. Yet, despite explicit recognition that needs and ambitions vary with men, in the last analysis capitalist thought was made meaningful and viable by a will to believe that human actions were overwhelmingly dictated by an uncompromising urge for pecuniary acquisitions. In response to this innate and unyielding drive, all other aspects of life were subordinated as man organized his whole existence for the purpose of reaping and accumulating personal riches. It is this general view of human nature which empowered a market-centered philosophy to dominate American and, to a lesser extent, European thought for the better part of two centuries.

Thus capitalist theory stereotyped man as an economic creature who, in employing his rational facilities, is forever concerned with maximizing his position. As producer, he is obsessed with desire for profits and as a consumer he is endowed with an almost "irrational" passion for painstakingly calculating what expenditure pattern would bring him the greatest joy and highest satisfaction. But although all men are to some degree hedonists, the theory emphasizes that although men, like flakes of snow, are generally very similar in nature, they are in fact quite specifically different and therefore want very different things from life. From this one might conclude that the ideal system would be economic anarchy, permitting each person to pursue his unique preferences.

This is exactly what capitalist theory prescribed. However, if this were all the theory had to contribute, it surely would have been rejected out of hand, for few men would have been enchanted with a doctrine that simply exhorted the individual to gratify his predatory nature by preying on his fellow creatures. It was, therefore, essential to convince man that through the promotion of his own self-interest, he not only rightfully earned happiness, but in so doing conferred wealth and benefits upon all of mankind. Given man's acquisitive nature, this proved to be not an insurmountable task, as market-oriented societies enthusiastically subscribed to the belief that the pursuit of personal riches was an aspiration worthy of the best of men, and as profit-making was hastily translated into a mark of grace to be interpreted by all as a dedication to public service.

Nor can one fault the logic supporting such a doctrine. For is it not true that the market is the place where each individual is permitted unlimited freedom in expressing his unique individuality? Is it not here that he is free to do as he pleases, spending his wages for anything that strikes his fancy, whether it be food, clothing, or something frivolous which gratifies an immediate whim or impulse? Is it not only through the market that the consumer can express his ever changing tastes and moods? What fascinated him yesterday is commonplace and dreary today; what he was willing to pay a high price for last week, he wants not at all this week; and what he didn't think about twice last year now stands high on his list of absolute necessities. All of these things the wise man understands and acts upon. Ever engaged in taking the pulse of the market, through experience he develops a keen sense of perception for interpreting signals forecasting new and exciting profit opportunities. With success comes glory, not only for himself and his family, but for the whole of society as friend and foe alike derive comfort and pleasure from his industry and contribution.

Much of this he does quite unwittingly. Intensely engrossed in studying the market and in enlarging his own stock of worldly treasures, he is little inclined to speculate on his contributions to humanity or to expound on his altruistic motivations. Surely here is the splendor of the market system, for in using the lure of purse to set his course in life, this self-seeker irrevocably commits himself to do the bidding of all, however base or insignificant, who would frequent the market place. Not only must he unquestioningly serve, but he must do it with dispatch and in a pleasing manner, or he will most surely be coldly and harshly dealt with. These things he knows, and knowing them, he can never relax.

From out of his and his fellow man's ceaseless vigil emerges then the economic activity and finally the goods which every society, be it centrally organized or free, must have if it is to survive and grow. But unlike authoritarian systems, out of the free market system flow automatically, without command or regulation, just the right volume and variety of food, shoes, television sets, and whatever, and all because men chase profits.

Should there be an overabundance of green bathing suits on the market (the public prefers red this year), the price of these suits would fall below cost, and men, appalled by the very thought of losses, would quickly shift their energies and attentions to making red bathing suits, or yellow shoes or purple lampshades, or whatever else may at the moment promise financial reward. Thus the market quietly and democratically coordinates all the many and largely unknowable forces, striking a perfect balance so that the multitude of consumers is supplied with the goods providing the "greatest good for the greatest number."

How truly beautiful are the laws of nature as revealed by the market and seen through the spectacles of capitalistic theory. But yet there persists a disquieting thought—that man, in his unrelenting drive for aggrandizement, might at every opportunity exploit and abuse by imposing exorbitant prices for the goods he makes and sells. Such fears, it was soon learned, were ill founded; for there was discovered yet another great equalizing force which, in ruling over the market, fairly and resolutely dispensed justice irrespective of caste or station.

This force, like most things in the market, is a product of man's drive for profits. It is the omnipresent and omnipotent law of competition, which has decreed that no man shall be permitted to exploit, take advantage of his neighbor, or long to earn more than his diligence and contribution warrant. Should any man be so fortunate as to have something left after he has covered his costs and paid himself an honest wage, his windfall is at best fleeting. The beguiling charms cast by high prices inevitably prove to be deceptive, because they seductively beckon enterprising suitors to desert their immediate activities in favor of the largess now bestowed upon a few. Alas, it cannot be otherwise. For the men who fall prey to the spell cast by high prices soon learn that profit demands ardent courting.

Would-be gain seekers, making every effort to supply the

market with additional goods, discover, much to their sorrow and after the damage is done, that the greater their ardor and the more they exert themselves, the colder, the more elusive are beauties of profit. In an effort to curry favor, these suitors have flooded the market with goods that previously had brought profits to a fortunate few only to find that because of their exertions, prices faltered and then fell drastically; instead of knowing the excitement that comes with the reaping and counting of profits, they number their blessings for having been able to sell at prices which cover their costs and leave a little to compensate them for the feverish labors.

Such then are some of the attributes of the pure capitalist market. A place where the terrible spectacle of deception and exploitation and the imposition of outrageous prices on the downtrodden masses can never materialize except as conceived in the fears of a twisted brain. None of these things can occur because, in a manner of speaking, the Archangel Competition stands watchfully over the market, pledging his infinite power to preserve a delicate balance, assuring that the price of goods can never deviate greatly or for long from the cost of producing and selling them. So it is that man need no longer concern himself with attempting, as in the past, to administer the nebulous and much corrupted concept of the just price. If only let alone, the market will compel man to pursue actions, the result of which must be a just price. For the just price is the natural price and, rather than the finite rationality and petty bumblings of man, it is the great unfailing laws of the market which must be relied upon to fix at once both the natural and just price.

Capitalist theory thus made intelligible how the splendid workings of the market system not only extracted from a begrudging nature just the right volume and variety of goods for maximizing human satisfaction, but logically demonstrated that prices in the free market automatically and forever gravitated toward and clustered at the long-sought but rarely attained ideal of the just price.

But cries against the market were still to be heard; some, for lack of knowledge, out of innocence; others out of a distorted will to pit man against a superior and unforgiving nature. In the main these cries were directed not so much against the admitted efficiency or the efficacy of the market, but against the manner in which it distributed the fruits of man's labor.

There is simply no denying that in all market-oriented societies, some men accumulated and commanded great personal riches and other men seemed barely able to lay their hands on the food and shelter necessary for keeping body and soul together. Although this was indisputable, these cries against capitalism nevertheless rested on misconception and misunderstanding, for the market system does indeed provide a logical and just basis for distributing the output of society. Assuredly, the market system cannot gratify the whim or fancy of each and every citizen it so faithfully serves. No system, given the niggardliness of nature, can hope to achieve this; and even the well-to-do man with an income of $20,000 a year cannot hope to satisfy his every desire. He may, of course, buy himself a Buick or a swimming pool, but in so doing he foregoes the long-planned trip to Europe, or the mink coat he half promised his wife as a Christmas surprise. There are, to be sure, men who, because of their success in the market, can afford to drive expensive cars, own fancy swimming pools, dress their wives in mink, and more; but of these there are few—very few. Many more in number are the men whose thoughts and energies are consumed not in choosing between luxuries, but in providing a meager diet and the simplest shelters for their family. Why this must have been so in the past and why this is true today, although to a lesser extent, capitalist theory makes clear.

There are diverse means for distributing the fruits of the economy. Industry, diligence, and good intentions all are virtues worthy of reward. But of all the conceivable measures for dividing wealth and comfort, surely there is none more just than the one which bestows and exalts according to the individual's contribution to society. And this, capitalist theory tells us, is precisely the measure that is operative when the laws of the market are free to work. For him who serves his fellow man well, the market provides abundant rewards; but for him who is rebellious and would disregard the wishes of his fellow man, as expressed in the market, the compensation is and indeed should be dolefully small.

Only, we are told, in the mechanistic, impersonal market are all men treated as equals. No favors are asked, no special privileges granted, and each man, like a loaf of bread, a ton of coal, or a bottle of ale is dispassionately measured to determine what, if anything, he has contributed and therefore is entitled to take from the economy. "Wages," wrote Professor Hicks, "are the price of labor; and thus, in the absence of price control, they are determined, like all prices, by supply and demand." If the individual is wise and industrious and heeds the will of the market, his effort will command high esteem and he will be provided with an income empowering him, should he so desire, to live in splendor. If, however, he is foolish and wastes his time and fritters away his energies, then the market must sternly instruct him—by placing a low value on his activities and supplying him with a meager and indeed often inadequate income—to the effect that he must mend his ways and convert his idle habits into those that are in keeping with the wants and needs of society.

Thus it is that the courageous, the diligent, and those clever in spotting and adroit at taking advantage of shifts in the market, are showered with riches, and the dullards, the indolent, and ne-er-do-wells are, in relation to their great numbers, accorded a pitifully small share of the economy's affluence. All this comes about because the Archangel Competition declared that he who would be affluent must meet the test of the market. What could be more fair or more democratic than to treat all men as equals, teaching each that the strain on his back, or the pull on his mind, is carefully weighed by the market to fix exactly whatever earnings he may be entitled to command? Surely such a system cannot be improved upon. For where there is success and the handsome income that goes with it, and where there is failure and its accompanying poverty, these, in the last analysis, are products of the individual's own making and should not and cannot be attributed to any perversity inherent in the system.

All this would seem to imply equality of opportunity or, to put it more generally, that the market automatically guarantees gainful employment to anyone who, through his own labors, would provide for himself. In short, the market economy, so capitalistic theory tells us, had built-in resistance to the scourge of unemployment. And the logic supporting this statement is irrefutable.

To be sure, some unfortunate individuals suffer the curse of physical crippling or mental derangement. Of these poor souls a few are so badly handicapped that they are unemployable and must be cared for by friends and relatives. Additionally, political and technological upheavals may for brief periods produce a state of unemployment that, at worst, is temporary. Even as these disruptive forces are exhausting themselves, the self-adjusting market is shaping the corrective forces necessary to return the economy to its natural state of employment. The logic demonstrating this is all quite straightforward, because once again competition and man's drive for personal gain are depicted as cooperating and benevolent forces pushing society toward a felicitous equilibrium.

If, for any reason, a certain number of would-be workers are unemployed, they can easily escape their idleness through the simple expedient of offering their services on the open market, which is another way of saying competing for the jobs that are available. Such action will, of course, automatically depress wages, which in turn will reduce production costs and temporarily, at least, give promise for high profits. But alas, high profits are not long realized in the competitive market; for as soon as news of their existence becomes widespread, new producers, anxious to share in the bounty, hasten to increase the supply of goods until prices once again are at the point where the producer does well to cover his costs and retain a small amount for his own labors. The glory of the whole process is that through the increase in the quantity of goods sold on the market, the unemployed workers are absorbed into the labor force and the economy once more operates at its natural level of full employment.

Thus the logic of capitalist theory compels the conclusion that an uninhibited economy is forever free of the appalling waste and human torment that is wrought by depression and unemployment. This must be so because free and able-bodied men genuinely anxious to secure work can, in the capitalist economy, always do so if only they are willing to sell their services at wages which are not in excess of what they are able to contribute. Only the intransigent who would demand more than his labors are worth need fall prey to idleness and this, rather than involuntary, is maliciously conceived and deliberately practiced unemployment. Fortunately, most men, if forced to choose between work and destitution or begging, would prefer gainful employment, even if their contribution, and therefore their wage, was low. Thus it is that under a true market system, where each man is compelled to rely on his own resources, involuntary unemployment cannot, without doing violence to logic, exist. To purport to measure and proclaim the evils, as some seem compelled to do, of something that cannot exist is not only foolish, but, because it confuses and deceives the innocent, mischievous. Only those who are unwilling to accept the just and objective verdict of the market would lack employment and income, and these by their own choice. Such is their right, as are the inevitable consequences that accompany it. Such is the way of freedom.

And still there are virtues unnumbered. Indeed, yet to be mentioned is the market system's greatest of all gifts to mankind: the promised fulfillment of man's hopes and aspirations for a better, more enjoyable life here on earth. Blessed, we are told, is the society that is willing to place its full trust in and abandon its destiny to the free and largely unknowable force of the market. For such a society shall be forever favored with rapid and automatic progress. On this score, as on all others, the logic of the system remorselessly draws its strength from the glorious conspiracy of man and nature— competition—which unendingly showers upon man the bountiful fruits emanating from the enhanced efficiency and expansion of worldly goods certain to be forthcoming from a price-directed and price-controlled economy.

Because of this conspiracy, as any man wise to the fickle ways of the market can tell you, the profit seeker can never sit idly by admiring the beauties of his creation. Always he must be plagued by the dreadful thought that on the morrow some remote competitor or some unknown tinkerer might carefully develop or accidentally stumble upon a startling new process or a remarkable new material that will revolutionize production, shatter prices, and bring ruin and catastrophe to him and his family. No matter how great his exertions, how advanced his methods, or how successful his past, he cannot for a moment indulge himself in the joy and glory of reflecting on his honestly won laurels.

Indeed, the greater his success, the greater the shadow of insecurity looms, for although prosperity has brought him luxury and public esteem, it also is an irresistible magnet attracting challengers who would wrench from him the very profits which are the distinguishing marks of success. Rest is not for him; the cycle is remorseless. The more strenuous his endeavors and the higher his achievement, the larger is the number who strain to dislodge him from his position of prestige and opulence.

Thus, if the profit seeker has any real hope for maintaining his position of affluence, he must each day selflessly dedicate himself to a renewed search for more efficient ways of doing things. Should his interest briefly flag or his genius momentarily falter, then he must pay and, according to the theory, properly so—through bankruptcy and financial disgrace—the just and implacable price exacted by the market. But if he continues to display, both through invention and enterprise, the diligence necessary to preserve his low cost position, then the market will reward him handsomely for both his single-mindedness of purpose and for the invaluable role he has played in advancing progress.

It is from the innovations and discoveries made by aggressive and independent leaders, and quickly copied by men at large, that the market derives fresh impetus for introducing, altering, and discarding the countless and minute complexities of the productive process. These are the fundamental changes responsible for the daily increases in efficiency and the ever expanding stream of fascinating and satisfying products. Further, these improvements are the only bricks and stuff from which true progress can be fashioned. Clearly the market not only automatically and benevolently confers social progress, but indeed carefully and fairly rewards each member in accordance with the extent to which he was responsible for bringing it about.

Such is the pure theory of capitalism. If nothing else, it remains a magnificent abstraction. But it is more. Breathing, as it did, vitality into the "American way," it is a spiritual force which, like a wise but aging warrior, is entitled to our respect and affection. Its primary contribution, of course, remains a political philosophy which, in glorifying the optimistic spirit and the robust energy fostered under a kind of economic anarchy, justified the free-enterprise system that altogether dominated 19th-century America. Fitting 19th-century man with spectacles enabling him to see his life in a natural order, it remains the wellspring of economic individualism.

If we are made more and more uneasy by the ever widening gulf separating 19th-century faith from our reality, our feverish search for a substitute ideology continues to be in vain. This should surprise no one, for the achievement of capitalistic ideology was monumental and indeed unique. Capitalist theory, by logic rather than revelation, navigated successfully the treacherous rocks—diversity (free will) and unity (determinism)—upon which other great systems had foundered. It permitted man to reap and enjoy the intellectual fruits of both.

Under capitalism, indeed, there must not be any state or church or superior authority whatever for shaping and directing one's wants, beliefs, or acts. Each individual is a divinely created sovereign who, being perfectly capable of governing himself, should be permitted unbounded latitude to pursue his own penchants and self-interest in the market place. Any force created for the purpose of curbing the individual's drive and self-interest is not only morally wrong, but contrary to the laws of nature, because it deprives man of inalienable rights to exercise his free will in developing his full human potential in the pursuit of happiness. Thus, under capitalist theory, society is a mass of diverse, separate, and unique individuals, each of whom does as he sees fit, each of whom is responsible for his own actions, each of whom is the master of his own destiny. If he achieves, it is of his own doing; if he fails, it is of his own making; obligated to no man, his fate, whatever it may be, is his responsibility and his alone.

If the society of capitalist theory is an economy populated by a vast number of independent and diverse individuals, it is also a world which enjoys the advantages of unity. The logical reconciliation of diversity with unity, a philosophical dilemma which tortured philosophers from Plato to Aquinas, remains, of course, the central contribution of Smith and capitalist theory. Providence, it seemed, had fashioned a beautiful system of natural order which caused private and public interest to coincide. Left to himself, wrote Smith, man, though "he intends only his own gain . . . is . . . led by an invisible hand to promote an end which was no part of his intention." The individual's pursuit of self-interest, Smith went on, "frequently promoted that of the society more effectually than when he really intended it."

Thus not only did the self-adjusting market solve the immensely complicated economic problems of production and distribution, but of even greater significance, it provided the rationale for economic and political freedom. For if in pursuing his own selfish ends, each man unwittingly, but nevertheless effectively, enhanced the common good, then individual freedom must surely be the foundation for the best of all possible worlds.

No one would deny, of course, that left to his own devices,

the individual, corrupted by self-love, will attempt to exploit his workers, deceive his customers, and accumulate wealth and power at the expense of the common good. Fortunately, he does none of these things, not because of his humanitarian instincts, of which, if he is to survive and the system is to work perfectly, he has none, but simply because he is without the power to effectuate these malevolent acts. For, according to theory, should he endeavor to deceive those who would sell to him, he will be without raw materials; should he endeavor to overwork or underpay his workers, he will be without employees; should he try to overprice his goods, he will be unable to sell them.

All of this logically follows because the market is ruled by an all-pervasive competition which altogether and forever precludes anyone from acquiring for himself the power essential for arbitrary action. In this sublime world of capitalist theory, all sellers and buyers, all workers and employers are, by the market, provided with an unlimited number of alternative opportunities and, therefore, no one person or group can ever hope to exercise the power sufficient to coerce another individual into making an unfavorable one-sided transaction. With power automatically precluded, exploitation and abuse cannot exist, and the political and economic freedom which man has always sought under the market system, once and for all assured.

Thus the age-old philosophical dilemma of free will and determinism is logically and beautifully resolved. Unlike the distinction between Plato's higher and lower reality, which to the average mind always seemed more mysterious than real, and unlike Aquinas' dualism of soul and matter, which to the ordinary mind appeared to be nothing more than poorly disguised Pantheism, and unlike communistic doctrine which, in proclaiming the inevitability of things, seems to deny man any power whatever over the shaping and altering of society, capitalist theory endows the individual with a full measure of free will, the use of which not only decides his own destiny, but indeed ranks high as an element in the alchemy determining the grandeur of his society.

Capitalist doctrine is, therefore, overwhelmingly optimistic in tone and outlook. Teaching that the free will of the individual is a prime mover of social welfare, it places a high value on education or training directed toward expanding the knowledge and sharpening the skills of the members of society. By elevating the intellectual powers and by increasing the physical prowess of the individual, not only is his worth and dignity exalted, but as his moral and physical fiber is strengthened and fully developed, he, through the exercise of free will, brings ever greater radiance to his already magnificent society. Thus capitalist theory has it that out of the multiplicity of diverse individuals, each pursuing his own destiny, the market delicately and infallibly fashions a harmonious unity which, like Plato's higher reality, although beyond full human understanding and measurement, resounds to the benefit of all men. Ruling the market is an unbending deterministic force that unfailingly converts all of man's actions, however wretched their origin or evil their design, into splendid acts of public interest. And although man is free to do as his conscience dictates, hopefully he will be passionately committed to exploiting his full talents, for the greater his exertions, the more grist that the beautiful, well-oiled market machine will transform into the benevolent energy so essential to the making of a better world.

The policy implications of this philosophy are unmistakable. Given man's incorrigible nature to seek power and advantage for himself, authority, whatever its origin or substance, can only wrong the individual and blight the society.

Of all the many forms of authority, none is more threateningly omnipresent or more bewitchingly dangerous than that which masquerades under the banner of the benevolent state. Always men will exist who will declare that only the supreme rule of the state can provide the unity of purpose necessary to attain the high spiritual and material values of which men are capable. Admittedly, by some rare and fortuitous combination of circumstances, the imposition of governmental powers may accidentally work some minor improvements; but, according to capitalist theory, the chances of good are slight, and the probabilities of damage are great.

Even more disturbing is the enervating toll that governmental action is bound to have on individual initiative and freedom. For the more towering the government becomes, the greater its resources for further expropriation, and the more it abuses man in the name of unity and mankind. Capitalist philosophy teaches that forced unity is calculated tyranny and that the only pure unity naturally emerges through the market where each individual is encouraged to pursue his personal objectives, develop his unique resources, and follow his own distinct morality. Thus, although capitalist ideology provides the rationale for the highly productive and remarkably efficient free enterprise system, its primary hold on the Western mind remains the freedom of choice and abundance of opportunities which over time it has promised and provided the individual.

If the ultimate test of a theory is direct practical application, then capitalist doctrine must be ranked a success. For it worked! Or at least men believed, and with good reason, that it was but a short jump from theory to reality. Not that the two coincided exactly; that was rather too much to expect from a complex and irrational world forever fraught with political and military upheavals. Man, to be sure, had not achieved the perfect society; injustice was still to be found, poverty was yet to be banished, and undeserving men, though fewer than ever before, waxed fat and grew decadent while some good men sweated from dawn to dusk, only to be broken by the disease-ridden squalor of their existence. Nor did prices slowly fall or hold steady, as theory said they would. Rather they rose spectacularly, only to fall precipitously, spreading financial panic, business catastrophe, and the want and sickness accompanying the ravages of unemployment. But for laying the blame, look not to theory, but to men. If the doubting Thomases and the world improvers would only approach the subject with an open and unprejudiced mind and if they would take the trouble to apprise themselves, they would discover quickly that the world's ills were products of foolish wars and the subordination of wisdom to greed as men deliberately contrived to subvert the natural workings of the market.

Indeed, given man's idle tampering and malevolent scheming, any progression stood as a tribute to the uncorruptible market forces that day by day and year by year carried America ever forward as a finer, more satisfying place to call home. Everywhere nature seemed less stubborn, more generous, perhaps even benevolent, as the nation grew fabulously prosperous and the individual learned to live affluently. No longer were men required to wear out their bodies and exhaust their minds fighting for the bare essentials of life. Common men, required to labor fewer and fewer hours at jobs that were safer, cleaner, and less demanding, were liberated to enjoy the endless shower of luxuries surpassing the wildest imagination of princes or pontiffs. But generosity was not the only virtuous characteristic of the market, for by openhandedly dispersing the fruits of nature to men of all walks of life, the market took on the airs of an unrepentant social leveler, erasing the sharp line that divided the poor from the middle class and slowly blending the middle class into the rich. The market did its work well, wiping out class distinctions and, to the untrained eye, making appearances deceptive and overt action misleading. Men began to resemble each other as they wore clothes of similar fabric and cut, ate food of equal nutritional value, drove cars of one manufacture, smoked cigarettes of identical tobaccos, and shared the same trains, theaters, newspapers, and hotels, as well as the conveniences and wonders of modern plumbing and electricity. And if all this weren't enough, after a few indiscreet and sometimes gaudy displays of wealth by a Vanderbilt, a Morgan, and other men of their station, the leveling process was further hastened by a social doctrine which condemned garish spending and ostentatious living as a sign of poor taste and the mark of the vulgar *nouveau riche.*

And freedom—how had the market fared on this score? It had promised much, which it gave, and more. No longer did tradition, command, or caste set the bounds or limit the heights of man's existence. With nothing more than a few bits of silver and some scraps of paper, man was now free to wander at home or abroad and to ask and expect friend and stranger alike to furnish to him the finest of food, the best of shelter, works of art, frivolous trinkets or whatever else might please his fancy. In return he felt no obligation to perform a specific service or impair his dignity by tendering profuse thanks; he was only required to relinquish a small fraction of his supply of silver and paper as he went merrily on his way, satisfying his curiosity and sampling here and there the infinite variety opened by his new-found freedom.

However, there is an omission. The morality of a materialistic society is both forged and found in the market place, or, as President Coolidge so aptly phrased it, "The business of America is Business." The market economy provides man with a clear and unmistakable purpose: to excel in the market place, which—when translated into common parlance—means the making and, although to a lesser degree, the spending of money.

Men of the arts and letters professing higher aspirations have always been prone to disparage the materialistic tendencies which seem to have dominated American thinking. Speaking of our failure to appreciate great music, art, and the contemplative life, they have little sympathy for the argument that the market system has the great advantage of providing distinct and unmistakable social purpose. Men who succeeded were rich, men who failed were not; all righteous men were expected to enter the race so all good men would be identified.

One can, of course, speak jestingly of such a measurement and one can argue forcefully that the purpose of life, rather than mere money grubbing, should be the pursuit of some sublime ideal. Perhaps so, but before condemning money-making as a foolish waste unworthy of human veneration, there remains one very important consideration that must somehow be weighed on the scales of humanity.

In some times past, economic activity was largely an individual affair. Each man was expected, as a solitary figure, to enter the market and, by drawing upon whatever talents or resources he could muster, extract whatever his individuality permitted. In a sense the market was one grand arena in which was conducted a deadly serious competitive contest requiring each individual to call upon and express his very last ounce of capacity. A Freudian might say that the human aggressiveness was to the profit of both the individual and society freely dissipated through the furious contest of the market arena. Perhaps the Christian concept of original sin or the capitalistic doctrine of self-interest better captures the nature of these innate tendencies, but whatever language is preferred, the Western view depicts man as an aggressive creature who desperately seeks to vent his unruly aggression through some socially approved cause which makes life meaningful.

Historically men have accomplished this identification largely through group action and by so doing have wreaked untold misery and destruction upon mankind. In the name of Christianity pious crusaders slaughtered and pillaged; in the name of holiness the terrible religious wars pitted Christian against Christian and bathed Europe in a sea of blood; in the name of primitive race purity Hitler preached the savage righteousness of untold horrors and the wisdom of scientific mass murder; in the name of communism the Kremlin proclaims the goodness of evil and declares that the high spirit of justice compels the imperiling of all human existence.

Capitalist theory is different. Disparaging group action as an abomination, it teaches that ultimate value rests in the individual and that no cause or movement, however inspired or idealistic, is superior to him. If the worth and dignity of the individual are to be perfectly exalted, each man must tend to his own affairs and give no thought to being his brother's keeper. He works out the inherent aggressions that drive him by going each day to the market place and pitting his skills against a host of ruthless opponents in one of the most fascinating and demanding of all contests ever devised by any human society. Here he can derive pleasure from being shrewd, from selling high, from buying low, from making a "killing," from piously and aggressively punishing and bringing misfortune to those who incur his wrath; and at the end of an exhausting day he can look back appreciatively on activities which, in addition to benefiting himself, have been blessed by society. Thus, however base, however wicked, or however evil his intents, man's aggressions and will for social approval, rather than the murder and devastation so often wrought by group action, are blended and converted by the workings of the market into a benign, even benevolent force bringing peace and comfort to his fellow man.

In the United States at least, men seemed content to find fulfillment through the exhilarating opportunities for self-expression offered by the profit system. There were, of course, a few bad moments such as the Spanish-American War and the embarrassing Panama incident, but these could hardly be interpreted as part of the grand imperialistic pattern forecast and outlined by a Marx or a Hobson; nor could these brief but graceless outbursts be compared to the shameless European colonialism which had so profoundly altered political geography and kept the map-makers busy during much of the 19th century. Rather than save the world, America wanted only to busy itself with affairs at home. Refusing to identify himself with any of the so-called grand unifying movements, the supreme hope of the American was to escape rather than to change history. Feverishly caught up in the excitement of the market, he was an isolationist by persuasion; only when an alien power forcibly threatened his felicitous society did he pick up arms to defend himself, and then not for the purpose of forcing his beliefs on other peoples in strange and remote lands, but for the purpose of crushing the evil that jeopardized his very existence. One can only guess the extent to which the market—by permitting the individual to vent his aggressions in the daily course of business—was responsible for America's pacific mood, but surely it was not without its influence.

Such, then, is capitalist theory; a magnificent doctrine in virtually every respect. Regrettably, it displays one rather serious deficiency: an ironic irrelevancy for the contemporary world. Inevitably, out of this irrelevancy has emerged a crisis in personal values and search for national purpose.

IV

Cries in the Wind

WHATEVER THE INTELLECTUAL SPLENDOR OF CAPITALIST theory, in the raw world of physical existence the unfeeling market often seemed possessed by some brutal force. Indeed the market's disregard for humanity was dramatically and tragically expressed even in 1790—14 years and five editions after the first publication of *Wealth of Nations,* while Adam Smith, the eternal optimist, lay on his deathbed. As death took Smith, it claimed also the preindustrial world that he had so eloquently systematized. Its replacement, a world he had helped to create, knew neither the optimism nor the felicity which he had predicted. Yet slowly his prescriptions were being adopted. Gradually the economic machine was being turned loose, free to do its work unhampered by mischievous, man-made fetters. Link by link the English Parliament unchained the market. First, it passed the Combination Acts in 1800, which forbade workers from forming associations of any kind; then it tightened the Poor Laws in 1832, and finally in 1846 it repealed the Corn Laws so that England stood foursquare for free trade. And as Smith had predicted, England grew proud and strong and rich. The system worked —mercilessly. It demanded an awful human price with every turn of the screw that imperceptibly but surely pushed England toward economic greatness.

The focus had changed. Now that wealth was to be actively

sought commercial England, unlike the medieval world which preached Christian charity to the poor, was determined to liquidate the begging class. To this end provisions were made for compulsory employment of all who would obtain poor relief. Thus England embarked upon its brief but tragic experiment in industrial slavery. At the same time that beggary was viewed as evil, the declining need for farm labor, the rising enclosure movement, and the "new husbandry" produced a marked increase in pauperism. Parish administrators, in an effort to lighten their financial burdens by finding work for those impoverished and dependent upon poor relief, negotiated with factory owners to assume responsibility for children in groups of 50 to 100.* In return for labor, employers pledged themselves to care for these children.

Robert Heilbroner, in *The Worldly Philosophers* (Simon & Schuster, Inc., 1961), gives insight into the kind of care provided these hapless creatures:

> In 1828, *The Lion,* a radical magazine of the times, published the incredible history of Robert Blincoe, one of eighty pauper-children sent off to a factory at Lowdham. The boys and girls—they were all about ten years old—were whipped day and night, not only for the slightest fault, but to stimulate their flagging industry. And compared with a factory at Litton where Blincoe was subsequently transferred, conditions at Lowdham were rather humane. At Litton the children scrambled with the pigs for the slops in a trough; they were kicked and punched and sexually abused; and their employer, one Ellice Needham, had the chilling habit of pinching

---

* Under the Poor Laws parishes provided "right to live" allowances. To reduce relief payments, parish administrators were anxious to find work for those on their rolls, even though the wage was below the allowance required by law. The difference between the wage paid and the legally established "right to live" allowance was made up by parish relief payments.

the children's ears until his nails met through the flesh. The foreman of the plant was even worse. He hung Blincoe up by his wrists over a machine so that his knees were bent and then he piled heavy weights on his shoulders. The child and his co-workers were almost naked in the cold of winter and (seemingly as a purely gratuitous sadistic flourish) their teeth were filed down!

Although conditions were never so cruel or savage in America—indeed it is hard to believe that such sadistic madness could have prevailed in England—it is nevertheless true that in the first half of the 19th century, the factory work force in the United States was composed of more children than women and more women than men.

Thus economic progress exacted a price, and during the early stages of the industrial revolution, a high one—by present standards, an exorbitant one. Not troubled by conscience and unconcerned by such moral concepts as "cruel," "savage," or "exorbitant," the market remains aloof, altogether insensitive to human costs of economic progress. Cost changes and shifts in market wants it weighs accurately and reflects quickly; but any accompanying social dislocation, be it great or small, it heeds not at all. Should there be perfected a new material or process which brings ruin to old established industries or which displaces large numbers of workers, the market, with ruthless efficiency, compels all would-be solvent men to adopt these cost reducing improvements immediately. About the fate of the ravaged industries or the beggared workers, the market remains blind and unconcerned. Dedicated to increasing efficiency and dispersing the benefits of progress through improved quality and quantity, the market is constitutionally incapable of showing either compassion or charity toward those on whom the heavy burdens of change ultimately fall.

In *The Great Transformation* Polanyi painted in vivid

colors the tragic social upheavals that fell on England as men seriously committed themselves to the frantic "race for profits."

> He writes: 'Enclosures have appropriately been called a revolution of the rich against the poor. The lords and the nobles were upsetting the social order, breaking down ancient law and custom, sometimes by means of violence, often by pressure and intimidation. They were literally robbing the poor of their share in the common, tearing down the houses which, by the hitherto unbreakable force of custom, the poor had long regarded as theirs and their heirs'. The fabric of society was being disrupted; desolated villages and the ruins of human dwellings testified to the fierceness with which the revolution raged, endangering the defenses of the country, wasting its towns, decimating its population, turning its overburdened soil into dust, harassing its people and turning them from decent husbandmen into mobs of beggars and thieves.'

However historians may think Polanyi guilty of embellishing facts and vulgarizing history, there can be no denying that the market is ill equipped to recognize the speed at which a society is capable of assimilating abrupt and profound economic change. Nor can the issue be evaded by arguing that once assimilated, improvements bestow greater prosperity upon all of society, for in truth the economic changes compelled by the uninhibited market may be so traumatic as to undermine the very foundations of the social order.

Rarely, of course, are the social costs of material advances so terrible as those imposed by the enclosure movements. Still, we are never free of them, although, to be sure, they appear in lesser dimensions and ever-changing forms. A dynamic society, a society which places its faith in science and the fruits of technology, if anything, is dedicated to unsettling the *status quo,* to fostering the very economic changes that create social disturbances. Increases in farm productivity, the introduction of diesel locomotives, improved printing techniques, and the importation of inexpensive Swiss watches are all developments which promote efficiency and enhance our standard of living. Had the market been free to respond fully to these developments, the American watch industry would have all but disappeared, thousands of printers and railroad workers would have been out of a job, and the agricultural sector of the economy would have suffered paroxysms of rapid contractions.

At some point, despite our passion for increased efficiency, we quite deliberately fashioned policies designed to frustrate the working of the market. The thought of tariffs or featherbedding or the sight of the embarassingly large stock of farm surpluses may be discomforting, but we have methodically erected barriers with the full intention of averting the market solution and thereby escaping the social costs that would accompany any such resolution of the problems. Thus, as the Tudors and the early Stuarts found it necessary to slow the enclosure movement, and as the British Parliament found it essential to enact the Health and Morals Act in 1802 forbidding children from working more than 12 hours per day, today we deliberately invoke measures which retard the pace of economic development and therefore lessen the strain of social disruptions.

Pure market forces show yet another disturbing tendency to debilitate. In exalting the present, they mortgage the future. Emphasizing efficiency at the expense of all else, the market demands an unremitting commitment to cost cutting. The low-cost producer is rewarded handsomely; the inefficient can expect only bankruptcy. Immediately lower prices may satisfy consumers, but at the same time may penalize posterity and damage future public welfare. For just as our ancestors in the quest for low-cost production "mined" the virgin soil, denuded the land of forests, and exhausted the seemingly unbounded supply of fish and wildlife, so conservation experts tell us that we, in our passion for efficiency, are consuming our soil, drinking, dissipating, or polluting our fresh water, and devouring our already inadequate supply of minerals at an alarming rate.

But market deficiency is not confined to the evaluation of natural resources. Indeed its greatest crime is its failure to evaluate adequately immense untapped human resources. For in the market the individual is worth what he can get, nothing more or nothing less. Thus the man, however great his strength or talents, is only worth what he is paid. That the individual, if given the opportunity, could make a much greater contribution, the market does not recognize. Nor is the market equipped to realize the fact that expenditures for training and education today lay the foundation for enhanced individual satisfaction and national wealth tomorrow. Inherently blind to these advantages and irrevocably geared to eliminate any expenditure not justified by immediate profit calculations, the market stands as a hostile force which, if permitted to operate freely, would strangle rather than encourage the existence of a free educated citizenry so essential to elevating individual dignity and productivity. It is in recognition of this fact that the nation, through political action and in the interest of education, deliberately moves to frustrate the market.

Thus the market, like any good machine, caring neither for history nor posterity, must, in the last analysis, be subordinated to some kind of political authority. As a great force it clearly has a pronounced effect on the society it serves.

Energized only by profit considerations as it is, there can be no doubt that the market is biased. As such it is quite capable of bestowing both personal tragedy and national catastrophe while it at once hastens and retards economic progress in the various sectors of the economy. And to say—as is not uncommon—that all these things are quite natural and consistent with the public good because they are the products of immutable law and the impersonal judgment of the market is to admit to the worst kind of ignorance, callousness, or self-deception.

Of all the policy implications of capitalist theory, none is more at odds with human nature than the one which makes a virtue of economic insecurity. Yet, in the shadowy world of capitalist theory, economic insecurity is assigned the primary role of infusing incentive. Indeed it is the haunting specter of poverty and financial disgrace that is to provide the motive compelling most men to commit themselves to excell economically. Remove this threat and the average man, we are told, becomes satisfied, indolent, decadent. No longer forced to drive himself, he not only loses interest in the market contest, but, having nothing to struggle for, he himself becomes lost. On these grounds unemployment insurance, social security, socialized medicine, and a whole variety of other welfare programs continue to be excoriated.

Some men do not need the frightening prospect of hardship and privation to spur them on. Enraptured by the mere thought of more and more profits, they can be counted on to stay at their post and give the very best they have to offer. But for most men, so the theory goes, this is not enough. Once, it seems, the average man has realized a tolerable standard of living and once he is assured by various welfare programs that the wolf has been forever driven from his door and that his position is secure, he deliberately takes steps to avoid the heartless demands imposed by the market. And this, according to capitalist theory, above all else, cannot be tolerated; for should this dangerously infectious attitude become general—and indeed there are disquieting indications that it has —then men would no longer give their lives to achieving economic excellence, and society would be deprived of the flow of benefits that springs from an unremitting search for economic improvements.

Ideally capitalist man would be endowed with at least a modicum of prescience which would permit him to call the coming turn of events. Unfortunately, clairvoyance is a rather rare trait possessed by few, and therefore the shifting of the market makes for a general state of uneasiness, which at best is discomforting to the individual. This, of course, is all quite proper, for under pure capitalism every man is expected to live with the disconcerting thought that his position, however exalted at the moment, is at best tenuous and insecure.

But even should the producer be favored with talents giving him a certain superiority in the efficiency race, the sweet satisfaction of peace of mind is still beyond his reach. Never confident that the market will continue to value his efforts, he is haunted by the prospects that his customers may desert him. A fickle lot, owing allegiance to no one, if they tire of his wares they will quickly and eagerly shift their patronage elsewhere in search of new and fascinating products.

But if the lot of the entrepreneur must always be distressingly uncertain, the position of the worker in the pure market economy is nothing short of precarious. For the worker can do little, if anything, to shape and control his economic destiny. At best his fate is cast by the success or failure of his employer. Should the latter blunder or be outmaneuvered in the market, he carries down with him all those dependent upon him for income and livelihood. Nor does a brilliant market performance by the employer afford the worker protection against the ravages of unemployment. Valuable to the enterprise only because of his productivity, circumstance, time, and the market conspire against him. He may fall ill, suffer an enfeebling accident, or lose efficiency with age; at any time he may be replaced by a younger, more vigorous man, or he may be dismissed simply because of the perfection of a machine which can perform his task more cheaply or accurately.

The employer is permitted no alternative. Indeed, should he be cursed with a deep humanitarian streak, should he feel a strong sense of responsibility for the welfare of his employees, he nevertheless must dismiss any of those who can be replaced by either man or machine capable of doing the job more economically. Failing this, his cost will rise above that of his heartless competitors and his entire enterprise will be placed in serious jeopardy. Thus, in the world of free markets, the worker, never sure from one day to the next of employment and income, is consigned to live in a state of nagging fear, because the tranquility afforded by economic security remains a luxury that the otherwise sensitive market system is impotent to confer.

There is no shortage of good men to defend the righteousness of this kind of personal economic insecurity. Emphasizing the virtues of adversity, they stress the deadening hand of security; citing prison life as the apex of economic safety, they protest that the individual relaxation accompanying peace of mind is directly contradictory to the development of self-reliance, independence, and the many other personal characteristics so necessary to the preservation of a free society. Retired generals, corporate leaders—especially those who head firms in which the stock ownership is widely dispersed—and men of inherited means seem, more than most men, to appreciate the wondrous advantages that a general state of personal risk confers on society. Coming as they do from various backgrounds and professions, these men have one thing in common: a position on high ground virtually impregnable to the surging tides of the market.

Not all men, of course, are in agreement with the pronouncements of these public spokesmen. Indeed it is the rare individual who, rather than actively courting the hazards of the free market, does not try to escape the rigors of unthrottled competition. Although the safe distance and the ethereal heights of high ground cause the play in the market to take on all the color and exhilaration of an athletic contest, the view is somewhat less romantic for those who are forced to submit to the daily hazards of the market. To the actual participants, the apparently random and therefore senseless risks imposed by the market often appear less challenging than frightening, less demanding than paralyzing, less the instillers of incentive than the killers of hope.

As such, men of all walks of life will go to almost any length to minimize or avoid these deadening insecurities. Business firms buy insurance, keep on hand large amounts of cash or negotiable securities, diversify operations, and develop elaborate means of forecasting, all in the name of minimizing risk. They universally condemn the evils of cutthroat competition and predatory pricing at the same time that they conspire to reduce, or better, eliminate price competition. Where private means are impotent—because the number of organizations is too large or because of the threat of new firms entering the industry—they turn to government demanding that legislation be enacted to mitigate the terrible uncertainty that stalks the market place. Tariffs, fair-trade laws, aid to small business, and government regulations covering the transport, the oil, and the communication industries all illustrate the cooperative efforts by business and government to curb the natural hazards of the competitive market.

As with the businessman, so with the farmer. Complaining that without government supports, farm prices fluctuate so wildly as to make efficient farming impossible and life intolerable, Congress understands the farmer's plea and enters the market to stabilize prices and reduce the risk of farming. Nor is the worker happy with his precarious lot. Helplessly buffeted about by an unreasoning power, the individual worker turns to the trade-union movement in hope of finding some small measure of relief from the poundings of a senseless market. Slowly group action has taken its toll. Gradually, as the market has been shackled, life takes on a whole new meaning.

Sheltered from the merciless perils of the market, men begin to know the personal confidence out of which emerges individual strength and dignity. Complete elimination of economic insecurity for labor—as for small business—is too much to hope for, but day by day new assaults are made on market generated risks. Seniority plans, retirement and sick benefits, unemployment compensation, and restrictions upon the introduction of laborsaving techniques and capital goods have worked to hold back the terrors of loss of job and income.

Thus we see that all men, whatever their status or profession, deliberately contrive to escape the ordeal of economic insecurity. Not that men are unwilling to expose themselves to certain kinds of perils. Indeed they actively seek the excitement and glory that go with courageously facing and conquering danger. Men test themselves in various ways: they go big game hunting; they cross oceans on a mere sliver of a raft; more recently they explore space in contraptions and at speeds which, in addition to being contrary to common sense, defy man's overwhelming instinct for survival. But the danger inherent in these kinds of tests is rather different from that found in the market. For when man pits himself against the elements or when his blood runs hot as he triggers a shot at a charging tiger, he at least knows his enemy and not only can he take steps to protect himself from injury and death, but he can, after a brief and exciting go at it, disqualify himself and return once again to the luxury of secure, civilized existence.

But the market is different. It is wily, it is unpredictable, and above all it is always there. Like a great cloud that is very real, it nevertheless is neither quite tangible nor wholly understandable. However diligently and carefully the individual may plan and strive to erect some kind of shelter as protection against hostile market forces, he is forever plagued by the thought that his solitary efforts can be little more than extraneous. From bitter experience he has learned that the goddess of the market is nothing if not fickle. One day she may favor a pious, simple farmer, the next a rather ill-kept provendor of curios, and on still a third she may have eyes for only the brightest of young engineers.

There is no escape for the solitary individual. The big game hunter, having demonstrated his courage and won his moment of glory, bids farewell to the risks of the jungle and the dangers of primitive living and returns to enjoy the kudos and comforts that his bravery has earned and high civilization can confer. Not so the inhabitant of a truly free market system; for the market in its truest form demands each day that the individual wager his wealth, his station, indeed his very existence on a game of chance, in which the participants are never quite sure of the precise rules, much less the ever shifting probabilities that are relevant at any moment in time. For most, if not all, men, such a perilous existence is not to be endured; the pressures are too unrelenting, the hazards too overwhelming, the adversity too gross. Finding life in the market intolerable, men take action— deliberate action designed with the direct and unmistakable intent of reducing, or better still eliminating, economic insecurity. To accomplish this, men band together and invent or contrive whatever is necessary to stifle the competition and halt the operations of the market forces.

Whatever the advantages of the competitive society, the pall of economic insecurity which inevitably broods over the free market place makes an exclusively price-directed economy unacceptable to virtually every social group. Unwilling to suffer the agonies of economic uncertainty, men turn to private and public means for the purpose of mastering the market and thereby winning for themselves a less anxious, more secure life. In effect, men—be they buyers or sellers— say: "We as a nation must be unwaveringly committed to the progress generated by heightened efficiency and expanding material output. But in our line of endeavor these gains can be harvested only if we as individuals are delivered from the incessant and paralyzing insecurity imposed by a free and senseless market."

While each segment of the economy is pledged to and works for the preservation of the virtues flowing from a general state of competition—tariffs, unions, price fixing, and farm supports are, in principle, all condemned as contrary to the public interest—each of the myriad of interest groups deploys whatever resources it commands in maneuvering to escape the rigors of a capricious, arbitrary price competition. Gradually these calculated efforts to foil the natural workings of the market were to have an impact; slowly the broad powers exercised by the Archangel Competition were circumscribed and then checked until finally the once mighty guardian and protector of the public interest was relegated to the position of a puppet ruler, the chief function of whom was to hold a make-believe court. But if his power was emasculated and his court little more than ceremonial, he nevertheless continued to be the focus of attention as he performed a service of incalculable value. For it was under the aegis of the Archangel Competition that men were to realize the Utopia of "eating and having their cake."

On the one hand, men learned to relish the satisfaction that comes from a moment of rest and the peace of mind that goes with economic security. At the same time, they were permitted to go merrily on their way without the need to face up to the shattering fact that their tampering with the price system had made the whole concept of the automatic self-adjusting market nothing more than a delightfully fraudulent fairy tale. Unfortunately, there were forces at work which one day would lay bare this incredible, if wonderfully useful fiction. One of these forces was an irresistible increase in economic power—an increase which no amount of disguise could long hide from even the most uncritical eye.

V

Corrupting Powers

OUT OF THE 1840's AND 50's EMERGED THE SPIRIT OF reform. Focusing on the slavery issue, it burned brightly and then exhausted itself in a violent struggle which strengthened the forces destined to convert America from a simple to a complex society. Fanned by a favorable tariff policy, a growing urban population, and the exigencies of all-out war, the country experienced a craving for manufactured goods. In such an environment a slowly unfolding industrialism was catapulted forward, carrying with it the factory-machine process, the routinization of tasks, and the aggregation of large amounts of capital. No group, class or section of the country was to escape the social change wrought as America was transformed from an agrarian to an industrial economy, from an intimate to an impersonal society, from a nation of essentially self-sufficient economic units to a country of specialists, each of whom contributed and was subservient to a highly complex, interdependent system of production, finance, and distribution. Through greater efficiency the machine process reduced costs. New and fascinating products were distributed through sprawling, telegraph-coordinated organizations and a rapidly expanding rail net, while national markets were prepared through advertising in the religious journals.

It all began with the railroads. Importing and employing

thousands upon thousands of foreign-born laborers, diligently cultivating and exploiting an expanding supply of capital, these creatures of iron and steam operated on a new and magnificent scale of economic grandeur that brought growth, prosperity, and pride to a young, ambitious nation. Their growth provided an immediate stimulant to quarries, lumber mills, carriage makers, and raw material fabricators, particularly those engaged in production of iron, steel, and coke.

At the same time lower cost and improved transport service made it profitable for manufacturers to turn to mass production techniques, the heart of which is standardization of process and parts. Learning from the pioneering efforts of Eli Whitney in gunmaking, producers of sewing machines, pumps, and clocks distributed devices made from interchangeable parts by workers who were compelled to follow precise standards.

As railroads opened more territory, as producers invaded markets further and further removed from the point of production, as mass production more and more became the *modus operandi* in everything from steelmaking to flour milling, as the small local mill was threatened and then eliminated by the efficiency of the large producer, the fortunes of the relatively independent enterprising Jack-of-all-trades artisan declined. The demand for the interdependent, specialist worker grew apace. The many jobs once performed by the single entrepreneur, such as the village blacksmith, were parceled out among increasing numbers of specialists.

Work was divided between managers and wage earners and every advance in technology and organizational procedure made the wage earner's role more precarious as he was driven to accept positions devoid of opportunity for self-expression and personal advancement. Having no other alternative, he resigned himself to performing endless, repetitive tasks re-

quiring little training and even less skill. No longer the prac-
titioner of a distinct and valuable art sought by many, he
could not proclaim himself as a sovereign identity who answered to no one but God and himself. Indeed, for work and
the wages it paid, he was dependent upon others with whom
his only link was the impersonal market system that at best
was subject to the vagaries of fluctuations, cycles, and panics
and caused him to suffer the combined agonies of impotency
and insecurity.

The farmer was not untouched by surging industrialization. From the factories poured a torrent of labor-saving farm
machines and implements which were to destroy and make
obsolete the simple methods of the frontier. Profits were to
be made from use of the steel plow, the reaper, and the self-
binder. And profits added a new and exciting dimension to
life. The "store-bought" dress, the surrey with the fringe on
top, and "real" factory-made furniture all could be had with
profits earned by growing a staple crop and selling it for cash
in the market. To do this the farmer had to discontinue
growing his own food, making his own homespuns, and
fashioning his own clumsy implements. He had to specialize,
to concentrate his efforts on those crops or livestock favored
by soil, climate, and particularly the market. By so doing, he
gained money and with money he no longer relied on his
own fumbling efforts and the few meager materials readily
available to him.

With the cash he received from his crops, he could call
on the entire world to provide him with whatever struck his
fancy in the mail-order catalogue. In return he had to relinquish only one thing—his economic independence. Once
he was committed to the use of farm machinery and commercial farming, he also became a specialist poorly equipped
to provide himself and his family with elementary necessities
of everyday living.

Thus the farmer, like his urban wage-earning brethren, had to live with the frustrating impotency and the bewildering insecurity brought about by being dependent upon a market system that escaped his control as well as his understanding. Compelled to compete in a seemingly capricious world market and to sell at prices that thwarted his most determined efforts and often drove him to the brink of financial disaster, the once proud, the once independent yeoman of the soil was now regarded as the "hick" and the "hayseed" by those who, because of an upper hand gained through control of supply or contractual agreement, viewed him with amusement and contempt as they manipulated this helpless creature in their scramble for wealth and power.

For those who did the manipulating, it was a glorious age —an age of opportunity and abundance, an age which by its very challenge encouraged man to scale new heights. And much like the elephant who danced among the chickens, the maxim of a Drew, a Gould, and a Vanderbilt became "each for himself." Nor was a Rockefeller or a Morgan anxious to deprive his fellow man of the joy and satisfaction that comes from economic freedom and self-reliance. Their prescription was straightforward and uncomplex: crush the budding trade-unions and discredit the muddleheaded reformers, who, in their utopian impracticality, would take away the pride and confidence that worthy men derived from standing firmly and resolutely on their own two feet and the principles to which they were committed. Perhaps it was true that for some life fell short of perfection, but the good men, the men that mattered, were perfectly capable of managing their own affairs and these men, through virtue, industry, and a firm position, would triumph over any unjust or unwarranted restraints or sanctions imposed by nature.

These rugged individualists were not troubled by the inconsistency of preaching one thing and practicing another.

They were self-reliant; they drove themselves ruthlessly; they were imaginative; they showed a remarkable willingness to assume risk. In short, they did indeed make their own way. In so doing they contributed to the industrialization and growth of the nation by fashioning a delicate balance that provided the stability and security necessary to the operations of large-scale, profit-making organizations. This is not to imply that these contributions were altruistically motivated, for such would be the grossest of perversions. Indeed their greatest contribution was to lump many smaller independent enterprises into single gigantic organizations. Not infrequently the only immediate advantage of these consolidations was the lessening of price competition and the increasing of profits. But this, they felt, in no way negated their creed of individualism. They were simply making their own way; any other man of similar persuasion and ability was equally free to do the same.

Whatever the intentions of Vanderbilt, Rockefeller or Morgan, these men, through the application of their talents and the pursuit of their own interests, created organizations of splendor and might. In so doing they, as much as anyone, unleashed the forces destined to undermine the very morality they aggressively practiced and even more fervently preached. By their very accomplishments they forged a state of extravagant inequality, making a mockery of economic individualism and the principles supporting it.

When the small operator began to die is really not so important. What is significant is that by the 1870's the typical small concern, owned and operated by a single person, a family or a handful of stockholders, was beginning to yield before the pressures of consolidations which had gained so much momentum during the Civil War. The painful depression of 1873 didn't brighten the outlook for the independent operator, and the general prospects of profits won through the introduction of expensive labor-saving machinery further heightened the interest in consolidation. All that was needed, it seemed, were markets to swallow up the torrent of goods that could be cheaply produced by large-scale production.

That these markets existed and were patiently awaiting someone to exploit them had been unmistakably demonstrated by a mild-mannered, pious Sunday school teacher named John D. Rockefeller, who, in his determined effort to integrate the entire oil industry, founded in 1879 the first authentic American "trust." His brilliant success caused admirers to apply his discovery to other industries. In steel it was Andrew Carnegie; in aluminum, Andrew Mellon; in tobacco, James B. Duke; in communications, Green and Vail. The Distillers and Cattle Feeders Trust became the Whiskey Trust; the National Cordage Company, through its virtual monopoly on the supply of manila hemp, firmly controlled the production of ropes and twines. Through intercompany cooperation, a Sugar Trust operated; the forming of the Diamond Match Company brought under common ownership virtually all the factories and mills on which this industry depended. And as a finale for one century and an opening for another, J. Pierpont Morgan welded together three-fifths of the entire nation's steel capacity into one vast economic unit. This new giant, the greatest concentration of economic power the world had ever seen, was appropriately called the United States Steel Corporation.

The justification for all of this was direct and forthright: it promoted efficiency; it furthered progress. Who could doubt the superiority of large-scale production! What more eloquent testimony could be found than the fantastically brilliant achievements of Henry Ford. Not only did this self-willed genius employ the principles of large-scale production to reduce the price of his cars from $950.00 in 1910 to $240.00 in 1924, but in so doing he offended most of the business world by announcing an increase in wages from $2.40 to $5.00 a day on the condition that his employees did not waste the additional income.

If few possessed the ingenuity or the pioneering spirit of a Rockefeller, a Morgan, or a Ford, common men nevertheless learned enough from the masters to hurry the nation ever forward on the path of economic concentration and power so that by 1932 Adolph A. Berle, Jr. and Gardner Means, in their celebrated and ground-breaking study, *The Modern Corporation and Private Property* (The Macmillan Company), ominously stated: "By 1899 the census reported 66.7 per cent of all manufactured products as made by corporations, and corporate increase in the 20th century has been most rapid; 87 per cent of goods were so produced by 1919 and it is fair to assume that over 94 per cent of manufacturing is carried on by corporations at the present time. Wage earners in the employ of manufacturing corporations have increased correspondingly from 65 per cent of those engaged in 1899 to 92 per cent (estimated) in 1929."

Within this sphere of power was a hard core of industrial might composed of between two and three hundred gigantic corporations which Berle and Means estimated controlled half of all corporate wealth and 22 per cent of the total wealth of the nation. In 1955, *Fortune* Magazine reported: ". . . almost exactly half of the U.S. output . . . is produced by about 500 corporations. Those 500 firms, all but two with net sales of $50 million or more, comprise less than two-tenths of 1 per cent of the 360,000 manufacturing (and mining) companies in the U.S. Yet they produce approximately one-quarter of the free world's total output of industrial goods." Commenting on the immense power of these giants, Berle, in a study for The Fund for the Republic on *Economic Power and the Free Society,* declared: ". . . not only do 500 corporations control two-thirds of the non-farm economy but within each of that 500 a still smaller group has the ultimate decision-making power. This is, I think, the highest concentration of economic power in recorded history. Since the United States carries on not quite half of the manufacturing production of the entire world today, these 500 groupings—each with its own little dominating pyramid within it—represents a concentration of power over economics which makes the medieval feudal system look like a Sunday School party."

In 1960, the Congressional Joint Economic Committee ranked both government and business organizations according to their economic power. Here are the ten leaders:

Business organization or political unit	Revenues Amount (millions)	Rank	Employees Number	Rank	Assets Amount (millions)	Rank
Federal Government ..	$69,117	1	2,405,000	1	$262,056	1
General Motors Corp. .	9,522	2	521,000	3	6,891	29
Standard Oil Co. (New Jersey)	7,544	3	154,000	8	9,479	15
American Telephone & Telegraph Co.	6,771	4	592,130	2	19,494	7
Great Atlantic & Pacific Tea Co.	5,095	5	145,000	9	647	164
Ford Motor Co.	4,130	6	142,076	10	2,962	60
General Electric Co. ...	4,121	7	249,718	5	2,398	72
Sears, Roebuck & Co. ...	3,721	8	205,609	7	2,036	84
United States Steel Corp.	3,439	9	223,490	6	4,437	39
State of California	2,965	10	114,675	13	24,308	5

Not that this concentration of power has gone unobserved or unopposed. Indeed the battle cry of Jeffersonian liberals had always been "down with the privileged." Nor were the many movements which were to march under Jeffersonian principles without influence. In 1887 the railroads were subjected to federal regulation and slowly brought to heel by the Interstate Commerce Commission, and in 1890 the Sherman Anti-Trust Act provided that combinations in restraint of trade were illegal.

Still reformers remained unsatisfied. Catching the spirit of the celebrated 1892 Omaha platform, Tom Watson declared the primary enemy of the Populist party to be "monopoly—not monopoly in the narrow sense of the word—but monopoly of power, of place, of privilege, of wealth, of progress." We must, he said, "keep the avenues of honor free," and to those who would advance themselves, America should call out, "The field is clear, the contest fair; come and win your share, if you can."

Along these same lines, the great Nebraska orator and reformer, William Jennings Bryan, as the Presidential candidate of both the Democrats and the Populists, spearheaded the most valiant and powerful assault that the farmers were ever to mount against a strengthening industrial system. Railing against the trusts and emphasizing his concern for loss of opportunity in America, he told an Iowa crowd, "I want it so that . . . [should a young man decide to enter politics] he will not find arrayed against him all the great financial influences of society unless he is willing to join them and conspire against the welfare of the people as a whole. If he enters business, I want him to be able to stand upon his own merits and not stand always in the fear that some great trust will run him out of business."

But if in 1896 the farmer's final effort in his battle against industrial concentration was inadequate, business was assailed from another quarter as the gifted reporter, Lincoln Steffens, began a series of articles that were to make muckraking fashionable. Following the pattern set by Steffens in *McClure's,* it was not long before virtually every mass circulation magazine turned a critical eye to the commercialization and corruption of capitalistic America. From the White House Theodore Roosevelt lashed out at the "malefactors of great wealth," threatening business with aggressive anti-trust action unless it took prompt and radical steps to change its ways. Finally the whole tone of Woodrow Wilson's New Freedom was hostile to industrial concentration. Repeatedly the President committed himself to "the application of Jefferson's principles to the present-day America" and "to the restoration of free competition."

The industrial tide was running too strong; however heroic the efforts of reformers, industrial concentration was not to be appreciably slowed. By 1900, the conditions which had been the wellspring of individualism had virtually disappeared. Industrialism and a spiraling population had changed the face of America. As World War I came to a close, America's population passed the 100,000,000 mark, almost half of which was crowded into urban centers. The number of people gainfully employed in agriculture declined steadily. Industrial and commercial employees outnumbered agricultural workers as manufacturing alone accounted for almost 10,000,000 wage earners, 8,000,000 of whom were employed by corporations.

Accompanying these changes in population and composition of the labor force was a growing sense of economic uncertainty. In an earlier age, honest and industrious pursuit of a profession guaranteed a stable, comfortable, and secure life. Now this was passed as millions of men, eager to earn and pay their own way, lived in the shadow of insecurity cast by the frightening prospect of unemployment. The workers, seeing themselves bought and sold like any other commodity, could never be sure of what was in store for them. Haunted by anxiety and insecurity that eroded away self-respect and impaired personal dignity, they became hostile to a corporation that could dismiss them whenever it felt like it. Their work became drudgery and their jobs lost their meaning as they restlessly searched for something that would provide them with a sense of achievement and security.

America had come a long way from the Jacksonian days of cheap and abundant land, chronic labor shortages, and small entrepreneurs. In one hundred years there had been a drastic shift in focus. The frontier was closed, more than 30,000,000 immigrants had come to American shores, and many a small business firm had been outstripped or absorbed by a Standard Oil Company or U.S. Steel Corporation. On the frontier men were essentially equal because they knew similar hardships and opportunity. They were economically free because theirs was the power to make their own way. Economic power, the antithesis of economic individualism, could not exist simply because of the abundance of raw materials and outlets which, by and large, enabled the common man to set up his own operations, be his own boss. But then a new dynamic, irresistible force appeared on the scene— industrialization. Born of the mind, it grew silently, spreading, taking shape, gaining momentum and gradually rolling over an entire continent, transforming, destroying and finally replacing the glorious age by which it was conceived and fostered with a radiant burst of magnificence and splendor.

Just how far America had come was dramatically illustrated by the famous lawsuit between Henry Ford and the Dodge brothers in 1919. The Dodges complained that Henry Ford deliberately followed policies that held prices and profits down. During the case Ford confessed that he did "not believe that we should make such an awful profit on our cars." In justifying his policy he pointed out that "it enables a large number of people to buy and enjoy the use of a car and . . . it gives a large number of men employment at good wages." To be sure, Ford admitted his interest in profits, for without them, he observed, "I would not be counted a success." But profits, he proclaimed, were not the ultimate goal, they were incidental to another end, which as Ford saw it was "to expand operations and improve the article, and make more parts ourselves, and reduce the price."

That the Court ruled against him meant little to this intransigent Puritan. For his convictions he would have submitted to being drawn and quartered. Nor is the outcome of the trial of more than historical interest to us. The case is not significant for what it concluded, but for what it highlighted—the immense power exercised by corporate leaders. Ford admitted that he was essentially free to pursue any one of a number of policies. Had he been so inclined, he could have raised prices, paid lower wages, reduced the number of workers he employed, and sold fewer cars. Fortunately, he did not choose to do so. Guided by a strong sense of moral responsibility, he worked for lower prices, a car for every man and a large number of workers.

Today, no doubt, the judge would rule for Ford. But this misses the mark, for if business organizations are not conducted for the purpose of earning profits, then what is their objective? In theory at least, as long as economic units were motivated by profit making, responsibilities were defined, objectives clear, and policies subject to evaluation. As long as they remained profit-maximizing institutions, they geared their methods to the rewards that come with pleasing the consuming public. But if corporations are not simply profit-creating instruments, what then is their purpose? To whom are they responsible? How are they to be judged? Indeed, are they to be judged at all? Or is the corporate leader a modern version of the feudal king generally dispensing justice according to the virtues and prejudices of his conscience, at once legitimatizing and condemning, enhancing and impov-

erishing, rewarding and punishing? Have indeed the great
corporate leaders attained such undisputed power and supreme eminence that the common man, like his ancestors
of the Middle Ages, can, as Adolph Berle in *The 20th
Century Capitalist Revolution* seems to imply, only cry
"Haro" while placing his trust and fate in the wisdom and
morality of "the King's Court"?

No one thought to ask these questions—at least not in
1919. America was committed to material progress; and bigness, as Henry Ford had irrefutably impressed on the common mind, was, if not the mother of this progress, then the
symbol. Whatever doubts or resentment the public may have
felt toward business in 1914, all was forgiven as postwar
America frantically tried to return to what President Harding called "normalcy." No longer was it in good taste to ex-
coriate business, and especially big business. Citizens clam-
ored to make Henry Ford—despite his tyranny and widely
discussed eccentricities—President of the United States; and
Bruce Barton, in his best seller, *The Man Nobody Knows,*
once and for all fused Christianity and Capitalism by making Jesus "the founder of modern business." Jesus, he wrote,
was the greatest of all executives. "He picked up twelve men
from the bottom ranks of business and forged them into an
organization that conquered the world . . . Nowhere is
there such a startling example of executive success as the
way in which that organization was brought together." His
parables were "the most powerful advertisements of all time"
and most certainly "He would be a national advertiser
today."

In this setting and under the sponsorship of a beneficent
White House and a benevolent prosperity, business more
than ever was elevated to the status of a national religion.

Despite a disastrous drop in farm prices and despite the flagrant "public-be-damned" attitude exhibited in the Teapot Dome scandal, the triumph of large-scale enterprise was all but complete. Under a cautious and *status quo*-minded Coolidge, a U.S. government publication referred to democracy as "a government of the masses," resulting in "demagogism, license, agitation, discontent, and anarchy." On Capitol Hill the reconquest of the American mind by orthodoxy gave the conservatives victory over the reformers, bringing additional pro-corporation legislation and causing Wilson's New Freedom laws to be suddenly seen as anti-union weapons, instruments for the preservation of pure Americanism as well as guardians of the prerogatives of free enterprise and the vast organizations that exercised them.

Underlying all this was the profound national belief that American capitalism—under the hands-off, prosperity-generating policies of a Coolidge and the delicate balance between great efficiencies and economic individualism sought by a Hoover—was moving toward its natural fulfillment. The "Hoover bull market," as it was sometimes called, well illustrated both the prevalence and the naïveté of this belief, as experts as well as the public at large were soon to pay dearly for their foolish, unbounded faith in the infallibility of business. But the high and rising stock market seemed to intimidate no one and least of all those who studied and purported to understand such things.

In *New Levels in the Stock Market,* Professor Dice of Ohio State University reassured the public by telling of "the mighty revolution in industry, in trade, and in finance." The stock market, he explained, was merely "registering the tremendous changes that were in progress." Hardly a day passed when some eminent figure was not quoted on the immediate health and the prospective vigor of the American economy. More than a month after the market had reached its Septem-

ber 3, 1929 peak, Irving Fisher, a brilliant theoretical economist, spoke of a " 'lunatic fringe'—madmen who lacked the
intellectual capacity to appreciate the basic soundness of the
economy"—proclaiming that the nation was moving along
"a permanent high plateau" which in a few months could
make stock prices "a good deal higher than today." On the
very eve of the great historic break in the market, Charles E.
Mitchell, Chairman of New York's staid National City Bank,
reaffirmed his earlier optimism when he reassuringly announced, "The industrial situation of the United States is
absolutely sound and our credit situation is in no way critical. . . ."

Dice, Fisher, and Mitchell, as well as thousands of other
good Americans, had placed their trust in theory that was
not applicable to the world in which they lived. For pure
capitalism, as a cohesive and meaningful body of thought, is
relevant only to the world of small autonomous units composed of free farmers, independent craftsmen, and single
entrepreneurs; of a world composed of giant business organizations, militant labor unions, and big and powerful governments, it can say nothing. In the capitalist world there is true
equality of opportunity, no one firm is large enough to have
any influence whatsoever in determining the price of its products, and the individual, rather than being a cog in a great
impersonal machine, is free and independent to steer his own
course and follow whatever endeavor suits his fancy.

But by the time the "Big Bull market" was born, this world
of small units had long since been laid to rest. To deny this,
one had to be overcome by the euphoria of the times or be
guilty of the worst kind of self-deception. And to gainsay that
U.S. Steel, or Ford Motor Company, or any one of more than
a hundred other large firms could sit down and calculate
what prices were to be charged, or to refuse to admit that
in the 20th century all men were not given the same oppor-

tunity to become presidents of large corporations, or attend college, or develop the innate talents and interests given to them by nature, was a frank admission that a make-believe world of opportunity and perfect balance was to be preferred to the one that ordinary men had constructed.

Most men, however, had in one way or another taken steps to make sure that such an imaginary fairy land could not exist. Their impairment of the natural workings of the market took many forms. Workers and businesses—the latter with early success—had used every instrument available to stabilize prices and therefore reduce personal insecurity. The government had frequently been called upon by men of all walks of life to curb predatory, if natural, practices, to take action to protect the nation's natural resources from being plundered and to guard the health and welfare of the nation's populace through provisions for education and better working conditions.

All of these acts imposed artificial barriers, all of these tamperings with the forces of the free market were signal fires indicating the existence of significant and growing centers of political and economic power. And power, whatever its source or dimension, is, by the inner logic of capitalist theory, inherently satanic; for power is a man-made evil which stands as an obstacle thwarting the flawless perfection promised by the free market system.

Under the doctrine of capitalism, each man is exhorted to employ whatever resources he commands for his own purpose and without regard for his neighbor. "To each his own" runs the maxim, and "May the devil take the hindmost." In a world of classical theory where no man is more powerful than any other, such an admonition can produce little harm and very much good. But in a world of growing organizations, where men are distinctly unequal in power and position, a code of behavior built on pure selfishness can bring fearful results. Once the contest is no longer equal, an admonition to maximize personal gain is nothing better than an exhortation encouraging the strong to prey on the weak, a justification for the powerful to shape and use society for the furtherance of their own interests.

In a world of great organizations, competitors can no longer easily move from one activity to another depending upon profit prospects. Business now requires huge sums of capital, expert technicians in production, finance, management, and advertising, and the small independent entrepreneur—whom capitalistic theory eulogizes and relies upon for developing the competition that will preclude the formation of power centers—has no chance whatsoever to challenge the mighty giants who draw their power from many products and far-flung markets. Without truly free competition—small entrepreneurs moving into the markets in which price is above costs—pure capitalist theory collapses.

For it is competition that ultimately transforms individual selfishness into social benefit. Destroy or emasculate competition or, to put it conversely, give some men power over others and the whole theory not only becomes extraneous, but fraudulent, if it is used to rationalize a society controlled by a limited number of power centers. Once the restraint of competition is gone, one cannot be certain of much of anything. No longer is there certainty that prices will be fair, or that a good man will find plenty of opportunities to give his best for a fair day's pay. Indeed if power exists, there is, so capitalist theory tells us, only one thing of which we can be fairly certain: that man will exercise his authority to take advantage of his fellow man by blocking the automatic workings of the free market forces. For if the seller—be he worker or vendor of goods—has power, he will most surely use it to improve his lot. If permitted, he will destroy worker mobility and fix prices which forces employment rather than price to be cut, thus bringing about unemployment and the threat of depression.

Yet despite all these imperfections, despite the fact that industrial power and government intervention harassed and diverted the course of the market, and despite the fact that men could no longer endure the personal insecurity compelled by an exclusively price-directed economy, it was not considered in good taste to dwell on these matters. Indeed such talk carried the ring of sedition; for the good American knew that if he worked hard, did a good job, and otherwise behaved himself, he would be rewarded with good fortune. All this was true because of the vigor and brilliance of American business and because of the wondrous, self-correcting markets which—by encouraging each of the millions of diverse and separate American personalities to set and follow his own course—automatically brought forth in the form of a social whole the best of all possible worlds. The millennium had arrived; man could find intellectual comfort and purpose in action by knowing that his destiny, written in the stars and controlled by benevolent nature, would be cloaked in glory as long as he himself did not prevent the forces of good from being triumphant in the free market.

In the fall of 1929, this imaginary world with its fairy tale orthodoxy toppled in one tragic crash. Everywhere men were lost, everywhere old standards fell and were smashed as disaster visited indiscriminately the energetic along with the feckless; the able with the incompetent; the virtuous with the irresponsible, and as without rhyme or reason, catastrophe was piled one upon another. Slowly and through bitter experience America was to lose faith in the world of Horatio Alger.

VI

Certainty Lost

NOT EVERYONE WAS TAKEN WITH ADAM SMITH'S NATURAL law of perfect liberties. In the United States Alexander Hamilton and his fellow Federalists spoke of "the rich, the wise, and the good," while Paris, the birthplace of the Enlightenment, became its grave as tolerance and the will to freedom became more crime than virtue under Robespierre. In England Edmund Burke and his *Reflections on the Revolution in France* won the day over Thomas Paine and the *Rights of Man* while Malthus and Ricardo—Carlyle's professors of the Dismal Science—had some hard second thoughts about the speed and inevitability of natural law in delivering men of common clay from a life of poverty and ignorance.

But the really devastating assaults on Smith's world of perfect liberty had to await the work of Karl Marx, a German Jew exiled in England, and Friedrich Engels, an apostate bourgeois, whose joint work the *Communist Manifesto,* appeared in 1848. Both products and admirers of the Enlightenment, they eulogized the enormous contributions of capitalism, only to proclaim that any future system which had as its cornerstone "perfect liberties" was incapable of furthering the peace, happiness, and liberty the Enlightenment could and should give to all mankind. As they saw it, the doctrine of "perfect liberties" might have been all right in its

94

day, but its day was over. And if things were to be set right —if the Enlightenment was to be put back on the track— a revolution was necessary. Out of the revolution would eventually evolve the classless society which, bearing a marked resemblance to Christianity's heaven, was to be realized here on earth.

These defections from the mainstream of thought were not without their impact. In England reformers had some success in forcing through social legislation, and in the United States the Grangers, the Greenbackers, the Single Taxers and the trade unionists, not entirely pleased with the tack "progress" had taken, called for major amendments to the social order. It is therefore not surprising that the 19th-century liberal, endowed with a reverence for the natural law of the social universe that far exceeded Adam Smith's, welcomed the unexpected support of a brilliant essay published in 1859 by Charles Darwin.

By drawing from a welter of facts, detailed studies, and ideas set forth by other paleontologists and geologists, Darwin, in his *Origin of the Species*, propounded an organic theory of nature not the least advantage of which was that it could be communicated to and understood by the man of average mind and education. As generally interpreted, Darwin's contribution proved that all living things, in their struggle to survive, were irrevocably committed to compete for the food and space necessary to existence. The product of this unending struggle was the imperceptible change from one generation to another which, over the span of eons, significantly altered the characteristics of the species. Thus in nature the hardy and the adaptable grew strong and flourished, while the unfit inexorably were pushed closer and closer to the margin separating life from death, until these weaklings perished and eventually became extinct. Through this natural selection process, then, the species forever continued to evolve characteristics which proved efficacious in the struggle for life.

Competition, always the touchstone of classical economics, now more than ever was given the force and status of immutable law. With the extension of evolution to the society of man, Spencer and Sumner made "struggle for existence" and "survival of the fittest" watchwords of the natural order. The implication of these words was clear. Nature demanded and provided an arena for competition. It rewarded excellence and punished mediocrity. Inherent within the divine order created by God was an automatic mechanism that guaranteed improvement and relentlessly pushed life, including the human race, toward some remote and unknowable Utopia. Unhampered by the clumsy contrivances of the social reformer, the progress promised by the Enlightenment was a certainty. State assistance of almost any kind was contrary to nature and the ultimate realization of the good life. Aid to the poor—the unfit—was the most heinous of all crimes.

Spencer, the founder and the most ardent exponent of Social Darwinism, although opposing tariffs and publicly-operated postal systems, was most effective in his enthusiastic condemnation of poor laws, public education, and government regulation of housing, working conditions and medical practices. In the eyes of God and nature, he declared, all men are equal. "If they are sufficiently complete to live, they do live, and it is well they should live. If they are not sufficiently complete to live, they die, and it is best that they should die. The whole effort of nature is to get rid of such, to clear the world of them, and make room for better."

To the world England gave Spencer; to Western civilization Spencer gave Social Darwinism; and to Spencer the United States abandoned its head and heart. The Age of Laissez Faire became an age of Social Darwinism; and the United States became the living validation of the theory of evolution. Unfettered by the customs, traditions, beliefs of the Old World, the competitive struggle provided the United States with a vitality and exuberance that brought startling growth, striking economic change, and a more prosperous and satisfying life for its citizens.

But economic change and abundance were not the only reasons for Spencer's American tour de force. It was as though Social Darwinism had been divinely tailored to fit the moral and religious philosophies of late 19th-century America. The religious fundamentalist, although somewhat uneasy over the orthogenic theory of creation, read into survival of the fittest and struggle for existence God's final vindication of both his faith and way of life. The survival of the fittest was simply a confirmation of predestination and the divine will of the Almighty, and the struggle for existence was simply a secular, and therefore imperfect, explanation of Calvin's holy doctrine of the Elect. Now the Calvinist was joined by the Social Darwinist; both viewed hard work and frugality as a mark of "grace"; in their hearts neither could find forgiveness for indolence or wastefulness. Life was a serious and demanding matter and those so foolish as to take it lightly deserved that which fate most surely held in store for them.

There were other forces at work propitious to the spread of Social Darwinism. Natural law, of course, guaranteed harmony and progress when the market operated under conditions of perfect liberty. Had it not been revealed to the oracles of the social universe—the classical economists—that nature's mechanics, unimpeded by the debilitating laws of man, would automatically produce this ideal state of equilibrium? Still, man must be on the alert for certain predatory elements. The prophet himself, Adam Smith, had cautioned against man's propensity to combine and conspire, and had, with certain exceptions, condemned the joint stock company as the enemy of society. Could it be that the powerful militant empires fashioned by a Gould, a Rockefeller, or a Morgan were antithetical to perfect liberty and guilty of frustrating the workings of nature? Surely not, for if so, how in the land of unswerving dedication to free enterprise could this be explained? And what of the automatism of nature which guaranteed progress and furthered the equality of men? If man is to be responsible for limiting the power of these empires, what action would he take? Where would he find the certainty of natural law? If neither religion nor nature offered universality or certitude, then where could man turn? These were the disturbing questions implicit in the swelling cries of the reformers.

Fortunately, these questions did not have to be faced, and if they did, Spencer supplied answers. His was a general theory of which classical economics was a special case. To be sure, the classical economists were correct in insisting that the market must be free from the tamperings advocated by malcontent reformers and the addleheaded do-gooders. Freedom was essential if the competitive struggle decreed by nature was to proceed as prescribed by the Almighty.

Still, the classical system suffered one fundamental flaw: it depicted the invisible hand as an equalizing force, which it was not. If man's uninterrupted march toward perfection was to proceed on schedule, the natural selection processes, working through the competitive market, instead of equalizing, must uplift the brilliant, the strong, and the superior. At the same time it must enfeeble and destroy the crippled, the unfit, the mentally and physically impoverished. Only then, through the normal course of social evolution, would the strong will get stronger and the weak, weaker; only then could the American nation and eventually all of Western civilization draw pride and comfort from the knowledge that it was being driven by the unexhaustible wheel of progress along the course of human splendor and magnificence. Action against the best interests of those who have amassed wealth and world power would therefore be the very height of folly, a crime against nature, and a sin against God.

In the struggle for existence these men had demonstrated superiority. They had proved their intellect, foresight, strength, discipline, tenacity, courage, industry, nerve. They were the elite, the guarantee, transmitted through their offspring, that tomorrow's promise would be realized. These men and the glorious edifices they had constructed—their powerful, splendid empires—richly deserved, rather than the abuse and invective showered on them by the malevolent or the well-meaning, the honor, prestige, and status that society had conferred upon them through wealth and position.

Once again the mechanics of nature had been vindicated. Man served society best by promoting the welfare of himself and his family. All other problems would in the fullness of time be ideally resolved by nature's machine. This splendid doctrine was universal; it made right unmistakable; caused certainty to prevail and faith to remain intact. The fact that Spencer's theory was one big empty tautology wherein wealth and power were used to illustrate the principle of survival of the fittest, which in turn was used to justify wealth and power, seemed to worry no one except a few dissident intellectuals and social reformers.

As the 19th century closed and the first decade of the 20th unfolded, Social Darwinism stood impregnable.

But then a note of discord was heard. Interpreting Nietzsche to serve their own purpose, the German militarists beat the drums of war to the lyrics of the superrace. War, they cried, was simply another manifestation of the struggle for existence and might was right in determining the survival of the fittest. War was the ultimate and most perfect expression of the competitive struggle. Worshiping violence and seeing themselves as a race of supermen destined to rule the world, they proclaimed that war was sanctioned by biological laws—the only mundane power capable of rendering a just decision. Warfare, they insisted, was a moral obligation of the vital, civilized race which in triumph would hasten the march of mankind toward the promised land.

Even the most devout followers of the faith were dismayed by these teachings. Surely this could not be the logical conclusion of Social Darwinism! But the damage was irreparable; American piety would never recover. Evolution talk was no longer popular or in good taste, and by the end of World War I it had disappeared as a conscious philosophy. Yet the idea was not to be dismissed so easily. Hanging on, if only in the subconscious, it played a vital role in producing a mentality which was to bring about the brief return to the gold standard, the abortive free-trade effort, the prevailing antilabor sentiment, and the trial and conviction of Sacco and Vanzetti for heresy rather than for the crime of which they had been accused. To those who in their hearts looked secretly back to the happier, more secure days of pre-World War I, America took on the symptoms of a society tortured by an eroding, all-pervasive, but indescribable force which was the source of the irreverence and immorality of "flaming youth" and the "roaring twenties."

Descending the church steps and contemplating the parson's vivid and frightening description of hell, more than one man must have been struck by the thought that such a place did exist and that his once orderly, once secure, once beloved society, in madness and impiety, was now racing headlong toward it. And he would not have been wholly wrong, for on October 24, 1929, amid the confusion of spent ticker tapes, the frantic shout of sell orders, and wildly plunging stock prices, certitude quietly and humbly made its way to an unobserved corner of the New York Stock Exchange where it peaceably but unmistakably died. By doing so on this "Black Thursday" in 1929, it was to make a mockery of everything certain men had believed and worked for. Finding life without faith unbearable, they tragically thought of hurling themselves from the great architectural monuments their faith had helped to create. These men may have been the more perceptive or simply the more confused. At any rate, before another score of years had passed, the American public and the world at large would come to know that secular certitude was forever dead.

Nothing seemed sacred. What was not swept away in the traumatic Hundred Days of the Roosevelt administration was subject to the unremitting erosion of domestic and international crisis. First there was the Depression, which, because it could not happen, could not be understood. Then World War II, and then victory, which thrust upon the United States a position of world leadership and responsibility it was ill-prepared to assume mentally, but which it could not reject militarily. To the faithful it seemed that the forces of evil had triumphed over the forces of good. In this short period of three decades signs of moral deterioration seemed to crop up everywhere. The nation had committed itself to poor relief, an army of unemployed had marched on Washington, the TVA was born and prospered, anti-trust legislation was briefly enforced, the national debt knew no bounds, the labor movement grew in strength and militancy, Social Security became a part of the American way, and the enforced wartime expansion of government was permanently frozen into the social structure. No longer was America willing, or for

that matter able, to await the good life that was to be ground
out by the immutable and ameliorating laws of nature. Nature was too slow, too uncertain, and except for the remaining secular fundamentalists, America embraced the concept
of the welfare state and in so doing dealt another fatal blow
to secular absolutism. To understand some of the forces
which brought this about, we must pick up certain threads
that in our haste we have overlooked.

Since the Renaissance, scientific inquiry had demonstrated
a disconcerting flair for disrupting the *status quo*. Researches
conducted during the first half of the 20th century proved
no exception to this rule. Among the many contributors to
the diverse, specialized and—to the layman—somewhat mysterious fields of science were Pavlov, Freud, and Einstein.
Pavlov and Freud were essentially psychologists; Einstein's
greatest accomplishment came in the area of physics. But our
interest here centers not on their professional contributions,
profound as they are, but on the impact of their research on
American thought. To the educated public Pavlov was famous for his dogs, Freud for his emphasis on the sexual drive
and Einstein for a new dimension—time. Each of these men
—quite unintentionally, no doubt—made scientific discoveries which slowly and indirectly would undermine the very
foundations of the Enlightenment.

The doctrine of the Enlightenment rested on nature and
reason. Man, it was assumed, is a creature of reason, the application of which, through the discovery of natural law,
would bring progress and a better life. It was an optimistic
faith. But suppose for a moment that it could be demonstrated that man was not essentially rational? What then?
Is man still perfectible or is this optimistic outlook misplaced?

Pavlov, an obscure Russian scientist, in his study of animal responses uncovered behavior patterns exposing some loose and untidy ends which had not been accounted for in the perfectibility-of-man thesis. The experiments, in which Pavlov conditioned his dogs to respond in a most "irrational" manner, have by now been assimilated into what we think of as the common body of knowledge.

Although not immediately apparent, inherent in Pavlov's findings was the genesis of thought that eventually was to undermine the very foundation of the Enlightenment. For as any sophomore student of psychology must know full well, what was true for Pavlov's dogs is also true, although to be sure in different form, for man. Conditioned reflexes induce, without resort to any rational process, automatic responses. Man, then, may be as much a creature of habit as he is of reason, if not more so. Nor are reflexes uniform. Men coming from different environments and living under different social systems are likely to show a disparity of responses to the same stimuli with the result that habit-determining behavior may vary from culture to culture and from place to place. If this is true, what then of reason and natural law?

But if Pavlov's work struck a blow, it was not a fatal one. His work was simply interpreted to mean that "reason's" task of remaking the world would be somewhat more difficult than originally anticipated. The 18th-century philosophers had perhaps been slightly intoxicated by their heady optimism, but there could be no doubt that their conclusions were correct. Perfectibility was still possible. Perhaps Hobbes's world, where by reason everyone would come to an agreement, now seemed somewhat more remote; but one could be confident that reason would rise to the occasion.

If the researches of Pavlov were to cause some uneasiness, the theories of Freud were to prove absolutely devastating. Most of the complex and esoteric work of this genius, which even today is the subject of controversy, need not concern us here. His description of man, however, does; for man, according to Freud, is governed by three masters: appetite, reason, and morality, or, in Freudian terminology, the id, the ego, and the superego. The id is an altogether unconscious, unreasoning, selfish force which, while providing the energy necessary to life, generates impulses directed toward the avoidance of pain and the immediate gratification of self. The superego, also unreasoning, is the seat of moral restraint and responsibility commanding the individual to act in a fashion that will bring social approval. Pangs of conscience are the price to be paid for ignoring the superego. Conflict between the id and the superego is one of the facts of life. A student, for example, wanting the respect and acclaim that go with academic prowess, is told by one impulse to cheat, by another that it is dishonest.

Riding herd on both these discordant forces is the ego. Responsible for conscious thought—reason—and perception of the real world of sound, smell, time, and physical dimensions, the ego is a link between the individual and reality. Obviously not all the impulses originating in the id and superego can be gratified. Some are in direct conflict; others must be ignored or repressed by the ego if the individual is to survive and adjust to reality. For example, no matter how strong the impulse, the ego must not permit the individual to jump from the top of a high building, just as it must not allow the gratification of the urge to commit homicide, if for no other reason than because of the punishment society will impose on the individual.

Freud's man, governed by three masters, bears little resemblance to the Enlightenment's "man of reason." True, reason plays a part in life, but man's basic wants and drives are unconscious and unreasoned. He is autistic, he distorts reality to serve his inner needs and then proceeds on the basis of this twisted view of reality to order his life. He is compulsive. He smokes although reason tells him it is harmful. He eats although he knows he has had enough. He buy things he neither wants nor needs with money he does not have. He is a slave to alcohol although he knows that drunkenness is destroying him. He desperately strives to achieve objectives which, once attained, turn to ashes. He seeks to dominate and be dominated. Fearing conscience and social punishment, he represses powerful and urgent wants, fears, and conflicts, only to have these latent impulses expressed in the form of resentment, tensions, ulcers, fatigue, skin rash, fantasies, gestures, blushing, dreams, or driving ambition. Sublimating his "wretched" and "depraved" impulses, he finds emotional outlets by displacing them with activities which bring him recognition and approbation. And all the time he uses ratiocination for rationalizing—makes up reasons for—his belief and conduct which, though he may consciously and earnestly will it otherwise, is designed to deceive himself and others.

Such are the attributes of Freudian man. Bearing the seeds of his own destruction, he is a far cry from the rational, the inherently good, the perfectible creature described by the 18th-century philosophers. Indeed the Freudian man, like the Christian man, is by nature more reprobate than enlightened. Of course, as man tried to learn more about himself, many of Freud's theories fell into disrepute and were discarded, some even by Freud himself. Yet he remains the father of the psychoanalytical method which, though discounted and, more often than not, deprecated by practicing psychologists and psychiatrists, continues to have a lasting importance in the treatment of mental diseases. His dramatic contribution—the concept of man driven by a latent, unreasoned, unconscious force—stands unchallenged.

The blow to rationalism was irreparable. After Pavlov and Freud, psychologists, physiologists, anthropologists, and sociologists saw man as an unconsciously driven creature responding to a world of custom, ritual, tradition, tabu, habit and superstition. Taking a Freudian analogy, the social scientists compared rational and conscious thought in the human personality with the small floating fragment which signals the existence of an irregularly-shaped, indeterminately massive iceberg.

If reason, one of the two foundation stones upon which the Enlightenment was erected, was made of sand, the superstructure, supported by the unshakable and impregnable footings of natural law, nevertheless remained sound—or so it seemed—as the march of science quietly unlocked the secrets of the universe. Born under the spell of Newton's causal universe, advances during the 19th century were moving slowly but surely toward the development of a single, unified system. The physical basis of chemical behavior was discovered by Dalton; the electrical by Humphry Davy. The critical link between mechanical motion and electrical current was supplied by Faraday, and Clerk Maxwell derived the mathematics which proved that all forms of energy are at bottom identical. Physics, it seemed, had reached the stage of perfection that Newton had given astronomy some two hundred years earlier.

There had been minor scares, of course. In 1846, for example, a remote planet, Uranus, seemed to misbehave and violate the timing of the causal laws of gravitation, but this problem was quickly resolved by Adams and Leverrier, who both independently deduced from Newtonian laws that some yet unknown planet was responsible for the seemingly erratic behavior of Uranus. And when a new German telescope groped further into unexplored space, the pristine, inviolable laws of gravitation were once again vindicated as the

previously unseen planet, Neptune, appeared right on schedule, patiently pursuing the orbit calculated by the English-
man, Adams, and the Frenchman, Leverrier.

Years later Leverrier was yet again to be fascinated by the
seeming independence of a planet. This time it was Mercury
that appeared to behave in a most disrespectful and disobedi-
ent fashion. Having explained earlier the apparent rebellious
behavior of Uranus, Leverrier felt there was no great cause
for alarm. Relying once again on Newton's system, he calculated that another planet—christened Vulcan—was responsible for Mercury's erratic and peculiar actions. But alas,
Vulcan has never been found; nor, to the great discomfort
of the fervent believers in natural law, is it expected to be.
For Newton had been found out. His wonderful system of
causation, nothing more than a felicitous approximation of
reality, was a fraud, a marvelous, useful fraud if you like,
but a fraud nonetheless.

To appreciate how Newton was found out, it is necessary to
take a brief excursion into both the world of the microcosm
and the world of the macrocosm. The former, quantum
physics, is the world of the atom, the electron, and the neu-
tron; it is also the world in which certainty was to suffer a
mortal wound. It all came about because this minute world
refused to conform to the Newtonian notion that elementary
particles of matter were simple miniature solar systems. Eventually, this obstinacy led scientists, early in the 20th century,
to abandon the classical mechanics of particles in favor of a
sometimes-wave, sometimes-particle theory of matter. From
these theories, Heisenberg, a brilliant young German physicist, developed his famous principle of uncertainty, which
asserts that it is absolutely and forever impossible to determine perfectly accurately and simultaneously the position
and speed of the fundamental particles of matter. In proving
this, he was to demonstrate that in the very act of measuring

position, speed was altered; in the very act of ascertaining speed, position became more indefinite.

To the layman Heisenberg's findings had little meaning, but to the world of science it was of immense importance. For if the scientist could not be completely certain of the present—and this is precisely what the principle implies—then most surely he cannot predict perfectly the future. Even more important, such a theory is a direct contradiction to the very essence of Newton's rigid mechanism of cause and effect. After all, Laplace, imbued with the 18th-century ideal of order, had asserted that if he knew the exact location and velocity of every atom in the universe he could look backward as well as forward in time and give the history and fate of every molecule, man, and society from the beginning of time to infinite eternity. Laplace's statement rested on the assumption that all events could be reduced to smaller and smaller parts, all of which obeyed some universal common law. Being obedient to a mechanical and inviolable law, the course of history is rigidly set, and, at least in theory, precisely determinable.

Men, of course, subscribe to different beliefs. Some believe that the eating of flesh is immoral, others hold that our society is superior to all others. Neither of these beliefs is subject to any final validation. So it is with the belief that there exists some beautiful, unobservable mechanism which inexorably pushes us toward some already predetermined destination. Perhaps if we had better measuring devices, we would, at bottom, find a rigid mechanism of cause and effect. But we don't and we won't. For man is like a child who, by his very touch in attempting to determine the shape and the texture of a snowflake, vitiates and dissolves that which he wishes to examine. Lacking complete knowledge of the present, our best hope is a future of probabilities and statistics—never absolute certainty.

Such is the status and legacy of quantum physics, the world of microcosm. It is a colorless, soundless, esoteric world of symbols and intellectual metaphors from which dualisms, indeterminacy, and paradox have driven once and for all Newton and secular certainty. But to the ordinary educated man this world has one very practical drawback. It is all but incomprehensible.

Unlike Adam Smith's perfect liberty, or Spencer's survival of the fittest, quantum theory is neither easily understood nor holds any special fascination for the thinking public. To be sure, we are told that world-shaking scientific breakthroughs have been made. Not fully understanding the significance of these discoveries, we are justly proud and interpret them as merely another illustration of the manifold signs of progress —which in a very real sense they are. As long as the new cosmology of the microcosm remains tightly locked in the private and secret world of the physicist and mathematician, the layman is secure in his ignorance and innocence.

At the other extreme of the continuum, however, lies the realm of the macrocosm—man's view of planets, stars, island universes, and flying galaxies. Here also a new threat to intellectual security was in the making. On May 29, 1919, eight years before Heisenberg formulated his famous uncertainty principle, scientific observation of an eclipse was to bring to the reading public's attention such disturbing notions as, "The Overthrow of Newton," "The Warping of Space," and "The Vanishing of Size." The chief architect of these ideas was Albert Einstein, a German-born Jew, who for his Special and General theories of relativity was to gain world-wide recognition and acclaim. So profound and original were his scientific contributions that his name must always be ranked with those of Archimedes, Euclid, Galileo, and Newton. A natural scientist, his work was necessarily technical and abstract. Yet it rapidly pervaded all social thought. His legacy to social thinking, in an oversimplified and vulgarized way, may be summarized in three words: Everything is relative. How this broad interpretation of his work came to be applied to the social universe needs some explanation.

When in our physical world we think of measuring devices, we think of absolutes: a yard, a cup, a pound, a gallon. Newton too had his absolutes, time and space, which Einstein was to show were not absolutes at all. As Einstein was to demonstrate, these so-called absolutes take on quite different appearances, depending upon the speed and location of the observer.

Take time for example. What is it; how do we calculate it; is it the same everywhere? Is time one thing on earth, something else on Mercury, different, in fact, on the billions upon billions of stars in the universe? Our conception of time is, of course, simply a measurement in space. An hour on earth is simply an arc of fifteen degrees in the daily rotation of our planet; a year, a record of the earth's trip around the sun.

Now what about Mercury? By our standards Mercury rotates on its axis once every 88 days; in the same period it circles the sun. Given our concept of time, a day and a year on Mercury would be identical.

And what about our universal concept of *now*? Anyone who has traveled the breadth of our land knows that California's breakfast time is New York's coffee break, that San Francisco's afternoon working period is Boston's hour for cocktails and dinner, and that the shank of the evening in Los Angeles is the time for sleep in Baltimore.

But *now* becomes even more elusive if we expand our horizons. Thirty-three light-years separate Arcturus and Earth. Should we receive a radio communication today from Arcturus, it would have been sent during our great depression; whether Arcturus exists today we cannot know until the end of this century. In such a context our universal and absolute concept of *now* is meaningless.

Nor can we dismiss this simply by saying that nature is playing tricks with our notions of absolutes, for as Einstein was to prove, relativity is the "substance" of which the universe is made. For what is true for time is also true for space and, like time and space, even mass, which for Newton had been a fundamental and indestructible basis of matter, proved to be variable with velocity. Indeed the grim spectacles of Hiroshima and Nagasaki are ghastly monuments to the fact that in the last analysis matter is just another form of energy. Thus space, time, and mass have exactness only in the context of speed; an observer traveling at one speed sees a different picture than one traveling at a much higher speed. But for the speed of light, everything is relative. Space and time are mere manifestations of intuition and can no more be divorced from the conscious than color, dimension, or size. Space instead of objective reality is nothing more than an arrangement of objects as man perceives them, and time has no independent existence apart from the events measured.

Einstein, to the end of his life, was dedicated to the search for a causal system which would replace the one he had helped so completely to demolish. His remark that "God is ingenious but not malicious" and his famous statement that "I cannot believe that God plays dice with the world," are both reminiscent of 18th-century deism. But whatever Einstein's personal beliefs, his work with both the atom and the stars was destined to destroy the remaining pillar of the Enlightenment: natural law.

In the gospel of the Enlightenment, man would find Paradise by reason of the discovery of God's immutable law. But science, the instrument of discovery, when seen in its true colors, was a treacherous betrayer. Instead of obediently performing its assigned task, it preaches a pernicious doctrine of relativity, denies the existence of universal laws, and revels in the impious creed that the only certainty is uncertainty. Thus in striving for unity, men of science had patiently constructed and carefully cared for a world of systems purporting to reflect the magnificence of nature. Slowly these pillars of perfection tottered and fell as the sharp outlines against the heavens were transformed into a settling dust which blurred the sight and deprived man of the clarity of vision of which he had once so confidently boasted. Alas, the world no longer was a place of precise distinctions, of sharp tones, of exact colors; as far as the eye could see and the mind could fathom, all seemed tinged with a perplexing, uncertain shade of gray. It was this thought that a celebrated student of science, Sir Arthur Eddington, captured when he wrote, "We have found a strange footprint on the shores of the unknown. We have devised profound theories, one after another, to account for its origin. At last we have succeeded in reconstructing the creature that made the footprint. And Lo! it is our own."

What psychologists and physiologists had done to reason, natural law was to suffer at the hands of quantum theory and relativity. Yet the death of reason and natural law was not meant to be an easy one, for if reason and natural law were to expire, what then of secular certainty? The very thought of life without certitude is bewildering, frightening, and unbearable. Without some higher authority, how is man to differentiate between right and wrong, good from evil, morality from immorality, progress from retrogression? Where can he turn for direction and guidance? Surely not to himself. This is too cruel, too demanding, too inhuman. Somewhere there has to be someone or something to tell him somehow what is worthwhile; without such direction this is a terrible world. Without natural law, who can prove that industry and conscientiousness are superior to indolence and irresponsibility? Besides, if everything is relative, then there is no essential difference between the drinking of alcohol and the chewing of betel nut, no essential difference between the noisy Fourth of July celebration and the Navajo rain dance, no essential distinction between the consecration of a balanced budget and the sanctification of a ceremonial fire. Indeed, without some guiding force, how can one be sure that the American society, for all its luxury and opportunity for self-expression, is superior to the early Melanesian culture, the mainspring of which was headhunting?

This is nihilism at its worst. Apparent in the Kierkegaardian as well as the Sartresque type of existential anguish, nihilism's most immediate and perhaps most tragic expression in America is the beatnik. In a more sophisticated form, its influence is apparent elsewhere. Cultural anthropology, philosophy, sociology, and more recently welfare economics have to a greater or lesser extent fallen under the spell of relativism. In an effort to be scientific the cultural anthropologist has in the past refused to pronounce judgment on the superiority of the society geared to headhunting or profit making, and any good upstanding economic welfare theorist —pleading inability to measure individual satisfaction— would never permit himself to admit that taking a dollar from a billionaire and giving it to a starving man would increase welfare. Whatever the merits or the demerits of the position of these hesitant academicians, men responsible for policy making are never permitted the nicety of the purist. Required by their position to act, these men, just as leaders always have, find it necessary to make decisions on the assumption that some things are good and some things are not.

The Enlightenment lives on, modified only in form. Despite unending international crisis and the growing specter of militant communism in the form of a powerful Russia and a rising China, despite an ominous jump in world population and the existence of thermonuclear weapons capable of destroying the entire civilized world, despite racial discrimination and the concentration of economic and political power, the American mood remains optimistic. For this we can be grateful. Having lost the unity and certainty of medieval Christianity, life without secular optimism would indeed be black.

But like Christians all worshiping one God in persistent disharmony, our society suffers a disagreement over the litany and the liturgy proper to the keeping of the faith. For want of something more exact, this disagreement may be characterized as a dispute between present-day 19th-century liberals, or conservatives, and 20th-century modern liberals. Both of these groups, of course, profess to serve the same ends: peace, prosperity, freedom, health, education, national defense, civil rights, truth, beauty, and goodness. Both groups seem to be equally endowed with divine powers and worldly virtues. Each has its share of ambitious, doctrinaire, militant, demagogic, remorseless, petty, incompetent members. All the important leaders of both groups are victims—benefactors if you like—of driving ambition. To both groups certain things are self-evident: life, liberty, and the pursuit of happiness are good in and of themselves and need no justification.

What separates these two groups is neither the goodness of their membership nor the ultimate goals to be achieved. It is rather a difference in faith. At bottom the 19th-century liberal or conservative has faith in and is loyal to—although he may deny this vigorously—natural law. He believes, to use the words of Hayek, that "especially in the economic field, the self-regulating forces of the market will somehow bring about the required adjustments to new conditions, although no one can foretell how they will do this in a particular instance." * He believes that if each man diligently and enthusiastically pursues his own self-interest, the law of nature —competition—will inevitably push us with the greatest possible dispatch toward the best of all possible worlds. Any governmental tampering can only retard the ultimate consummation of the millennium.

Although on the defensive, the conservative forces have influence. Indeed at the moment the conservative movement seems to have found renewed vigor. Senator Barry Goldwater criticizes liberals for subscribing to collectivistic precepts, however unwittingly, with the intention of hurrying progress and compelling human advances. In so doing, he believes, "they fight against nature" while wanting "to play God with the human race." In setting forth the conservative creed Senator Goldwater states, "The laws of God, and of nature, have no dateline. The principles on which the conservative political position is based have been established by a process that has nothing to do with the social, economic, and political landscape that changes from decade to decade and from cen-

---

* Actually Professor Hayek strongly resents the conservative label. Classifying himself as a true liberal, he differentiates between conservatism, liberalism, and modern liberalism. Modern liberalism he sees as nothing short of disguised socialism, while he describes conservatism as an attitude which, in professing a profound opposition to social change, exalts the doctrine of the elite. According to Hayek the distinguishing characteristic of the true liberal—now commonly referred to as the 19th-century liberal—is his unquestioning faith in the natural law of the market. Using Hayek's definition, conservatives in the coteries of William F. Buckley, Jr. and Russell Kirk would not qualify as 19th-century liberals at all. Fearing the irreverence of the insensate market forces, these men, in speaking of great transcending, cosmic truths, condemn economics for being too materialistic, too mundane. This distinction between 19th-century liberalism and conservatism is not wholly without merit. For our purposes, however, 19th-century liberalism and conservatism will be used synonymously.

tury to century. These principles are derived from the nature of man, and from the truths that God has revealed about His creation." Thus Senator Goldwater and the conservatives who join him hold that the canons of truth have been forever found.

What are these eternal truths? First, let us say they are attractive both for their ease of understanding and for their appeal to the American's belief in the worth and dignity of the individual. At bottom the principles of the conservative teach the virtues of individual autonomy and the excellence of freedom of enterprise—pure capitalist theory. Armed with these principles the conservative is able to pronounce judgment on virtually all public policy. Specifically, he speaks with authority on the follies of an unbalanced federal budget, on the excesses of labor unions, and on the dangers of federal economic and humanitarian programs. He can also expound with confidence on the merits of abolishing progressive taxation, on the need for drastically cutting governmental expenditures, and on the wisdom of returning to the doctrine of states' rights as the means of guaranteeing individual civil liberties.

But more than any specific policy recommendation is the conservative's conviction that we as a nation must accept the irreducible fact that man is, through collective action, impotent to alter or shape the laws of nature. Government, of course, has its functions. It must preserve law and order. It must restrict the power of business organizations—a feat, we are told, largely achieved through antitrust laws. It must crush the belligerent and irresponsible labor unions which even today threaten our very way of life. Beyond this, the federal government must not go, for man cannot, through the use of government, ever hope to direct or master the forces of nature. Should he try, his efforts, however well-meaning, however well conceived and administrated, must perforce be perverse, self-defeating. For God had ordained that whosoever would, through pride and impudence, ignore his limitations and rise above the true order of the universe must surely suffer the implacable penalties imposed by nature. But for all this the conservative tells us that we have nothing to fear, that it is true that progress is inevitable if only we once again adapt our behavior to conform with the immutable law of divine providence. Unfortunately, we are told, America in very recent years has, in its impatience, seen fit to disregard this basic truth; but if we hurry, there is yet time to turn back the tide before the damage becomes irreparable.

One need only point to the burgeoning welfare state to show that the conservatives have suffered some shattering defeats. Replacing the creed of the conservative is modern liberalism—a pragmatic belief that man, through his own efforts, is capable of altering the state of affairs in such a way as to make the world a better place to live. Where there is misery, squalor, and poverty, there must be opportunity; where there is discrimination, there must be equality; where there is disease, there must be health; where there is ignorance, there must be education; where there is economic insecurity, there must be security; where there is degradation, there must be human dignity.

If this can best be accomplished with the mechanics of the market, the price system will be relied upon. Where the price system is inadequate or too slow, then other means will be devised to achieve objectives. If there is unemployment, or economic growth is sluggish, federal expenditures must be manipulated, interest rates fixed, taxes adjusted, budgets unbalanced, and money created. If the price of full employment and rapid growth is inflation, then so be it, for the sound dollar in and of itself is a false god. If the senior citizens of the nation lack the wherewithal for drugs and medical attention, then they shall be provided with them. If local and state governments are laggard in providing sufficient modern educational facilities and the funds necessary to attract bright, intelligent, and vigorous people into the teaching profession, then the federal government must step in. If certain minority groups are depressed and suffer discrimination, coercion backed by legislation shall be employed for the purpose of giving all men the full rights guaranteed by the Constitution. There is no one right way; one day liberalism may cherish, the next day it may challenge; in one age it may seek more economic intervention by government, in the next, less; in one time it may be hospitable to labor or to business, in the next, hostile; in one time it may propose tax increases, at another condemn.

Humanist by persuasion, the modern liberal believes that he is a product of his own efforts. If there be poverty, misery, and slavery, they are of his making; and man, and man alone, must bear the responsibility. There is no natural law, no supreme being, no blind historical force that decrees man must suffer the lot of ignorance and squalor. In his humanism, he is democratic, believing in "the masses"; he bows to the majority rule. He is optimistic, believing always that through education man can be lifted above his primordial and bestial instincts. He is experimental, believing that the world can be remade; he refuses to subscribe to any determinist doctrine. He is rationalistic, believing that he can, through hard work and intelligence, increasingly expand his mastery over his environment. He is relativistic, believing that problem-solving involves the here and now. He is of the conviction that what was fine yesterday may be quite unsatisfactory today. He is egalitarian, believing that the doctrine of the "elite" was manufactured for the purpose of protecting special privilege. He is scientific, believing that the findings of science rather than time-honored "truths" are the instruments of progress. He is a statist, believing that the state must take an active role in redressing inequities and promoting the dignity of the individual. He is progressive, believing that the gradual altering of existing and the adding of new institutions is essential to increasing welfare. He is a vigorous defender of civil rights—more so than his conservative counterpart who, with his higher susceptibility to elitism, can be intolerant of alien ideas. But for all of this, he is not a revolutionary. Impressed by the vitality and efficiency of private production, he is in fact firmly committed to the private enterprise system as a means of supplying most daily requirements.

Skeptical of the doctrine of automatic progress, the modern liberal, committed to man-is-the-measure-of-all-things philosophy, chafes at the bit to get on with those things that need doing. In his impatience, exuberance, and flexibility of method, his apparent inconsistency of approach seems to bother him little. In the introduction to his public papers and addresses, President Franklin D. Roosevelt wrote, "In these volumes those who seek inconsistencies will find them. There were inconsistencies of method, inconsistencies caused by ceaseless efforts to find ways to solve problems for the future as well as the present. There were inconsistencies born of insufficient knowledge. There were inconsistencies springing from the need for experimentation. But through all of this I trust there will be found a consistency and continuity of purpose."

However one may view modern liberalism, its chief virtue is neither consistency nor constancy. If anything, with age it has become even more incorrigible. Lacking unity of purpose and constancy of method, it suffers from apparent, if not real, infidelity. Sponsoring on the one hand research and services for increasing the agricultural output, it administers acreage allotments and marketing quotas for decreasing production on the other. Federal Reserve bank policy and treasury policy are often at odds, and while the Anti-Trust division rails against the concentration of industrial power, defense contracts and war plants are dispensed to make the powerful even more powerful. But even if all the many seemingly irreconcilable policies and practices were somehow reconciled, the modern liberal in resolving one set of difficulties is immediately confronted with a new and more complex set of problems. Like a prisoner frantic to escape the confines of his prison cell, he painstakingly fashions a key to the door of freedom, only to find that he is irretrievably trapped in a bigger, more frightening, more bewildering cell, for which there is no apparent door, much less a key.

Ineffective in his efforts to chain industrial might, the modern liberal naïvely sought to neutralize old power by creating new power. But when his creations, the labor union and the governmental agency, reached maturity, he found they paid him no more heed than did the powers he had hoped to destroy. And when the great giants of labor and industry come to do battle—as surely they must—he can only stand on the sidelines helplessly wringing his hands while the nation he pledged to serve and protect suffers the inevitable paroxysms of all-out war. All around him are governmental agencies which, for all his good intentions in launching them, practice, in their vigor or senility, petty tyrannies. When on those rare occasions a gross perversion of objectives enrages him and he would through the democratic process call his bureaucratic tormentors to account, he is confronted by obsequious, yet patronizing, experts who with all their technical competence and fatal reasonableness educate him to the justice of their position. Overwhelmed by the complexities of the problem and the knowledge of the experts, the modern liberal refuses to admit that the slave has become master and disguises his impotency and frustrations by defending his tormentors or postponing action to some date that will never come.

But for all of this, his greatest struggle is with himself. Having denounced divine will, natural law, and blind senseless forces, the liberal can cite no superior being or power to prove either to himself or to others that his position is correct. In a land desperately searching for unity, the disunity and confusion he has helped to foster make him the center of an unrelenting barrage of criticism and attack. Lacking higher authority to which he can appeal, his only defense is his moral convictions.

The intellectual font of 19th-century liberalism—today's conservatism—is the Enlightenment and more specifically the doctrines of pure capitalist theory. 20th-century liberalism, also a child of the Enlightenment, in addition to reflecting the loss of certainty in the natural sciences, draws energy from the change in public sentiment wrought by the great Depression. It is to the conditions that brought this change in attitude and the economic thought that grew out of them that we must now turn.

VII

A Luther Named Keynes

THERE HAD BEEN A NUMBER OF WARNINGS. A SHARP BREAK IN early September and another in October, however, merely caused people to speak of bargains in the market. Steel, for example, once $261 per share could be picked up for $204, and Radio was down from $114 to $82. Still, despite the prevailing state of optimism, things did not seem quite right. At best the market appeared listless, not quite able to throw off its lethargy and break through the old highs. It made several valiant attempts, the last on October 22. But then on the next day, October 23, 1929, the market suffered a sharp setback as heavy sell orders caused trading to go over the 6,000,000 share mark. The drop in prices was precipitous, so much so that people who held stock on small margins— paying only a fraction of the price of stock they had purchased—were compelled either to sell their securities or give their brokers additional money to hold them. To men who understood these things, the market situation had assumed a grave and ominous tone.

The next day, October 24, 1929 was destined to become a watershed date in American history. The bottom fell out of Wall Street. Before the day was over, the ticker tape would lag an unprecedented four hours and on the New York Stock Exchange an incredible 13,000,000 shares would change hands. As a wave of low margin holders flooded the market with forced sales, fear and then panic caused men to stampede with the hope of unloading before the entire market collapsed. Losses were staggering, big and little speculators from all parts of the nation were driven to the wall and then wiped out, while throughout Wall Street and thence the country, wild, incredible rumors spread like wildfire.

On October 25, *The New York Times* wrote, "One of the reports was that eleven speculators had committed suicide. A peaceful workman atop a Wall Street building looked down and saw a big crowd watching him, for the rumor had spread that he was going to jump off. Reports that the Chicago and Buffalo Exchanges had closed spread throughout the district, as did rumors that the New York Stock Exchange and the New York Curb Exchange were going to suspend trading. These rumors and reports were all found, on investigation, to be untrue. . . ."

It might have been much worse except for the efforts of major banking houses, which let it be known that they had full confidence in both the soundness of the economy and the strength of the market; and that, in addition to uttering such reassuring words, they would use their combined resources to restore order on the Exchange. Quickly word spread that the major New York banks, led by the house of Morgan, were buying heavily. Before the day was through, a spirited rally caused most of the pivotal stocks to regain a measurable part of their losses. On this optimistic note things held firm on Friday, October 25, and for the early part of the session on Saturday. But on Monday a cascade of new liquidation orders once again caused the ticker to fall behind and the market to break sharply. Again brokers found it necessary to make frantic calls for margin money.

But Monday proved to be only the prelude to the fury that was to engulf the great Exchange as the gong struck at 10:00

the next morning. Almost at once the great hall became a bedlam as brokers frantically offered to sell at almost any price; by 10:30, trade exceeded three million shares; by noon eight million, and at the end of the day, more than 16 million. The banking support which had courageously and successfully restored order on "Black Thursday" was swept violently aside as block after block of various issues deluged the exchange. On the New York Stock Exchange losses were estimated at almost ten billion dollars and in lesser markets such as the Curb and the over-counter market, near panic set in as investors sought to get out from under.

The pathos of the situation was portrayed in the October 30 issue of *The New York Times*:

> Groups of men, with here and there a woman, stood about inverted glass bowls all over the city yesterday watching spools of ticker tape unwind and as the tenuous paper with its cryptic numerals grew longer at their feet their fortunes shrunk. Others sat stolidly on tilted chairs in the customers' rooms of brokerage houses and watched a motion picture of waning wealth as the day's quotations moved silently across a screen. It was among such groups as these, feeling the pulse of a feverish financial world whose heart is the Stock Exchange, that drama and perhaps tragedy were to be found . . . the crowds about the ticker tape, like friends around the bedside of a stricken friend, reflected in their faces the story the tape was telling. There were no smiles. There were no tears either. Just the cameraderie of fellow-sufferers. Everybody wanted to tell his neighbor how much he had lost. Nobody wanted to listen. It was too repetitious a tale. . . .

Still the market had not reached its low point for the year. Not until November 13, several weeks later, would the market hit bottom. Only then, after the carnage had been cleaned up and the debris swept away, could the nation sit back and assess the wreckage. The sight was a fearsome one. In two insane months the market had dropped nearly 50 per cent, losing all that it had gained in two preposterous years. But the death of the Big Bull Market was only the beginning, for as markets faltered and then came thundering down, the Bull carried with it the confidence, the ideals, the hopes and eventually the prosperity of a distinct historical period. A decade was gone; the postwar era was going; a new age was about to begin.

It was not to be a pleasant decade. On the domestic scene, in the ten years between 1930 and 1940, the nation was to suffer and learn to live with a new experience: the fear that the bountiful opportunity of the old America was forever lost. Even today, more than thirty years later, we are not clear as to the reasons; but there are certain broad outlines which mark the nation's tragic descent from "normalcy."

Within the mood of 1929 lay the seeds for its own destruction; from the pervasive confidence that ordinary men were meant to be wealthy came the rampant speculation that made both the rise and break in the market inevitable. Although it is true that the Wall Street debacle affected only a small fraction of the public, and although both business and political spokesmen pronounced that the market was neither an accurate nor reliable barometer of the economy's soundness, it was soon apparent that the economic indicators were following the lead that was set by the market, if less precipitously. Indeed in the June before the crash, the Federal Reserve indexes of industrial activity and of factory production had peaked and begun to show signs of slipping, and by October literally all the standard barometers—freight-car loadings, factory payrolls, department store sales—were signaling a general lessening of economic activity.

Any one of a number of things may have triggered the shift in direction. Perhaps a faltering consumer demand caused a reduction in inventories and new orders; or perhaps a lack of dispatch in reinvesting the lavish profits generated by prosperity may have been responsible for the turning point. Whatever the initial cause, it was the dramatic shock of the market collapse that led ordinary men to wonder whether their orthodoxy had betrayed them, whether the gods, in which they had placed their unquestioning trust, had failed. No longer did men of Main Street exude confidence or speak with respect or admiration of the captains of industry or the titans of Wall Street. Opinion had changed, men became cautious, questioning, fearful as the psychological pendulum shifted from unbounded optimism to one of suspicious pessimism.

In an interdependent society where virtually every man is dependent upon the economic whole for even the most elementary requirements of life, such a profound downward psychological shift can only bring disaster. It was not long before the business indexes began to tell the story of a sick economy which day by day grew sicker. Unemployment shot up; from 1.5 million in 1929 to 4.5 million in 1930, and finally to a tragic high of almost 13 million in 1933. During the same period national income plummeted from $104 billion in 1929 to $56 billion in 1933. Twelve long years would elapse and the United States would enter World War II before America would once again know the opportunity and prosperity that come from full employment.

But economic measurements are cold abstractions which have nothing to say about the human suffering, the humiliation, or the despair wrought by depression; of the vacant-eyed, forlorn men shuffling through a bread line; of the loss of farm capital and self-respect engendered by disastrously low farm prices; of the sickness and disease that flourished because of squalor and undernourishment; of the undermining of confidence produced by a rash of bank failures, or of the loss of human dignity that comes from being compelled to beg. Of these things economic indexes can tell us nothing. Nor can the indicators tell us the way the ordinary man responded to these shocks: how he engaged in hunger riots; how he marched in the Bonus Expeditionary Force on Washington; or how he—in such a stronghold of conservatism as Iowa—dragged a judge from the bench, beat him and hung him until he fainted, in order to alert the lawmaker to the practical necessity of changing mortgage foreclosure law. Mostly, ordinary men listened and hoped; they listened to the calm reassurances of public spokesmen, hoping that their promises would soon be fulfilled.

From Washington the eternal phrase, "the economy is fundamentally sound," was later augmented by "prosperity is just around the corner," but for President Hoover the Depression was a bewildering, terrifying ordeal. Committed as he was to traditional economic theory, he could do little more than certify that the economy was fundamentally sound. Mechanistically inclined, he believed that the market system was self-correcting, that full employment was guaranteed and that tampering with the economy could only make matters worse. Placing his trust in an automatic market as the ultimate shaper of the good society, he was paralyzed by a fear that the significant use of federal funds to relieve unemployment would create dangerous political centralization, undermine the integrity of the recipients, and violate "nature's" law that the national debt could not exceed a low fixed amount without bringing bankruptcy to the government and catastrophe to the nation.

Within the context of these principles, Hoover made a

genuine and sincere effort to dispel the awesome economic blight that had beset the nation. In November of 1929, upon realizing that the crisis was something more than a shake-out in the stock market, he announced a tax cut and exacted a solemn promise from leading industrialists that they would neither reduce wages nor discharge employees simply for the purpose of maintaining profits. At the same time, the President wired state and city officials throughout the nation, asking them to cooperate in alleviating the emergency through expanding public works programs. Having done this, the President sat back and awaited the self-correction guaranteed by the automatic market mechanism—prosperity, so the theory told him, "was just around the corner."

But as the President waited and anticipated, the situation grew more desperate, the outlook more bleak. Finally, after almost a year of nothing but disappointment and disillusionment, the President's Emergency Relief Organization was established. Set up to coordinate already overtaxed relief at the private and local levels, by 1931 the effort gave way to the pathetic "Give a Job" campaign wherein private citizens were exhorted to give the unemployed jobs washing windows, mowing lawns, polishing cars and other odd chores. With unemployment running at 7,000,000, the absurdity of such a trivial effort for dealing with a national emergency of such immense proportions emphasizes how completely pure capitalist theory had become the shaper of American economic thought and policy.

Yet even this fails to convey how conclusively Mr. Hoover's thoughts were dominated by economic orthodoxy. The most tragic display was to come in the battle over aid to a drought-ridden area. Recognizing the devastation worked by the drought, President Hoover favored the appropriation of some 25 million dollars for providing such things as fertilizer, seed, and livestock feed. When Congress proposed to increase the appropriation to 60 million dollars, the President was incensed and publicly reprimanded the legislature for its disregard for public funds. But more than the prospective waste of public monies, the President was profoundly disturbed by the provisions authorizing the purchase of foods for unfortunate human beings. Such legislation, the President felt, might set a precedent which could do irreparable damage to the moral fiber of the nation. Should the reformers and unemployed become enthralled with the notion that federal appropriations could be made for the purpose of feeding hungry citizens, then the entire social structure was in danger of crumbling. Such a proposal, thought the President, threatened the very heart and substance of the economic doctrines which in capturing the American mind had taught that the purpose of life was to pursue and accumulate stores of material goods. Through personal riches and the recognition they provided, not only was life made meaningful, but the individual was permitted the satisfaction of self-fulfillment.

For the government now to provide the basic necessities to those incapable of or unwilling to make their own way would be to profane the very foundation upon which the American culture rested. If goods were free, how then could one distinguish the deserving from the undeserving or, without the means to discipline the weak and the indolent, how could one be certain that pursuit of material goods would continue to be the primary object of life? Relief, and particularly federal relief made a mockery of the whole system, for to give help to the incompetents—and a good man, so the saying went, could always find a job—was tantamount to an admission that the frantic race for economic advantage, instead of being a deadly serious matter imposed by an unforgiving nature, was nothing more than a contrived contest, the rules of which were artificially fixed by man himself.

Rather than admit this or back any program in which such

a heresy was implicit, Mr. Hoover courageously stood by his principles, although he gained a reputation for being a callous monster who remained unmoved by the suffering endured during this critical period. By ignoring public clamor for action and by refusing to compromise his ideals, Mr. Hoover and his party courted the certain and overwhelming political defeat they were to suffer in the election of 1932.

In the campaign there could be but one issue—the Depression. Its mark was everywhere. Panhandlers plying the streets were a common sight; transients slept in public buildings, on park benches, and along highways; once prosperous factories stood stark and empty, their windows broken or boarded up; mines operated at a fraction of capacity, if at all; trains carried as many tramps as cash-paying passengers; freight shipments fell off to a dribble, and the once proud symbol of American superiority and wealth, the automobile population, deteriorated into a mass of aging jalopies. Retail stores were hard-pressed for lack of bill-paying customers; the restaurant, hotel, and other industries catering to the luxury trade fell victims to bankruptcy; and while disease and illness continued to exact their toll, hospitals stood half empty because people could not afford the cost of medical care. In such an atmosphere the public, believing that conditions could not possibly be made worse and that any action was better than none, voted for the change which brought Franklin D. Roosevelt to the White House.

A gracious patrician blessed with an illustrious family name, an abundance of energy and captivating charm, Franklin D. Roosevelt pledged himself to champion the cause of the "forgotten man at the bottom of the economic pyramid." Yet for all his biting criticism of the old order, as the campaign waxed hot and as he promised the country a "New

Deal," his word carried the distinct ring of orthodoxy as he extolled the virtues of a sound currency, a balanced federal budget, and the absolute need for governmental economy. What all this meant voters could do little more than guess as they trooped to the polls and registered their malcontent with the existing state of affairs.

As it turned out, Roosevelt was by temperament ideally suited to assume the responsibilities of the Presidency. Virtually free of any doctrinal commitments and impatient with uncompromising people who were ruled by a systematic economic philosophy, he was a self-confessed pragmatist who placed his trust in the power of the human mind to discover and invent means for curing the malady which had fallen upon the nation. The country needs, he observed in a major address at Oglethorpe University, "bold, persistent experimentation. It is common sense to take a method and try it. If it fails, admit it frankly, and try another. But above all, try something."

The nation was not to be kept waiting; quickly it learned that the President intended to use whatever was at his disposal to shake off the lethargy which had beset the economy. On the day following his stirring "the only thing we have to fear is fear itself" inaugural address, the new President met the creeping monetary and credit paralysis head on by declaring a four-day bank holiday. At the same time he summoned Congress for a special session, while at the White House day and night conferences were devoted to drafting emergency bank legislation. Within three days a bill was introduced into Congress; the House debated it less than an hour; the Senate less than three; by the end of the fourth day the President signed it into law. The celebrated Hundred Days had begun; the New Deal was in full swing.

The details of the precedent-shattering early New Deal days are part of a familiar story: how the President, through his radio "fireside chats," conveyed a spirit of serene assurance which promised hope and instilled confidence; how he formed and was influenced by his Brain Trusts; how a President-dominated Congress rammed through a welter of hastily conceived and improvised bills; how the sacred price of gold was deliberately desecrated; how federal deficits piled up as half a billion dollars was distributed by an ardent Harry Hopkins "to feed the hungry and goddam fast"; how TVA, the CCC and the AAA launched bold new programs; and finally how the economically secure raved and cursed, complaining that the country had fallen under the spell of a mad tyrant in the White House who, in satisfying his mania for personal power, was determined to crush everything and everyone that stood in his way.

But the affliction that beset the nation was fearfully tenacious. Despite the best efforts of soothing reassurance and aggressive federal action, it stubbornly refused to release the nation from its crippling influence, and the economy continued to sink lower until bottom was finally touched late in 1933. Yet much had been accomplished. There was, to be sure, some anxiety over whether capitalism could survive, but the profound mood of unrest and disillusionment had been dispelled. And except for a few dissenters, the talk of revolution which weighed so heavily on the minds of many Americans had subsided. But there was much to be done, for as long as ordinary men saw but knew not why idle capacity and human want stood side by side, both reactionaries and radicals would find abundant food for nourishing resentment and discontent—an explosive combination which could lead to violence and revolution.

In the December 31, 1933 issue of *The New York Times* there appeared an open letter written by an eminent economist to the President of the United States:

You have made yourself the trustee for those in every country who seek to mend the evils of our condition by reasoned experiment within the framework of the existing social system. If you fail, rational change will be gravely prejudiced throughout the world, leaving orthodoxy and revolution to fight it out. But if you succeed, new and bolder methods will be tried everywhere, and we may date the first chapter of a new economic era from your accession to office. . . . I lay overwhelming emphasis on the increase of national purchasing power resulting from governmental expenditure which is financed by loans and is not merely a transfer through taxation, from existing incomes. Nothing else counts in comparison with this. . . . It is beyond my province to choose particular objects of expenditure. But preference should be given to those which can be made to mature quickly on a large scale, as, for example, the rehabilitation of the physical condition of the railroads. The object is to start the ball rolling.

Few men took any special note of the words contained in this letter. Economists being what they are, an intimidating lot, and economics being what it is, a forbidding subject, this should not be a surprise, as few men could be expected to discern that within these words lay the ideas for a revolution in economic thought. The writer of this letter was John Maynard Keynes, a man of remarkable energy, versatility, and genius. When this letter was written, its author already enjoyed great eminence.

Both a thinker and a doer, he defied simple classification. A teacher, a scholar, and a theorizer, he was never satisfied to be merely an ivory-tower academician. An erudite Cambridge don who taught and mastered, as few men have, traditional economic theory; a public figure who had a unique and important hand in shaping British monetary and foreign policy; a patron of the arts who was a power in shaping his country's cultural life; the chairman of a great insurance company; the

Bursar of King's College, Cambridge; a successful businessman in his own right; the chairman of a magazine read by the
intelligentsia; the editor, for more than 30 years, of the very
learned and highly respected *Economic Journal;* the author
of a number of highly praised books as well as countless articles covering a variety of diverse and unrelated fields, Keynes
was the antithesis of the prototypal academic specialist who,
in spending his life studying and writing stillborn treatises
on sterile trivialities, loses all contact with the everyday world
of reality. For most men, any one of his numerous roles or
achievements would have been enough to fill an ordinary
lifetime. But his record is all the more astonishing because of
his incredible performance in undertaking simultaneously
both a variety of posts and personally initiated projects, all
of which he carried through with force and brilliance.

In 1919, at the relatively tender age of 36, he was suddenly
vaulted to international fame as the world read his relentlessly analytical, yet genuinely human *Economic Consequences of the Peace.* Written with the perspective afforded
him by his position as principal representative of the Treasury at the Paris Peace Conference, it was a masterpiece of
logic and literary style. Frustrated by his impotence and
appalled by what he called the "murder of Vienna," he resigned from the Conference in protest and despair and set
forth to tell the world how the Council of Four had shame-
fully abandoned the cause of fashioning an honorable and
viable peace in favor of gratifying their passion for settling
old political scores and imposing crushing reparation payments on a defeated and bewildered people. Within the
Treaty of Versailles, he discerned the seed for the resurgence
of an aggressive and hostile German militarism.

In retrospect, the *Consequences of the Peace* carried another and perhaps even more unsettling message for the student of economics. It stated that laissez-faire capitalism, that

"extraordinary episode," had in August, 1914, met its end. Briefly summarized, Keynes' explanation was essentially this: The circumstances which enabled business leadership— driven by a rapidly expanding population and limitless opportunities for profitable investments in the exploitation of new sources of food, natural resources and an incessantly advancing technology—to pile one success upon another had burned themselves out. In the old order the bourgeoisie jealously garnered and quickly converted savings into the productive enterprise which brought personal profits and national prosperity. But in the postwar period, with the weakening of these impulses as investment opportunities diminished and the aggressive spirit of private enterprise flagged, the savings habit of the middle class had lost its social significance; indeed the persistence of this habit, because of the difficulty of returning savings to the income stream, posed a serious threat to maintenance of a smoothly operating, prosperous economy.

To the America of the 1920's, flourishing under the stimulus of the radio and automobile boom, talk of surplus of saving could only sound like arrant nonsense. It was not until after World War II that the economic stagnation thesis was to achieve popular currency and men would begin to appreciate the full implications of the economic system briefly sketched in the *Consequences of the Peace*.

In 1921 Keynes turned his energies to an entirely different field and published *A Treatise on Probability,* a work which the celebrated mathematician-philosopher Bertrand Russell described as a book "impossible to praise too highly." It was almost as if he felt that economics was not quite intellectually honest or at least not sufficiently rigorous or demanding to provide any real test for his mental powers. Accordingly he turned to the most esoteric and abstract of subjects: probability. Here he breathed the rarified air of epistemology and learned first hand of the treacheries of unpatrolled logic. Not that he ever lost his appreciation of the symmetry or the beauty of a neatly framed logical system—for this he was too intelligent—but the mastery of methodology given to him by his work in probability and his overwhelming preocccupation with policy matters soon caused him to tire of a purely logical nicety. Impatient with the doctrine of logic for the sake of logic, he was blessed with a freedom of mind that enabled him to rise above traditional thought and see his world from a new and different perspective.

But mathematics was only a side excursion; his first passion remained as always the society in which he lived, and more particularly Western capitalism. He continued to write and in 1931 published *Treatise on Money,* a two-volume work written for his profession. A technical and scholarly work reflecting solid and sometimes brilliant research, by ordinary standards it was an extraordinary performance. The object of some rather damaging criticism, it was nevertheless not only well received, but generally lauded as a truly great effort by those for whom it was intended. Reiterating and elaborating the economic vision he sketched earlier in the *Consequences,* he conceived of the economy as one gigantic mechanism plagued by an unruly force which impaired the operations of an otherwise efficient and smoothly running machine. As in his early writings, the villain was savings. The ingrained habit of savings, he emphasized, was one thing; the decision to invest, something quite different. Each was separate from the other; each was a distinct activity; but while everyone was expected to be imbued with the virtues of thrift, only the enterprising businessman possessed the power to return savings to the income stream through the process of capital accumulation.

Herein then lay the Achilles heel of the capitalist machine. For while any community of good, honest men always tried to lay something aside, businessmen could not be expected to undertake new ventures unless the prospects for recovering the original investments plus earning some profit were favorable. And if for any one of a number of reasons investment did not measure up to savings, then some funds would not be returned to circulation with the result that sales would fall and fewer workers would be needed to supply the wants in the market. All of which conspired to reduce the general level of economic activity and the size of the national income. Here lay the ominous threat of depression—a threat from which the freely operating capitalist economy could never quite escape.

Somehow the *Treatise* did not quite come off; somehow, Keynes felt, it had missed its mark. Wanting to reach his professional brethren, he had painstakingly backed it with scholarly research, liberally laced it with the conventional trappings, and carefully grounded it in traditional analysis. The result was a cumbersome, entangled effort—an overburdened system that floundered under the weight of the message he hoped to convey. All this Keynes saw and understood. There was but one thing to do: abandon the effort and begin afresh. Resolutely turning his back on years of work, he decided to depict the workings of the economy in the form of a rigorously logical system, free of the clutter of conventional scholarly trappings. To this end he turned his remarkable talents and in late 1935 completed *The General Theory of Employment, Interest, and Money* (Harcourt, Brace & Company, Inc.).

This was and is a dreadful book: abstract, forbidding, obscure, just as Keynes meant it to be. "This book," he wrote, "is chiefly addressed to my fellow economists. . . . The matters at issue are of an importance which cannot be exagger-

ated. But, if my explanations are right, it is my fellow economists, not the general public, whom I must first convince.
At this stage of the argument the general public, though
welcome at the debate, are only eavesdroppers at an attempt
by an economist to bring to an issue the deep divergences of
opinion between fellow economists which have for the time
being almost destroyed the practical influence of economic
theory, and will, until they are resolved, continue to do so."

Ultimately Keynes' objective was not so much the fashioning of ivory-tower abstractions as it was to influence the practical world of policy making. But as long as the Western
world's foremost minds remained captive of traditional capitalist thought, the kind of action necessary for crushing the
Depression lay beyond the pale of acceptable behavior.
Economic thinking, if not by the public, at least by its leaders,
had to be radically revised. Old concepts which until the
onslaught of the Depression had stood the test of time and
served the nation well had to be junked and replaced with
new and untried theories.

The first obstacle to any such profound revision of thought
was the economics profession itself. For more than a century
and a half after Adam Smith, respectable economists had
patiently labored in the construction and perfection of an
elaborate, intellectually demanding, logical apparatus which
explained the wonders and extolled the virtues of the naturally functioning free market system. To Keynes fell the
task of convincing his colleagues that their life's work had
been in vain, that the doctrines they had so unerringly taught
the young were now both false and mischievous. But if the
mission was formidable, the prospects for rewards were great.
If he could convert members of the profession, he could
count on a body of disciples to spread his view of the economy throughout the Western world. Through fellow econo-

mists he could catch the ear of highly placed public officials, through the writings of professional economists the intelligentsia could be reached and gradually influenced, and through the classroom the open-minded and the youthful could be enlisted.

And so Keynes set forth to change the mainstream of economic thought. To accomplish this, not only would he have to undermine conventional thought by underscoring its inadequacies and perversities, but he must devise a new system demonstrably superior to the one it was to supplant. First came a devastating polemic directed against what he called classical economics. Upon the ruins he erected, brick by brick, his edifice. To make certain that his message did not fall on deaf ears or that his fellow economists did not merely give it a passing nod, he resorted to both skill and craft to force the profession to sit up and take notice. He shocked, he exaggerated, he oversimplified, but most of all he eschewed the familiar, the known, the comfortable—even where it would have served him well—and created a new and perplexing lexicon which placed Western capitalism in a different and, for most, a disturbing light.

The success of the *General Theory* was immediate and sustained. Almost immediately Keynes was elevated to the position of a master surrounded by ardent disciples who pledged themselves to the teaching and spreading of his doctrines. In the *General Theory,* they proclaimed, was a scientific diagnosis of the malignancy that threatened to extinguish the free enterprise system. No longer, they declared, was it necessary to deny the existence of grave depression, to temporize on such matters as unemployment and privation, or to resort to the unconvincing and worn counsel that with a little more patience and optimism, the market would automatically right a badly listing economy. Nor did Keynes stop at diagnosing; he prescribed for the ailing economy and in a manner which, when translated by his disciples, an intelligent person could understand and appreciate.

The message was at once simple and revolutionary: the wondrous automatism of the market was nothing but a fiction. To be sure, a freely operating market would direct production, allocate resources, distribute income, and generally determine the pace and direction of the economy, but there existed no inherent guarantee that it would provide either the full employment or the continuous progress promised by capitalistic theory. Indeed the natural workings of the market may foster boom or bust, depression or inflation, stagnation or progress.

Why was this so? To answer this question Keynes returned once again to a vision which appeared repeatedly in his earlier economic writings, the heart of which was the separation of saving and investment decisions. In the past he caught glimpses of the tensions wrought by this separation only to find that in his reconstructed mental image, much as with an uncompleted jigsaw puzzle, certain pieces would not quite fit and the picture always remained unfinished. Now he had recaptured and duplicated the vision, and when the last piece was neatly set in its proper place, the villain in the economic drama was revealed. The key to it all lay in interest rates.

The observation that savings and investments involved independent decisions was scarcely new and most certainly did not orginate with Keynes. Yet this separation gave little cause for worry, for according to high doctrine, these seemingly distinct and unrelated acts were in fact bound together and perfectly balanced through the adjusting mechanism of the interest rate. Businessmen, in their unceasing quest for profits, were forever on the lookout for favorable opportunities to borrow money, for which they went to the market and paid a price—the interest rate. Like all things in the free market, the price of money was determined by the supply of and the demand for investment funds. If a community was poor or prodigal and savings were in short supply, interest rates would be high and businessmen would curb both their borrowing and their expenditures for such things as plant, equipment and inventories; but if the populace was frugal, causing savings to be large and interest rates favorable, businessmen, eager to take advantage of the low cost of borrowed monies, would accelerate their investment activities. Thus a delicate balance was promised; never could savings and investments be long out of joint. Through the fluctuation of the interest rate, an equilibrium was struck; savings through the investment process were automatically returned to circulation, causing the income stream to flow on unimpaired and the economy to run at full throttle.

Implicit to this explanation of the functioning of the economy was the assumption that businessmen never lacked for profit opportunities, or, to put it more precisely, that the profit prospects in a capitalist society were always sufficiently attractive to induce businessmen to absorb any amount of savings that might be accumulated. It is on this critical point that Keynes centered his assault not only by uncovering and openly parading this deeply buried assumption, but by questioning its very validity.

Suppose, he asked, that profit opportunities, for one reason or another, suddenly dropped to nothing; or still worse, that investment prospects promised losses rather than profits. For a wealthy society well schooled in the virtues of saving, he pointed out, this is not as far fetched as it might immediately appear. Indeed, the richer a bourgeois society grows, the larger becomes the proportion of income that it is likely to lay aside, and the smaller becomes the percentage that it is wont to spend for the gratification of immediate need and wants. The business sales and profit outlook is thus dimmed and there exists a paradox of sorts. For the greater the savings, the larger is the need for expanding investment programs which return unspent sums to the income stream; but the more that is saved—not spent in satisfying consumer desires—the less propitious are the prospects for business profits. Thus while a growing effort to accumulate savings makes necessary accelerated investment activity, this very effort dampens profit prospects and thereby works at cross purposes with the heightened capital expenditures necessary to keep the economy running at full speed.

It was, said the Keynesians, just such an imbalance of savings and investment activities—which no possible change in the interest rate could correct—that lay at the roots of the great American Depression. In the fall of 1929, economic confidence had suffered a shattering blow causing business interests all over the country to reassess their investment plans at the same time that consumers were jolted into taking a hard second look at family finances. This conspiracy of consumer prudence and business retrenchment was quick to leave its stamp on the market. Construction work slowed, manufacturers' orders fell off, and workers in capital as well as consumer industries became unemployed. Compelled to pull hard on the purse strings, workers without jobs and income curbed their expenditures on everything from food to furs, driving market demand still lower. In response to this unfavorable turn of events in the market, businessmen, already operating at reduced output, were forced to slash work forces further and shelve plans for enlarging capacity. And so the downward spiral grew in scope and momentum until the nation suffered the ravages of want and privation, while everywhere the instruments of wealth and luxury stood idle.

According to established theory, this was neither very shocking nor serious because an automatic adjustment in interest rates would soon be forthcoming which, in brightening the profit outlook and raising investment sights, would cause the economy to generate a full head of steam. It was at this point that Keynesian theory deviated from the traditional. With factories idle or operating at a fraction of capacity, with banks of machines untended and mines unworked, with vendors overburdened with stocks of goods that did not move, it was, said the Keynesians, foolish to assume that businessmen would be cheerful and optimistic about investing in expansion programs, even if the interest rate fell to nothing. And indeed there was a floor below which the interest rate could not fall. It couldn't drop to zero; such a rate would tear at the very vitals of capitalism. Without interest payments on loaned funds the banking system would collapse, the insurance industry, among others, would not meet its legal commitments and the operation of the entire monetary and credit structure would be placed in jeopardy. Moreover, centuries of tradition had placed thrift and frugality among the most exalted of human activities, evidencing self-denial and discipline worthy of a just reward in the form of interest payments.

Thus bank vaults could bulge and insurance companies could be swamped by surfeit of unloaned funds, but interest rates would always remain well above zero. Yet in an economy racked by unemployment and living in the shadow of idle productive capacity, few businessmen would be willing to borrow funds at a zero interest rate, much less at some minimum floor imposed by institutional factors. Keynes concluded that the economy may, for prolonged and tortured periods, operate at a level far below full employment. Only when profit opportunities improved would a surge of new investment provide the economy with the stimulation necessary to begin the arduous climb out of the deep depression into which it had fallen. In 1933, when Keynes wrote President Roosevelt his open letter, as during all the years that he worked on the *General Theory*, profit prospects remained distressingly dim, as did the outlook for a robust recovery.

For all this, Keynes was intellectually and temperamentally committed to capitalism. He had little faith in either socialism or the masses, and had no wish to see capitalism either atrophy or suffer a violent death at the hand of revolution. And so, accompanying his diagnosis was a prescription which he declared would not only restore the patient's health, but would, if faithfully administered by prudent and honest men, elevate the economy to previously unscaled heights. All that was needed to get the economic machine running again was vigorous investment activity, and because it was not in the immediate best interest of businessmen to expand old or initiate new ventures, some other institution, at least temporarily, must assume this responsibility. The only agency that could do this on the necessary grand scale was the federal government.

At once blasphemous and perceptive, Keynes wryly observed, "If the Treasury were to fill old bottles with bank notes, bury them at suitable depths in disused coal mines which are then filled up to the surface with town rubbish, and leave it to private enterprise on well tried principles of laissez faire to dig the notes up again . . . there need be no more unemployment and with the help of the repercussions, the real income of the community would probably become a good deal larger than it is. It would, indeed, be more sensible to build houses and the like; but if there are practical difficulties in the way of doing this, the above would be better than nothing."

Though the words carried a facetious ring, the spirit was deeply sincere. Somehow the economy must be jolted from its calamitous resting place. Profit opportunities must be sharply enhanced, and there was no more expeditious and less disruptive means of doing this than through the fiscal and monetary policy. The immediate need, said Keynes, was massive doses of public expenditures to be financed by funds largely obtained through the sale of government bonds. Money so secured and spent, whether it be for such make-work projects as leaf raking or such constructive improve-ments as dam and road building, could bring only good. For in return for their work, employees would receive and spend income, causing private business to hire and pay workers who in turn, by satisfying their needs in the market, would fur-ther stimulate business activity. The spiral which had blindly pulled the economy into a terrible state of depression could be deliberately reversed and directed by man as it pushed the nation at an accelerating pace along the road of material progress.

That was Keynes' message. One might suspect that it brought joy and elation to whomever learned of it. It had something for almost everyone. For the theorist, who de-manded above all an internally consistent, mechanistic system, he built a neat and tidy model liberally laced with esoteric jargon far beyond the reach of even the most inquiring lay mind. To the policy maker he offered a straightforward ex-planation that squared with both experience and common sense and provided the basis for decisive action. It was op-timistic; flushing no live villain from the economic wood pile, it identified no evil men plotting against society; nor did Keynes single out and chastise malevolent monopolists, conspiring radicals, scheming foreign elements or any other class as the source of the economic crisis. The fault he found was in the machine itself. Fortunately, the defect was minor, the mechanism fundamentally sound. But it did bear watch-ing and whenever it manifested signs of running down—as it was prone to do—gentle but firm pressure applied by the hand of government would promptly restore its smooth precision.

Keynes was confident that he had found the permanent means of dispelling the menacing shadow hovering over the free enterprise system. Furthest from his mind was any notion of undermining or destroying the bountiful and felicitous system which he genuinely admired.

From the beginning his work was so interpreted by a few. Carrying a fresh message, it provided disenchanted men with an intellectual home. As time passed, and his work was studied by the young and the uncommitted, his followers increased and his influence spread. But to a substantial and influential portion of those men who concern themselves with such things, Keynesian economics would be considered a pernicious doctrine. Although Keynes talked of exorcising the depression demons and thereby saving capitalism, by instinct these men detected the unmistakable scent of danger— a danger so grave and so evil that it threatened to make a mockery of everything they had lived and fought for. Even President Roosevelt, a self-confessed pragmatist, a willing experimenter and a social innovator, blanched at Keynes' matter-of-fact statement that huge federal deficits were absolutely essential if the economy was to enjoy both freedom and a swift restoration of sound health. Pump priming, as it was popularly known, was of course haltingly tried, but the effort was uncertain and the results, though beneficial, limited as the economy continued to languish at a fraction of capacity. Only the pressures of World War II forced a policy of deficit spending on a sufficiently broad scale to push the nation to the heights of full employment and then—used to excess in financing the war—beyond into the potentially treacherous world of inflation. In the postwar period, an unbalanced federal budget was commonplace; the federal debt, with minor interruptions, climbed steadily, and in 1959, as the nation was momentarily staggered by a sharp and painful recession, the government, in an agonized decision to keep economic activity high, applied the policy implications of Keynesian economics and ran a deficit of some $12,000,000—the highest annual peacetime deficit in the history of the nation.

If Keynesian economics was accorded academic respectability* and became a potent if not quite honorable power on the banks of the Potomac, many honest, influential citizens throughout the land linked the Keynesian with the radical and the left. Indeed the Keynesian, it was publicly said, masquerading under the guise of public welfare, bored from within and was more to be feared than the self-admitted agents of communism.

If the analysis was deficient, the instinct was unfailing, for inherent within the new doctrines was a heresy so fundamental that it was to shake the whole social and intellectual edifice. In essence Keynes refuted the perfection of capitalism and implied that the entire rationale underlying the American business civilization was nothing short of a fraudulent apologetic. The capitalist machine was not, he emphasized, automatic; it did not with precision push society inexorably toward a secular millennium. Left to itself, it was erratic and unruly and unless carefully tended and controlled by man himself, it most surely would drag mankind through muck and misery and eventually give impetus to authoritarian powers which would one day rise up and wipe out the forces of freedom.

---

* The first general elementary textbook in economics to present the Keynesian system appeared in 1947. Today there is little, if any, demand for a principles text that fails to elaborate in detail the Keynesian framework of analysis.

By making man rather than the machine the master,
Keynes had opened the door to a corridor at the end of which
lay a terrifying philosophical conundrum: What is the meaning and purpose of life?—a question which for almost two
hundred years had lain dormant. Voltaire had written,
"Work keeps at bay three great evils: boredom, vice and
need." The message was clear: If each man cultivated his own
garden, each would find happiness in his own talents and the
world would be a place of honor and abundance.

The spirit captured by Voltaire in his classic *Candide* was
formalized by his contemporary and acquaintance, Adam
Smith: If finite man would abandon his quest for the infinite,
if he would sublimate his yearnings for knowing the unknowable, if he would overcome his authoritarian compulsion to
discover and establish the sublime society, if he would strike
all this from his mind and concentrate his physical and mental energies on tending his own garden, then he would find
peace of mind and the world would be spared the terrible
and senseless violence and misery that man throughout history has brought upon himself. What Voltaire knew intuitively and told in an amusing, yet serious, parable, Smith,
by resolving the diversity-unity dilemma, proved analytically
in his masterpiece. As time went on, lesser men further elaborated and refined Smith's framework until capitalist theory
was a towering complex of logic, capable of dealing systematically with any objection that might be raised. Under the
freely operating natural law of the market, prices would be
altogether just; men, both rich and poor alike, would be
fairly rewarded according to their contributions to society;
workers eager to work would never suffer from want of employment, and, above all else, the multitude of forces operating in the market—which no mere human mind could know,
much less comprehend and organize—would be carefully
weighed and measured by an "invisible hand" uniquely qual-

ified to fashion an ideal balance out of which would emerge a perfect movement toward moral and economic progress.

By implication Keynes was to make this all romantic nonsense: it is not enough for each man simply to tend to his own affairs; someone must see to it that the economy is running properly. And by saying this, Keynes lifted the lid on Pandora's box, which Smith had tightly secured, with his belief that man holds in his hand power over his own economic destiny and that ultimately he must decide what is right or wrong, good or bad, just or unjust.

As long as man works his own isolated plot, secure in the knowledge that the laws of nature unfailingly transform individual effort into a benevolent force pushing society ever forward at just the right speed, he lives in a simple and intellectually comfortable world which, in addition to conferring unprecedented personal freedom, imposes a minimum of individual responsibility. Shatter this faith and life becomes almost unbearably complicated, as man, from the whole vast welter of disorganized daily experiences, must somehow draft a social blueprint which is right and proper and good. To demand this is to ask mortals to transcend mortality. And yet this is exactly what the Keynesian conclusion implies. For if, as Keynes said, the economic machine is not geared to exalt automatically the lot of mankind, then nothing is fixed or sacred and whoever controls the economic machine has the power to guide it according to his wants and fancies. Should he want the machine to turn out more goods and services, he need only run it faster; should he want more and better medical services, then he must set the mechanism so that more doctors, hospitals, and drugs are provided; should he want the rich to be richer and the poor poorer, then he must adjust the control regulating the distribution of income.

But things are not always as simple as they seem. At best

the economy is an imperfectly understood mechanism that appears to be willfully perverse, refusing to comply with even the most reasonable demands. No sooner, it seems, is one crisis resolved than one or two or a dozen others cry for immediate attention. There is no help for it; alone the machine is incorrigibly irresponsible; man must do his best, however inadequate that may be.

What is man's best? Is he running the machine too fast, too slow; is it set for optimum economic growth; for progress, should the secure, catered-to business executive earn more in a week than the grimy, physically-endangered coal miner is paid in a year; are honest job seekers without work while still other men are employed at menial tasks not equal to their talents and creative powers; should the federal government finance public housing, education, urban renewal, farm prices, free lunch programs, medical aid to the aged, electrical power, flood control—and if so, to what extent? Just a few years earlier, in theory, if not always in practice, the answer to such questions, if they were asked at all, would have been the stock response, "All that shall be done shall be done by the infallible market." The great Depression and Keynes made such a reply, if not ludicrous, then certainly irrelevant—and therein lay the tragedy.

At first, of course, the full implications of the new thinking in economics was not fully revealed. The spirited Keynesian placed his faith in science and expertise. Hire an expert, a competent economist of the right persuasion, and the seemingly intractible problems would become pliable, readily lending themselves to easy solution. Through fiscal and monetary policy, through governmental spending and taxing, through the easing and tightening of the money supply, the machine could be managed nicely and the economy could go on functioning much as before. So it seemed, at least at first; afterward, answers came less easily, resolution more slowly. Spend, the new theory said, but for what? Surely not for foolish leaf raking; much better for something constructive, such as public works that would not compete or interfere with private business.

But how much should the government go into debt; how does one know when the economy is operating at full employment, and what is a satisfactory rate of growth? Besides, what twisted logic is it that restricts governmental activities to strictly public works such as flood control and road building, when there is misery, poverty, ignorance and sickness? Should these things be permitted to persist when they could be eliminated with no more effort than is required to flip a switch or turn a screw? The market is for man, not man for the market; therefore, let us employ it as the servant it was meant to be; let not one man be hungry or sick or lack opportunity because of the superstitious notion that the market is some natural or holy force which is beyond the grasp of even the best of mortals.

Thus man set out to master the economic machine, to adjust and enlarge here, to repair and delete there. No sooner had he done this than those in essential agreement began to argue among themselves. Some said the machine was operating much too slowly while others claimed that it was overburdened and would surely burn out if the preposterous pace was long continued; some, pointing to strikes, farm surpluses, and inflation, cried out against "calculated" and "managed" inefficiencies, while others derisively dismissed these complaints with a wave of the hand and talked only of how the economy moved swiftly forward and how the individual was blessed with prosperity, security, and dignity.

Of the people who concern themselves with such things, most stood on the sidelines, watching and wondering. Some found it fascinating and believed that man had finally found the means for realizing his worldly destiny; others, puzzled and unsure, viewed the goings on with mixed emotions, while still others saw the whole proceedings suffused with a kind of universal and unconditional evil and cried "a plague on all your houses." Indeed, in this latter group, there were men who found a certain sadistic satisfaction in seeing the experts become more and more entangled in their desperate and frenzied efforts to keep the machine working satisfactorily.

The source of their rancor was a staggering blow dealt to orthodoxy. They spoke of freedom, of opportunity, and of efficiency. But these are abused, threadbare words. Having been freely expropriated by tyrants of all ages to mask and justify the most vicious and inhumane crimes, they have lost much of whatever emotional appeal they may have once carried. These bitter men turned to logic, or at least to simple concepts which readily lent themselves to easy measurement.

On the dangers of the unbalanced budget and inflation, they waxed eloquent; on the outrageous inefficiency and the immense and identifiable powers of government, they talked interminably. But these issues are at best pale reflections of the sinister force that aroused their warrior instincts and caused them to view the new economics with fear and trembling. These were practical men; hard, seasoned professionals who buckled on the sword to defend something they had so often and so contemptuously boasted they knew or cared nothing about: a philosophy. The practical significance of the new theory they quickly grasped: that the government might need to spend to reverse the direction of the economy and that the standard price indexes overstated actual price rises, these men of quick wit and high station swiftly mastered. Any school boy could see all this, but what the school boy did not and could not understand was that the new thought threatened to undermine the entire structure of

American beliefs and values. All this these men knew intuitively and, recoiling in horror, they rose up to do battle.

For some two hundred years America lived and prospered under the philosophy of the Enlightenment. The creed was uncomplicated, optimistic: Cultivate your own cabbage patch and all will be well. To the average American this was translated into: Concentrate on economic activity, or better still, profit opportunities, and forget the problems of the world. If anyone should doubt the wisdom of this, let him go to the great book, the *Wealth of Nations,* where he would find it said that if each man minded his own affairs, the market would automatically create from the countless and diverse parts a sublime unity which exalts man to ever mounting heights. Man was to know perfection on this earth, perhaps not in Europe where the idea had originated only to wither for lack of application, but certainly in America where men placed their hopes, their dreams, their faith, even their love in a benevolent Nature.

How wonderful it all was; in America there could be no formation and unleashing of the terrible forces that wracked Europe and the rest of the civilized world. Let man concern himself only with his own garden—particularly profit making —and all would be well. Think not of existing injustice, of the discrimination against the Negro, of the young who are deprived of adequate education, of the children born to brutally depraved parents, or destined to bear the scourge of the city slums or the curse of the isolated poverty-stricken hills. Think not of the maimed and crippled who must forget about such lofty thoughts as dignity and self-respect in their begging to satisfy their daily requirements, think not of the millions upon millions of hapless people in strange and remote lands who live and die in ignorance and poverty. Think not of these things, they are too unsettling, depressing, embarrassing. Evil has always existed in the world and there is

nothing the individual can do to alleviate or erase it except
through minding one's own affairs, letting Nature resolve it
in her own inscrutable way.

Certainly it would be better if the world were a place of
flawless splendor; but who can make it so? Man has tried
again and again; but each time he lays claim to infinite good
and ultimate truth, it leads to zealous authoritarianism and
then human degradation and wretchedness, out of which
emerges savage destruction and senseless mass murder, all
justified in the name of truth, beauty and justice. Except for
World War I, when we foolishly became intoxicated with
saving the world, and World War II, when we were compelled to defend our gardens, America has been largely
spared the awful calamity of piety and hate that has plagued
the rest of the world. And this wondrous peace and prosperity, this unequaled freedom and happiness all flowed from
a unique American social structure under which each family
unit looked to its own interest and expected others to do the
same.

The lesson is unmistakable; the course of action decisively clear: do with your life as you will, I shall neither
trespass on your property nor violate the sanctity of your
thoughts; in return I ask only the same of you. I hold no
claim that I know the shape or dimension of perfection for
of these things I do not think. The world is too vast, too
complex, too contradictory for any petty rationalist human
mind to apprehend in its entirety. The only truth is that man
cannot know ultimate truth. All that I or any man can do is
to give myself unsparingly to my chosen vocation while placing my full trust in the unfailing laws of the market.
Whatever is mine I have earned through honest labor and
therefore richly deserve. If you and everyone else did as I,
all men would be healthy, prosperous, and secure. Don't
question the make-up of things, and don't wonder why some

are blessed and some are not; these things you cannot know, much less understand. Believe only that the system is infallible and that if each man had the courage and the pride to make his own way, then surely mankind would march swift and true along the road to human perfection and secular progress.

This then is the creed of orthodoxy—a creed which flows from an uncompromising faith that the free market is geared to produce a state of human splendor. The unsophisticated economic determinist has a simple, ready-made explanation for the unbending tenacity of those who cling so desperately to this creed. Such orthodoxy, they declare, provides the apologetics for rationalizing disparity of income and position and is absolutely essential to the justification of the narrow interests of the rich and powerful. Certainly no one can dispute that the inner logic of traditional capitalistic theory concludes that the rich are deserving and that the poor and unfortunate are in one way or another inherently inferior. But to limit orthodoxy to such an inconsequential role is to fall far short of the mark.

For men of all walks of life—and particularly those in positions of leadership—need and demand social approval and to an even greater degree must be guided by some inner light that tells them that they are in fact fighting the good fight. Without this, man suffers a sense of guilt, making life a terrible ordeal. Thus it was that by giving purpose and meaning to life, traditional economic theory made its greatest contribution. It spelled out unmistakable goals, the achievement of which was easily measured. Fasten your power and skill upon economic endeavors, it preached, and to the extent that you succeed, you will be rewarded with personal riches and public glory. By following this course, not only will you find satisfaction through developing and expressing your own unique and sovereign personality, but you will confer benefit

upon the whole human race. Here then was an easily understood, optimistic "eschatology" which, while liberating the
individual to pursue vigorously his own destiny, freed him
from any worry over the social consequences of his action
on the theory that whatever he did would hasten man in his
step-by-step travel along the route to human perfection.

Keynes, by teaching that the automatism of the private
enterprise system was nothing more than historical fiction,
belittled this wonderfully happy perspective. This was heresy
in its most base and disquieting form. For if it was frankly
conceded that the free market was nothing more than an
unruly force which, with equal indifference, could deprave or
perfect man, then the American culture rested on an illusion
that made both individual goals and the future of mankind
terrifyingly uncertain.

If Keynes were right, then some centuries back man must
have taken the wrong turn, for which he has no one to blame
but himself. Fired by a passion to improve his creature comforts, his gaze and his aspirations slowly shifted from the
other world to this as he was caught up in the exhilarating
and absorbing experience of constructing for himself an
earthly paradise.

This was not accomplished through some deliberate plan
—that would be too much like the authoritarian structure
against which he rebelled—but by individual exertion and
contribution which the divine workings of providence would
coordinate and fashion into a magnificent whole. Gradually
an irreverent science heightened the tensions between Christian cosmology and secular observations; and Western man,
proud of his newly acquired health, riches and knowledge,
thought less and less of the divine and the transcendental and
placed his trust in his own mental and physical powers to
create a secular heaven. This was to become his focus, his
dream, his life. And now the new economics would take this
away from him. For the faithful there was but one course of

action: to deny the validity of these pernicious doctrines; to identify, isolate, and condemn the evil that they were. Under no circumstances could they be accorded respectability; to do so would make the whole of life empty, meaningless, and unbearable.

Having ordered his life on the certainty that man was a selfish creature motivated by the self-love of original sin, and being confident that man was impotent to abstract and create a finite good from an inscrutable and infinite universe, there was no alternative but to fight any doctrine which implied that some form of central authority was necessary to direct the course of the economy and the nation. At best, authority was a barren artifact or an impediment that impaired the individual's capacity to contribute to community welfare; at worst, given man's compulsion to promote himself and the cause he championed, a rapacious force that would not be stilled until it had enslaved the human race by stamping out the last spark of individual originality and creativity.

Paralyzed by this spectacle, the true believer steadfastly thinks only of the wonders and virtues of the natural law of the market. As for objective reality, this he quotes, refutes, or distorts according to what is essential to peace of mind. In retrospect, the Great Depression becomes a much needed restorative, a kind of health-inducing cathartic. Identifying and crushing inefficiency, it cleansed the system of creeping decadence and substituted a stern but necessary discipline, enabling America to preserve her heritage and move forward in the realization of her manifest destiny. When confronted with immediate and obvious examples of malfunction, the true disciple stands ready with a whole battery of standard replies. "A good man can always get a job, and the superior one cannot be held down." "If there is fault, it comes from power—power exercised by the labor unions and the government, both of which foolishly tamper with and impede the workings of the market." "As for a General Motors and U.S. Steel, these engines of progress are precluded from abusing power by competition and anti-trust legislation, which make impossible or illegal the holding and exercising of business power."

In one breath governmental expenditures are excoriated for overstimulating the economy and fostering rampant inflation, and in the next breath they are chastised for undermining business confidence and inducing a depression. Foreign aid is soundly condemned for its futility and waste, but even more so because governmental expenditures are equally disruptive on an international scale as they are injurious to the free enterprise system on the domestic scene. "Except for expenditures in defense of our gardens against alien agression, the ultimate hope for world peace and prosperity resides in the operations of an internationally free market."

Such is the picture. It depicts an imperfect society which revels in a false, sinful prosperity, a community racing headlong toward its own destruction. Yet all is not lost, there is still hope; but we must mend our ways and time grows short. And what shall be done? Direct action; of the sort for which America is renown? A frontal assault on the problem? Of course, but before action is taken, there must be some contemplation of the true nature of the good life. Only in this way can man begin to realize that the waxing and waning, the endless waste and repair—which preoccupy and offend the mundane senses—are merely transitory and insignificant aberrations unworthy of man's attentions or energies. Only when the purity and splendor of the free market system is religiously perceived and becomes the moving force determining the course of life is there hope for reversing the tide and achieving the good society. When this is fully appreciated—as surely it must be—then the world will return once more to the Golden Age, wherein lies truth, beauty, and justice.

However one may react to intellectual systems or grand ideologies, I would suggest that even the most hardened American cynic can never quite escape an occasional twinge of longing for the untroubled thought enjoyed by the disciple of capitalist theory. I would think that the most profane iconoclast is not without a certain uneasiness which causes him to resent, if only subconsciously, the heresy formulated by nature and articulated by Keynes. For to the Western mind, capitalist ideology has much to offer. Its heart remains the supreme value of human life, its life's blood the worth and dignity of the individual. At the center it emphasizes that no cause, no canon of truth, no movement is worthy of the destruction of the most unworthy of individuals. In the good society of capitalism, free, intelligent, and self-reliant men, by pursuing separate goals and developing individual talents, find meaning and happiness in life through self-expression and creativity.

That these principles are less than immediately applicable and that the goals of capitalist theory are less than perfectly realized in the hard world of everyday life is, of course, an undeniable fact. Yet a society with free enterprise for a mainspring is not without certain built-in protective measures for the individual. For the private enterprise system remains— although it bears little resemblance to that depicted by capitalist theory—a society of diverse and conflicting elements which always guarantee some level of mobility and multiplicity of opportunities. Business organizations themselves, while anxious to protect their own flanks by various restrictions on competition, desire sufficient maneuverability to alter their operations as they see fit, to drop one product and add a new one, to close one plant and open another.

To this end business organizations commit themselves to an open society and by so doing provide a measure of protection for the individual, although not the kind of protection found in the world of pure theory or that enjoyed by our pioneer forefathers. For this we cannot hope; still, through the safety conferred by the numbers of pluralism, the individual is permitted a latitude of decision that cannot be tolerated by a society unified under a central agency for the purpose of achieving some single, predetermined goal.

There remains one other advantage. Capitalist theory—as with all ideological systems—lends itself very nicely to widely differing interpretations and even the most devout apostle can, with a minimum of discomfort, accommodate all sorts of operational deviations from the pure theory. Public education, social security, and a modest amount of foreign aid can, with a bit of mental forcing, be made to fit into the building of the ideal republic.

Anthropologists tell us that man must have his metaphysics and that the society must have its ideological cement, or the community will fly to pieces. If this is true, we might do well to accept on faith capitalist ideology, rather than critically laying bare its traits and weaknesses, thanking our Maker for providing us with an intellectual system which makes the individual the center of the universe. In another world, or in our world at another time in history, I would think this view appropriate. But in this world of science and technology and organization, in the world in which we must live day by day, I am saddened and made fearful by the thought that this once vital and appropriate philosophy is tragically pathological and that in the world of the future it is geared to destroy the very values it is designed to preserve and exalt.

The source of this fear is not so much the domestic scene, where the power of the government and other conservative organizations, such as business corporations and labor unions, are much too well entrenched to be overturned by violence and where the exceptions to the theory are sufficient in number and broad enough in scope to preclude any traumatic change in the social structure through the ballot box. It is in the deadly serious international race from which America cannot, however she may desire, escape, that this system of beliefs works its severest damage. However one may wish otherwise, the world, touched and infected by Westernization, is tortured by turmoil and conflict as the less civilized and economically backward areas strain against tradition and fight to overthrow established order in an effort to improve life here on earth. In Latin America there is an ominous stirring; in Africa, social and political ferment; in Asia, the searing fire of force; Laos, South Vietnam, and India hang by a thread as communism denies the validity of the individual and seductively spreads the gospel of history, progress, and mankind. Throughout much of the world the authoritarian spirit is gaining acceptance and momentum as more and more people are victimized by an ideology which teaches that the individual must subordinate himself to the will of an inexorable and indifferent whole.

Yet America, still the greatest power of all, shackles and cripples herself with a system of beliefs that places such matters as a balanced budget and a slowly rising price level above fighting an evil which arrogantly stalks the world, openly ridiculing and, wherever possible, crushing the very foundation upon which our civilization rests. Our obsession with finances, a stable price level, and a compulsion to prove the existence of a market automaticism which is forever lost, deprive us of using immense, untapped resources, not only for the defense of our gardens, but for the teaching of the world, through education and genuine economic development, that ultimate social values rest within the sovereign individual. In this context, pure capitalist orthodoxy is incurably pathological, and the doctrines articulated by Keynes are a liberating force enabling America to do serious battle in protecting and spreading the values of the West.

VIII

The Final Heresy

THE YEAR 1930 WAS CHARACTERIZED BY NEITHER ELATION nor high expectations. As the economy sank deeper and deeper into the Depression and men solemnly spoke of an exhausted economic driving force, America knew a growing sense of despair. Yet from out of this darkness was heard a voice of enthusiasm and optimism, talking not of poverty and unemployment, but of abundance and luxury. The voice spoke of the recent past, telling of the fruits of the industrial revolution, of the increases in human productivity, and of how, through further mastery of his environment, man would transform the world into a veritable cornucopia. This means, said the voice, "that the economic problem is not— if we look into the future—*the permanent problem of the human race.*"

The voice was that of the same man who some years later was to identify the origin of and prescribe the cure for the Depression: John Maynard Keynes. Unlike many others who found it amusing or fashionable to speculate on Utopia, Keynes viewed the coming age of opulence with mixed emotions.

"If the economic problem is solved," he observed, "mankind will be deprived of its traditional purpose." Posing the question, "Will this be of benefit?" he answered, "We shall be able to afford to dare to assess the money-motive at its true value. The love of money as a possession—as distinguished from the love of money as a means to the enjoyments and realities of life—will be recognized for what it is, a somewhat disgusting morbidity, one of those semi-criminal, semi-pathological propensities which one hands over with a shudder to the specialists in mental disease."

At the same time Keynes was disturbed, remarking, "Yet there is no country and no people, I think, who can look forward to the age of leisure and of abundance without a dread. For we have been trained too long to strive and not to enjoy. It is a fearful problem for the ordinary person, with no special talents, to occupy himself, especially if he no longer has roots in the soil or in custom or in the beloved conventions of a traditional society. To judge from the behaviour and the achievements of the wealthy classes today in any quarter of the world, the outlook is very depressing!" *

When Keynes wrote in 1930, the Western world lay prostrate under the scourge of poverty and men could not be expected to take seriously this fantasy of the dangers of wealth and prosperity. Keynes had demonstrably erred in his predictions. He had estimated that it would be a full century before the West would suffer a plague of plenty. In America this was to be accomplished in barely 25 years.

Documenting this transformation is a veritable flood of literature, the most provocative of which include David Riesman's *The Lonely Crowd,* William Whyte's *The Organization Man,* and John Galbraith's *The Affluent Society.* All of these works elaborate the thesis that man in recent years has slowly shifted his point of reference, that as a dynamic social force the "dollar race" is fast losing its primacy and men are turning to other things for charting the course of life. Riesman is a self-taught sociologist, and Whyte an employee of one of the nation's largest publishing companies.

* *Essays in Persuasion,* The Macmillan Company, 1931.

Both men, however, not without a certain amount of painful nostalgia, speak of a lost society populated by inner-directed dollar chasers; both depict a new social order composed of individuals who look to the formal group and the hierarchic organization for direction and purpose. Galbraith also sees the doctrine of "wealth for the sake of wealth" falling from grace—but ironically much too slowly. Rather than pleading for a re-energization of the still powerful but fading dynamism of money making, Galbraith, the only economist of the group, speaks derisively of our irrational tenacity in clinging to the trappings of a once useful but now largely spent social purpose. In a society where the economic problem is essentially solved, he argues, centering life on the remorseless pursuit and accumulation of material goods is not only foolish, but mischievous. Depicting affluence as a liberating force, Galbraith sees in America an opportunity for men to turn their attention and energy to those things that provide inner satisfaction and self-fulfillment.

It is this doctrine of declining economic urgency that I have designated "the final heresy." Although articulated only recently by social philosophers, it evolved slowly out of a world of reality until it pervaded our everyday thoughts and became an integral part of the body of common sentiment. All about us there are signs of the hold this heresy has upon the public mind. In conversation we hear ourselves say, "Money isn't everything"; "It doesn't pay too well, but I do like it"; "After 20 years in the service, I will be able to retire on a good pension," while in our literature we read that the decline of economic urgency is undermining conventional materialism and causing traditional economic forces to lose potency in determining individual destiny and social direction. Reflecting a search for security in an insecure world, these expressions indicate that the once powerful money-making motive is only one of many variables in the contemporary formula for the good life.

Perhaps the security-minded college student—so often the despair of those who preach the virtue of freedom and individuality—best illustrates the extent to which "the final heresy" has influenced the American mind. Amused by and contemptuous of the Horatio Alger spirit, the contemporary college student entertains few thoughts of setting out alone and unaided to meet and conquer an eagerly awaiting universe. The world is much too big, and complex, much too unmanageable for such foolish dreams. Speaking with concrete assurance, he tells of his goal to become an executive of a large, prominent firm. Not immediately; this would be expecting too much. First, he must join the ranks of an aggressive company, prove his worth as a diligent worker and faithful servant, one day to be rewarded by a position of honor and stature.

Not that the young college graduate is contemptuous of either money or the comforts it will buy. It is simply a matter of alternatives. To set out alone, as a single soul, in pursuit of wealth and glory requires an extraordinary combination of personal traits and rare assets. Included among these are money, experience, knowledge, imagination, and a sort of reckless irresponsibility in the weighing of moral obligations to family and creditor alike. A few men doubtless are so endowed, but of these most see the world as a place carefully staked out and ruled over by well-established, powerful organizations. To court open battle with a General Motors or a Westinghouse or a Macy's is to invite economic disaster and personal disgrace. Reminded by his parents—who bear the scars of the Depression—of the wisdom of prudence; told by

common sense that without a haven of refuge, an impersonal
society can be a cold and savage place; and taught by his
teachers that the modern business organization is the product
of numerous and diversely skilled specialists, the job-hunting
college student has no alternative but to pledge his services
and his loyalty in return for the money and position offered
by one of the great organizations that populate modern
America.

Nor has this change gone unreflected by the great centers
of learning. Thirty years ago the aspiring young undergraduate interested in learning something about business spent his
time trying to fathom the mysteries of the economy. In so
doing he was taught that the individual was the center of the
universe; and that the whole social order, and particularly
the economy, was geared for but one purpose: to gratify the
wants and fancies of the individual. Today, except for a required course in elementary economics—often seen by the
student as a trackless wasteland of arid charts and meaningless
functions—students spurn economics in favor of subjects that
exalt the organization and, if only by indirection, instill
within the individual a sense of personal inadequacy.

And so the typical young graduate goes out to join the
forces of some well-established business, political, or social
institution. With a bit of luck, as he masters his assignments
and apprehends the operations of the organization, his income and position advance as he is given growing responsibility. How fast or how far he will rise is a product of many
factors, many of which are beyond his control. As a person he
may be happy or miserable, productive or barren, creative
or dreary, as different men have always been in all times and
all societies. But there is a difference, if not in man himself,
then in the society in which he lives. For not only is present-
day man blessed with material comforts and conveniences of

all sorts which make life easier and pleasanter, but, unlike his counterpart of 50 or 100 years ago, he experiences real difficulty in attuning his activities to the pursuit of material goods, or more specifically to dollar making.

Not that the American is oblivious to either money or the advantages it confers. Indeed the "organization man" ever looking forward to a more generous paycheck is wont to discipline himself to tend to business, to develop the habit of studied diligence and, with an eye to advancement, to think ahead. But alas, the relationship between dedication and reward is often a distant and distressingly tenuous one. Promotions are unpredictable and agonizingly slow, and the correlation between "virtue" and advancement is something considerably less than perfect. Also at odds with resolute dollar chasing are the intimate subcultures which are the bricks and stuffs of which great organizations are made. As distinctly personal societies they demand loyalty and impose on the worker a set of norms and ethics which to a greater or lesser degree reflect Christian values. Unlike the hard-swinging, free-market operator who is expected to put business before friendship, the white-collar worker is taught to develop a sense of warmth and affection for his fellow workers. The weaknesses of others are to be understood and forgiven; an unwritten law commands that the individual sacrifice personal interest before doing damage or injustice to either friend or colleague.

As an integral part of a subdivision, the worker's first responsibility is to his peers, and he gives little thought to linking his position with the financial welfare of the whole. To be sure—whether a personnel manager, a publicity director, or division statistician—he is pleased to learn of healthy company earnings; but since his immediate efforts can be related to company profits only indirectly, he finds purpose through the use of other standards, which make his efforts meaningful. In so doing he may very well exalt a program which is at cross purposes with those of money making. He may, for example, set a course which will expand his department, inaugurate a new function, or take over a job already quite adequately performed by some other division within the organization. Frustrated by the widening gap between performance and immediate monetary rewards, the organization man is impelled to invent largely parochial, nonfinancial standards for assessing conduct and bestowing success.

But there is still another energy which gives further momentum to the final heresy. Ironically the origin of this emerging force is nothing less than America's triumphant transition from rags to riches. When the necessities and comforts of life are scarce, man treasures them and will give his life to the winning of them; but when essentials abound and luxury is commonplace, material goods lose their luster and man searches for other distinguishing marks. In a society where the commonest of creatures possesses an abundance of food and clothing, owns a house full of mechanical wonders, and can speak with authority on the advantages of travel, men who would make known their individual superiority must turn to other avenues for prestige.

Such then is the conspiracy of forces which, through a steady erosion of the traditional economic drives, has caused America to be stunned and bewildered by a growing sense of loss of purpose. But now we are ahead of our story; before proceeding further, it is essential to leave the world of everyday senses and enter the realm of thought where contending doctrines clash in a fight for the supremacy of the mind. If we are to understand the changing American attitude, it is necessary to examine, however hastily, some of the intellectual battlegrounds along the route from orthodoxy to heterodoxy, from high doctrine to "final heresy."

Grand ideologies die a slow, lingering death, and orthodox economics is no exception. Three wars, a calamitous depression, the conversion of the federal government from a neutral to a primary economic force, and a basic transformation of the character of the business organization have all played a role in compelling the individual to search for and live by a different set of values. But at the level of social philosophy, change comes harder and when we think or speak of such things as farm subsidies or union activities, we fall back, as if by nature, on a slightly battered but nevertheless still respected economic philosophy.

Despite remarkable staying power, orthodoxy is today on the defensive, resisting as best it can a pitiless assault on all fronts. It grudgingly surrenders ground as its chief spokesmen learn that theoretical foundations make imperfect weapons in the battle of everyday crises. Of course, as long as responsibility is not theirs, as long as they can stand on the sidelines and expound sacred principles while carefully hedging on specific courses of action, these apostles of orthodoxy can speak with uncompromising authority. They, however, no longer go unchallenged. In a free society there are always men who, wanting to change the order of things, find nothing more gratifying than to level a cold and withering eye on high doctrine. Of those who show contempt or aggression, none are more hostile toward orthodoxy than many of those persons who are so cavalierly lumped together and classified as intellectuals.

The term *intellectual* is at best fuzzy and confusing. The stereotyped intellectual does not exist; and although intellectuals tend to cluster under a favorable climate of opinion, they are to be found throughout the professional world. Nor is position or work performed a satisfactory criterion. A history professor whose only passions are baseball and the strategy of General Lee would not qualify, but a popular novelist

who elaborates the conflicts of values underlying the Civil
War most surely would. Perhaps the most that can be said
about the intellectual is that he is fascinated by the study of
one or more social or value systems. As a bitter social critic
or a disciplined defender of the *status quo,* he may be a
narrow, self-righteous cynic who is tormented by the immediate state of affairs. Lacking power in a world of power,
he is often acrimonious, believing that his talents are not
adequately appreciated and that society could be a magnificent place if only men would take heed of the ideals so carefully elaborated by him.

But whether a bitter authoritarian personality or a happy
individualist cursed (or blessed) with an incorrigible curiosity, many such men have had a corrosive effect on the prevailing ideology, whatever it may be. Forever asking embarrassing questions, they display a flair for contrasting the ideal
with the actual and highlighting the gap separating them.
Although the reins of power are beyond their grasp, they are
not without influence. Indeed, as any good absolutist knows
full well, and as Hitler and Stalin demonstrated with terrible
thoroughness, intellectuals are a potential menace and warrant screening of the most painstaking kind. In the absolutist
regimes, those irrevocably committed to high doctrine deserve recognition and exaltation; but those opposed, or even
worse, those who would lay it bare in the cold light of day,
must at all costs be silenced.

In an open society the intellectual enjoys freedom for
making his presence known and, to a greater or lesser degree,
influencing the turn of events. As a researcher or idea man, he
has access to the ear of leaders invested with decision-making
responsibilities; and as a university professor, he impresses
the fruits of his investigations and thoughts on the minds of
those who are preparing to make their way in life. Important
as these roles may be, the intellectual exercises his greatest

influence by means of the pen, through which he can vent his wrath or detail the results of his study. Of the published materials of intellectual origin, only a very small fraction finds its way to the outside world, but more often than not it is blatantly or subtly at odds with commonly accepted ideology.

There have always been a fair number of intellectuals who have preached that life is much too precious to be thrown away on the materialism of Madison Avenue. But by the populace at large, such men are regarded as amusing curiosities or effete and repulsive malcontents everlastingly mumbling something about music, art, literature, or religion. There exists, however, a kind of unspoken agreement that a free society must tolerate such harmless eccentrics, even if normal people cannot make sense out of their incoherent mutterings, much less take them seriously. If most of these voices went unheard, new forces were gathering in the realm of thought which, before they exhausted themselves, were destined to tear at the very roots of social theory. Certain members of the intellectual class saw and spoke of this rising force; and, by so doing, they unwittingly set out upon a course that would lead the social mind further and further from established doctrine.

The 1930's was a time of anguish and trial, but it was also a decade of great change, particularly in economic thought. We have already observed how during this period the Depression and Keynes conspired to alter man's view of the economy. Although Keynes' system must be ranked as the outstanding contribution of the decade, other ideas were taking form which were to have an equal, if not more profound, influence in modifying man's conception of his economy, indeed his whole society.

Matters came to a head in 1933, when two academic economists independently published systematic works evaluating the changing nature of competition in the market place.* Starting from the obvious fact that competition in the market was nowhere near as pure as theory implied or orthodoxy asserted, these writers raised disquieting questions about the capacity of the real world to deliver the results promised by the world of theory. In traditional thought everything turned on competition or, to put it another way, on the complete absence of market power. Now as long as competition is in fact pure—no person or group enjoying any discretion whatsoever in setting prices—then logic dictates that the free market will forever work toward a sublime harmony of maximum consumer satisfaction, just prices, full employment, and economic progress.

But what if competition is imperfect? It was to this question that these writers turned their attention. In the main their focus was technical. Concentrating on the effects of reduced competition on prices and production, they wrote their books in the esoteric style of their profession. For a while at least, the philosophical implications of their probings lay safely buried under a logical edifice of formidable terminology and geometric functions. Only some years later, after the technical had been mastered and elaborated, was there anything like a general reading of these books for their philosophical content. And only then was it apparent that within these works dwelled certain embryonic ideas that were directly antithetical to the prevailing belief that the market was an inexorable force geared for the perfection of society.

If the full meaning of the breakthrough in theoretical analysis was long obscured to even the dedicated scholar, the

---

* *The Theory of Monopolistic Competition* and *The Economics of Imperfect Competition*. The former was written by Edward Chamberlin, an Amercan; the latter by Joan Robinson, an Englishwoman.

significance of empirical studies made during this period was widely appreciated. In 1932 Berle and Means published their ground-breaking work, *The Modern Corporation and Private Property,* and later in the same decade the highly regarded Temporary National Economic Committee conducted investigations further exposing incredible and alarming concentration of power. The documentation of the existence and use of immense economic power which emerged from these diggings in the real world was, to many, a disconcerting revelation. Having learned from the mainstream of thought that desire for self-gain is a primary human motivation, logic compelled thinkers to condemn these exposed seats of power as instruments of the few for impoverishing the many.

Here was evidence demonstrating beyond all doubt what some men had suspected but few had had the courage to face: the existence of an evil so all-pervasive that it threatened to corrupt the whole of society. In *Monopoly in America* (The Macmillan Company, 1955) Adams and Gray observe:

> Monopoly . . . is an abomination in a free society. It can come into existence only by the destruction of economic freedom; it can perpetuate itself only by the continued suppression of economic freedom. Thus, by the necessities of its own being, monopoly is the antithesis of competition. But monopoly, in order to preserve itself, can do more than merely destroy the free market and restrict competition; it can, transcending the narrow confines of the market place, reach out to suppress both social and political freedom. Monopoly is not, as many assume, strictly an *economic* phenomenon, the influence of which is limited to the market. On the contrary, it is a power system—and power is a social institution, indivisible and all-pervasive.

In this context monopolistic power is a specter driven by need to "dominate the entire society and suppress all freedom." The source of this dread is, of course, capitalist theory itself. The pure theory teaches that competition is the single agent mighty enough to convert individual instinctual drives for self-gratification into a high order of social good. Lacking the kind of competition that precludes the power to set or influence prices, pure theory teaches that the economic system is inevitably geared to work in a perverse and malicious fashion. Without competition, not only are powerful, self-seeking men equipped to impose callous injustices on the weak, but, even more important, the entire system of private property is placed in theoretical if not actual jeopardy. For as the theory has it, competition and competition alone compels the establishment of the just price, the assurance of equitable rewards, the guarantee of full employment, and the ceaseless unfolding of economic progress. Remove competition and all intellectual certainty is lost. Most surely there can be no guarantee that any of these beautiful ideals will be realized; and indeed, if theoretical analysis can be trusted, it is all too clear that the exercise of economic power is unfailingly antithetical to the hope of achieving the millenium so successfully adumbrated by pure capitalistic theory.

Man can live in a state of tension and shock only so long. Continually faced with a disturbing situation, he will correct it either through action or thought. During the crisis of the 30's, his response was a spontaneous cry for immediate and decisive action. As would be expected the initial reaction to the documentation of economic might was a dramatic condemnation of the malevolent monopolists who suddenly were identified as the agents of depression. Once again the battle cries of the 90's were rediscovered and men rallied to destroy the industrial giants who would make mockery of the very doctrines which justified their existence.

But if the clamor for correction came easily, action did not. It was soon obvious that men of power did not take kindly to the suggestion that they relinquish their "hard won" prerogatives. Not surprisingly, the "power elite" was entirely militant on such matters and marshaled all available resources to preclude governmental action designed to lessen its scope of influence. In the democratic arena, where good intentions abound and power is the shaper of policy, these men of strength skillfully deployed their forces, and the reform action so feverishly called for was never permitted to materialize. Instead of breaking up the power centers, extant power begot new power, and the industrial giants grew only greater and mightier.

Thus it was that man was compelled to make a choice. He could be stoical and learn to live with the belief that his was an imperfect and decadent society, or he could adjust his theory to conform with certain stubborn realities. Finding only mental agony in the former alternative, he had no choice but to pursue the latter.

A change in social focus is at best a slow process, and this new perspective was not to be achieved without many a bitter and hard-fought battle. But after the findings of Berle and Means a modification seemed to take place, when it became fashionable to speak of the separation of ownership and control. After an initial reaction of horror, men began to see advantages in this separation. For, it was said, when the owner is in control, all the might of the giant organization is ruthlessly focused on profit and there is no room for such lofty virtues as human kindness or social responsibility. When the ownership is dispersed, we were told, the operation of the organization is conducted differently. Under these conditions the business organization is directed by a new breed of men who, like civil servants, work for salaries rather than profits. These professional managers, unlike the entre-

preneurs of old, are not the victims of the profit fixation and
therefore would listen to their Christian conscience, to the
benefit of both the firm and society. Just how this change in
control was to bring about an advancement of the common
good was not always made clear except that these professionals would not be singularly motivated by selfish instinct.
As such they would be in a position to take whatever action
seemed necessary to make all of human life a richer, more
meaningful experience.

To many this reasoning seemed plausible, but to those who
pondered seriously, a number of nagging questions remained
unanswered. For example, if, as both Christian and economic
thought had always taught, men were forever cursed with the
sin of self-love, how was it that these professional managers
were somehow uniquely blessed with goodness? And how, if
some men are good and some bad, does one distinguish? Has
it not always been a fundamental tenet of liberalism that
finite man could never know infinite good; that each man
must find his own separate good, and that only the natural
law of the market could sum up the countless individual
goods into one grand social good? Does not placing trust in
business statesmanship deny Smith's resolution of the diversity and unity dilemma? Does it not imply that personal
pursuit of self-interest is contrary to the public good and that
certain individuals, specifically professional managers, are to
stand aloof and arbitrarily impose their will on all of society?
And if this be the case, why are business managers uniquely
suited to direct the course of events? Should not this responsibility be delegated to public servants who are forced to submit to the will and inspection of the public?

These are the questions some men asked, and in so doing
tormented themselves and others who would listen. Suddenly
a new line of reasoning erupted that was to make all of these
queries seem remote and largely irrelevant. The rise of this

new outlook was heralded in a 1941 book entitled *The Managerial Revolution* (The John Day Company, Inc.). "The present," wrote the author, James Burnham, "is in fact in a period of social revolution, of transition from one type of society to another. I shall present a theory . . . which is able to explain this transition and to predict the type of society in which the transition will eventuate." The heart of Burnham's theory was that industrialization compelled a jerky but inexorable movement toward The Managerial Society.

The origin of this transition, he observed, was inherent in the nature of the productive process: "The growth of large-scale public corporations along with the technological development of modern industry have virtually wiped . . . [the individual entrepreneur] out of the important sections of the economy; with a few exceptions, they remain only among the 'small businesses' which are trivial in their historical influence." In explaining the transformation of economic institutions, he wrote, "There is a combined shift: through changes in the technique of production, the functions of management become more distinctive, more complex, more specialized, and more crucial to the whole process of production, thus serving to set off those who perform these functions as a separate group or class in society; and at the same time those who formerly carried out what functions there were of management, the *bourgeoisie,* themselves withdraw from management, so that the difference in function becomes also a difference in the individuals who carry out the function."

In describing the new class—the managers—he said, "We may often recognize them as 'production managers,' operating executives, superintendents, administrative engineers, supervisory technicians; or, in government (for they are to be found in governmental enterprise just as in private enterprise) as administrators, commissioners, bureau heads, and so on. I mean by managers, in short, those who already for the

most part in contemporary society are actually managing, on
its technical side, the actual process of production, no matter
what the legal and financial form—individual, corporate,
governmental—of the process."

As a dispassionate scientist Burnham talked repeatedly of
"what is and what will be" rather than what "ought to be."
Yet he professed to see certain distinct advantages in the
managerial society. In addition to the resolution of the op-
pressive unemployment that haunted America, he believed
that "under managerial economy there will be a greater total
output of material goods in relation to the total population
than under capitalism, including such goods as supply the
needs of warmth, food, shelter, and so on. This would seem
to indicate that the masses on the average (not necessarily any
particular section of the masses, and the result is not guaranteed) would have a somewhat higher material standard of
living."

Painting with bold, broad strokes, Burnham did not limit
himself to the economy; he addressed himself to the monumental task of depicting the whole social landscape. What he
portrayed, however, held appeal for neither the eye nor the
mind. Dominating his entire scene was a matrix of mechanistic forces producing unmistakable deterministic pressures
that forever worked to push the civilized world further toward a managerial society. In the final stage of this inevitable
evolution the managers as agents of the state would control
and direct literally all organized activity. When his work was
finished in 1941, it was Hitler's Germany that was depicted
as the prototype—although in an early stage—of the managerial society.

For most Americans, who are optimists by nature, such a
dismal prognosis could only be rejected as appalling. Perhaps
Burnham's analysis would have been more palatable had his
investigations been purely economic. But they were not; and

the dreadful picture he painted provoked a damaging barrage of criticism. He was indicted for being a bad historian, an ill-informed economist, and a political journalist who would hide his admiration for a criminal Germany under the guise of scientific investigation. With America's entry into World War II, Burnham's analysis was swallowed by the tide of everyday events. It would be some time after victory and international order of a sort was restored before there was a renewed interest in his work. And then it would become common to rail against the managerial society and a concomitant loss of individual freedom and initiative.

Despite wars, some men continue to study their society and ponder the hopes and prospects for the human race. One was Joseph A. Schumpeter, an imaginative political economist and a thoroughgoing aristocrat in the European tradition who was emotionally and spiritually committed to capitalism. As the war raged on all fronts in 1942, he published his social science classic, *Capitalism, Socialism, and Democracy* (Harper & Row, Publishers) wherein he attributes virtually every important development in the postfeudal world to the capitalist mind and spirit. Captivated by the heroics and glamor of the adventuresome entrepreneur in the capitalist arena, he was as scornfully opposed to Marxian socialism as he was contemptuously indifferent to the dull gray world of socialistic democracy. To Schumpeter, the daring and courage of the innovating entrepreneur in the risk-bearing and profit-taking capitalist society represented the summit of cultural evolution. Anything that might come after this could be only retrogression.

Schumpeter's conception of capitalism was very unlike that of many of his colleagues and very different from that adumbrated by the competitive model. Depicting capitalism as an evolutionary process, he methodically focused the light of history on traditional theory and conventional ideology. The mainstream of economic thought, in his opinion, idealizes a static, atomistic, antlike society. In essence, Schumpeter branded such thinking as mischievous nonsense. For, he declared, it is not the effete competition depicted in the textbooks that counts, "but the competition from the new commodity, the new technology, the new source of supply, the new type of organization (the large-scale unit of control for instance)—competition which commands a decisive cost or quality advantage and which strikes not at the margins of the profits and the outputs of the existing firms but at their foundations and their very lives."

Attacking the traditionalists who were forever decrying the evils of such power concentrations as U.S. Steel or the Standard Oil Company, he defended the large corporation and observed, "As soon as we go into details and inquire into the individual items in which progress was most conspicuous, the trail leads not to the doors of those firms that work under conditions of comparatively free competition but precisely to the doors of the large concerns—which, as in the case of agricultural machinery, also account for much of the progress in the competitive sector—and a shocking suspicion dawns upon us that big business may have had more to do with creating that standard of life than with keeping it down." Instead of a fixed set of relationships populated by an unnumbered quantity of milling and powerless organizations, capitalism, he insisted, is a process of industrial mutation "that incessantly revolutionizes the economic structure *from within,* incessantly destroying the old one, incessantly creating a new one. This process of Creative Destruction is the essential fact about capitalism. It is what capitalism consists in and what every capitalist concern has got to live in."

Thus Schumpeter's economy, unlike the neat and orderly one envisaged by the traditionalists, was energized by a number of aggressive and identifiable industrial giants who, one with the other, were engaged in a death struggle. His notion of competition was distinctly different from that which peacefully and automatically operated to assure a just price, the establishment of a fair wage, and the elimination of undeserved profits. Indeed in Schumpeter's theory profit was the life blood of economic progress; from it were fashioned the major weapons of battle, out of which came the "perennial gale of creative destruction." With high profits, firms were in a position to experiment, to develop new products, to improve the quality of old, to venture high stakes on price reductions, to explore the hazardous fields of untried methods and unproved equipment, and generally to undertake projects of large risk which the small firm, lacking both talent and financial reserves, could not begin to imagine, much less actively and continually initiate.

It is this fierce competition to discover, to innovate, and to grow that Schumpeter believed gave robust vitality to the American economy. Always unyielding, this competition between titans was, he felt, a far more profound force in accelerating the pace of progress and raising the standard of living than conventional competition ever was or could be. In speaking of the existing state he remarked, "This kind of competition is as much more effective than the other as a bombardment is in comparison with forcing a door, and so much more important that it becomes a matter of comparative indifference whether competition in the ordinary sense functions more or less promptly; the powerful lever that in the long run expands output and brings down prices is in any case made of other stuff." Along these same lines, John Kenneth Galbraith in his *American Capitalism* (Houghton Mifflin Company, 1953) some years later observed:

> The bituminous coal industry, apart from a handful of very large operators; the cotton textile industry, apart from a few very large groups of mills; the clothing industry, the lumber industry and the shoe industry do

very little research. None of them are thought of as technically progressive industries. All of them (apart always from the few large firms they contain and which help prove the case) roughly meet the specifications of the competitive model. They also conform to the ideal which the American economist has had anciently in mind. No firm in these industries (the few special cases again excepted) has appreciable influence on prices; each is forced by circumstances which it cannot control to search for the greatest efficiency of operation; in most of them entry and exit are admirably free; few of the firms in these industries engage in extensive competitive advertising and salesmanship. Yet almost no one would select them as a showpiece of American industrial achievement. The showpieces are, with rare exceptions, the industries which are dominated by a handful of large firms. The foreign visitor, brought to the United States to study American production methods and associated marvels, visits the same firms as do attorneys of the Department of Justice in their search for monopoly.

Such then was the state of American economic thought during much of the 1950's. Not that there was unanimity or that the transition from conventional thought to the evolutionary view came as a clean break with the past. But as time passed, talk of the concentration of economic power and its concomitant abuses faded as public interest turned to inflation, unemployment, and economic growth.

It was popular to discuss the wonders of dynamic or workable competition, a phrase implying that many of the things promised by conventional competition and more were to be realized from the endemic struggle among the engines of progress—the business empires. Having essentially accepted and rationalized the existence of economic power, talk of the social structure gradually blended into the background as policy makers focused their attention on balancing social stability with economic growth. The new thought was on these lines: Let us not worry about the organization. It may be true that the industrial titans, in frustrating the automatic workings of the market, do momentary injury to low prices and full employment. But even if this is so, the day-by-day piling up of benefits in the form of an extravagant stream of remarkable products and incredible efficiencies dwarfs any minor and temporary deviation that might be traced to strategic, short-run use of power. Look around, the new voice said. Without Dupont there would be no nylon; without IBM and its mighty competitors the marvels of the electronic machines and the digital computer would be beyond the powers of man; without General Motors and a handful of other integrated auto-makers there would not have been the research and development or the automation and cost-cutting methods that make the automobile an American birthright.

Now, admitted a small voice, some of our large firms may suffer a kind of paralysis of bigness; a few, no doubt, have grown beyond the point of optimum efficiency. But surely it must be agreed that ideal size varies from industry to industry, from area to area, and even from firm to firm; and that no one has yet found or is likely to find anything that resembles a commonly accepted measure for assessing which firm suffers a sickness of bigness. Therefore we should dispense with this foolish speculation and permit the market through "workable competition" to resolve this problem if, indeed, a real problem exists. For if it is true that some organizations are crippled by a sort of creeping elephantiasis, they will be unfailingly disciplined by the market, and eventually they will adapt internal operations to outside realities and remain healthy, viable contributors; or they will fall before an indifferent "perennial gale of creative destruction."

Surely, the new thinkers said, it must be apparent that a movement to return the economy to something approaching textbook competition would be nothing short of lunacy. It is only fortunate, they argued, that the romantic souls who preach such preposterous idealism are the source of more amusement than policy; but let those obsessed with the simplicity of bygone days understand that the implementation of their impractical yearning would exterminate economic progress and make a travesty of the whole economic process.

In rallying around Schumpeter and preaching his doctrine of dynamic competition, these enthusiasts neglected only one thing: Schumpeter's vision of an internally generated capitalist evolution which, in eroding the capitalist spirit and undermining capitalist institutions, would ultimately enfeeble the very motive power of the capitalist engine itself. At the end of the evolutionary process—forty, sixty, perhaps even a hundred years away—Schumpeter saw only socialism.

The theory of dynamic competition is attractive in many ways. It frankly admits the existence of bigness and proceeds to convert it into a benevolent economic advantage. For those who are unconvinced, for those who complain that economic power is an impediment producing short-run distortion, the knights of dynamic competition explain that minor aberrations can easily be offset through the application of "Keynesian" policy.* The procedure, they say, is simple and

---

* Not Schumpeter, however. Seeing government as a threat to his beloved capitalist order, he was, although not intractably so, suspicious of even emergency antidepression measures. To the very end he maintained that the capitalist engine alone and unaided could have satisfactorily resolved the issue of the Great Depression.

painless. If there is unemployment, if the economy is not growing fast enough, this can be swiftly remedied through further injections of federal funds into the economy. Being able to borrow from commercial banks and the Federal Reserve System—which in theory has unlimited power to create money—the government's source of funds is without bounds. There need be no reason why corrective steps cannot be taken to alleviate whatever unemployment might arise. The important issue, therefore, is not the composition or the structure of the economy, but the action that must be taken to assure the optimum rate of economic progress. Rather than wasting our talents by speculating on the state of market competition, we must fasten our thoughts on significant issues: inflation and economic development.

Thus it came about that policy interests shifted from the discussion of competition as the regulator to the government as the energizer. It was not long before an inflammatory debate spread until attention centered on one primary question: What degree of inflation should the nation be willing to bear for the purpose of stimulating economic growth? Congressional committees addressed themselves to this question, special bodies were commissioned to study it, and established organizations issued reports and conflicting recommendations for resolving the issue. The economic journals blossomed with familiar thoughts in new dress, and articles in the popular magazines and the financial pages of the newspapers alerted the laity to the economic dilemma which had beset the economic thinkers.

Finally, in the 1960 presidential campaign, the nation saw the two candidates grapple with this issue. Both candidates, of course, pledged themselves to promote economic growth and protect the price level. But fate had decreed that Vice President Nixon must underscore the ominous dangers of inflation, while history assigned Senator Kennedy the role

of pointing to Russia and expounding eloquently the virtues
of economic growth. With the election of Kennedy to the
White House, the die had been cast—or so it seemed at the
time.

Even as this debate was moving toward its dramatic culmination, a gentle, yet chilling breeze sprang up and gained
strength and intensity. To those who took notice, it carried
a familiar and disturbing whisper which repeatedly asked,
"To what purpose is this much-praised economic progress?
Is it sacred unto itself, or is it to somehow benefit mankind?
If the latter is the case, then must we not consider not only
the amount and rate of growth, but also the composition
and distribution of its fruits? If it is to render the highest
good to mankind, must we not chart its course and channel
its direction?" These questions quietly infiltrated the world
of thought. Most men, sensing profound blasphemy, ignored
them and turned their thoughts to less disturbing matters;
but a few, possessed of courage, faced them squarely, gave
them serious thought, and tried to respond with honest answers. One such man, endowed with a rare combination of
economic knowledge, a creative imagination, and a literary
turn of mind, was John Kenneth Galbraith. In *The Affluent
Society* he turned his talents to answering these questions and
in so doing skillfully and eloquently framed a most disturbing picture.

His message is an absorbing, if, some say, a wicked one. In
substance, he holds that America is the captive of an ideology
which makes man the slave and the system the master. He
further identifies this ideology as the theory of the market,
and although he praises this intellectual force for serving
man well for so long, at the same time he condemns this
"conventional wisdom" as an outgrown ideal that serves no
purpose but to enervate social vitality and to maim the
powers of the individual. In emphasizing that change in

thought has failed to keep pace with the changes in the state of wealth, he points out that in all of history the world has always been compelled to fight the curse imposed by a niggardly nature, that man was without the means to provide himself with sufficient food, clothing, and shelter. But this now is past, at least for America. Ours is The Affluent Society, a place where the basic requirements are a birthright, where luxuries have become "necessities."

Out of this blessed abundance, even extravagance, has emerged a new way of looking at American society. It is to the elaboration of the thinking and values implicit in this new line of inquiry that a large portion of the remainder of this chapter is devoted. To no little degree the source of this rising vision can be traced to Keynes, Alvin Hansen,* and, from a different quarter, David Riesman, to mention a few. Still, in the stream of economic thought, the work of Galbraith is of singular stature in popularizing this view. Having given credit to these men for inspiring this social focus, it would do a great injustice to assign them responsibility for the specific interpretation and elaboration that follows. With this in mind, let us turn to an examination of what I have chosen to refer to as "the final heresy."

When the essentials of life are scarce, they are prized as highly as life itself, and man must bend his back and exhaust his talents in pursuit of them. But when they are plentiful, then one would think that man would turn all his greatness

---

* Often called the Dean of American Keynesians, Professor Hansen is famous for his stagnation thesis. Similar in focus and tone to much of *The Affluent Society*, it long antedates the contributions of Galbraith. Hansen's influence on his fellow economists has been great. Unfortunately, his work, being directed to his colleagues, was necessarily more esoteric, his rhetoric less dramatic, and it therefore did not command the attention of the educated laity as did Galbraith's.

to some more edifying and satisfying activity. Regrettably, such a shift is not easily accomplished. By training and education, we have been imbued with the notion that the primary function of life is to solve the economic problem. It is, so our system of values tells us, in the economic arena that we are to excel, to demonstrate our worth, to make our mark in society. Having accepted this as truth, we have organized our society around a set of institutions and laws, the origin of which is the market itself. In such a society the ultimate test is a financial one. Success is measured in money, undertakings in profits, and high station and public esteem is accorded to those who win rich rewards.

This is so because of a belief that without this standard, the bulk of the population would not be willing to commit itself to the unremitting pursuit of material goods, without which it would be impossible to realize the ultimate goals of liberalism: the perfectibility of man. If goods are more or less free, the thrill of the chase is gone, economic incentive is dissipated, the economy is threatened with disastrous production failures and much of life, as most Americans have been taught to know it, becomes painfully absurd.

That such a statement is barren of neither logic nor emotional appeal does not alter the fact that America is a victim of one of the familiar ironies of history—the very act of meeting and conquering an obstacle enervates the philosophy from which society derives its strength and radiance. By thwarting the niggardliness of nature and harvesting vast wealth, America unleashed a force that tears at the vitals of materialism, sapping its once boundless energizing powers, and transforming it from a benevolent into a mischievous doctrine. To understand why this once wondrous driving force is now found wanting, we must examine closely our system of values.

To begin with, it should be noted that the always uncertain method of measuring everything in monetary units is perhaps more unreliable today than at any time in our history. At best such a measurement misleads and not infrequently frustrates the very objective it is designed to promote—material progress. If we are genuinely committed to the proposition that sublime reality resides in an expanding outpouring of possessions, then we are guilty of an inexcusable failure to advance the public welfare. To no little degree this flows from our fixation on the dollar as the final unit of measure. If instead of concentrating on balancing income with expenditures—which, except during wartime, has precluded the economy from running at anything close to theoretical capacity—we focused on running the economy full throttle, we could, without doubt, create a veritable surfeit of both consumer goods and productive capacity.

On this score there is no room for doubt. The capacity of the industrial economy is nothing short of incredible. To the doubter of this proposition I recommend a look at West Germany which in fifteen years converted a twisted mass of wreckage and rubble into one of the strongest of Western economic powers. Nor is there anything particularly miraculous about the German experience. Should the United States be so inclined, it could unleash a burst of energy and production that would make the German record pale by comparison.

Assimilation of unemployed workers, a perennial source of national embarrassment, into the productive stream would be a beginning; but if the last ounce of production is to be the ultimate goal, then the labor force should be expanded by making jobs more plentiful and attractive. From the vast pool of the underemployed, such as Southern agricultural workers who make little or no contribution to total output, could be mustered new production personnel, and incentive for research and development could be furthered through government fiscal reforms.

Such a basic change would strain the economy. But the challenge, rather than hampering output, would be a stimulant for higher production levels. Caught between shrinking pools of available labor and a rising demand for goods, private firms would be motivated to invest heavily to satisfy new demands and substitute machinery for a faltering supply of human resources. All of which would further increase the nation's productive capacity.

To the observer of the wartime economy, all this is the tritest of common sense. Having witnessed the power of youth spent in war-making, he also saw a rise in national total output. Much of the new-found strength was, of course, exhausted in military operations; but even as the war effort picked up momentum, the volume of both producer and consumer goods rose. In constant dollars—1954—the Gross National Product increased from $238 billion in 1941 to $314 billion in 1945; in the same period Personal Consumption Expenditures advanced from $154 billion to $171 billion. With the close of hostilities and the gradual easing of postwar demand for consumer durables, the U.S. economy once more settled back to operate at a more leisurely pace as shortages disappeared, deliveries were immediate, and the unemployed found job opportunities less plentiful.

While the U.S. economy quickly lost much of its postwar steam and floundered as one enervating recession followed another, West Germany, with each passing day, gained strength and vitality. The change was startling. At the end of the war Germany lay prostrate, its people scarred by a nightmare of horror and destruction. The marks of battle were everywhere. Whole cities had been virtually wiped out; much of the transportation net had been gutted; the once powerful German industrial might had been laid waste. Momentarily bewildered and lost, the Germans felt a sense of hope in the will to begin anew, to rebuild Germany into the powerful and productive society it had been. Although the task seemed monumental, if not impossible, the opportunities for initiative were unlimited. Everywhere existed a pressing need for the most elemental requirements of life— houses, simple tools, clothing, machines, food, factories, toothpaste, liquor, appliances—everything that goes into the making of life in a highly complex and interdependent society. The demand for goods was unbounded, the prospects for profits propitious. Further charged by generous amounts of American aid, the economic climate provided all the raw materials for a brilliant burst of national prosperity and production.

If buoyant optimism inspired a will to restore and surpass prewar Germany, U.S. thinking made prudence the watchword as it struggled under the paralyzing fear of overproduction. Embarrassed by a mounting stock of farm surpluses—the bane of both Democratic and Republican Secretaries of Agriculture—U.S. thought was sobered by the possibility that similar spectacles might be repeated in other sectors of the economy. Even at the lethargic pace of the 1950's, the automotive industry was flayed for irresponsible overselling and monetary proposals for speeding lagging residential construction were soundly condemned, not because the nation was adequately housed, but because the sin of overbuilding would ultimately precipitate depression and unemployment. In the meantime, we have been taught to count the blessings flowing from the international tensions and the unrelenting arms race that threatens to extinguish all of civilization.

In the October 30, 1960 issue of *The New York Times* T. Coleman Andrews, former Commissioner of Internal

Revenue and now president of an insurance company, is reported as telling a business group, "The threat that faces America today is the chance that Russia's Nikita Khrushchev may come forward with a genuine peace proposal that cannot be refused. If the Soviets should present a sincere and reliable proposal for peace, "it would throw us into an industrial tailspin the like of which we have never dreamed." This, he went on, "would result in the greatest depression America has ever known because our arms industry, coupled with foreign aid, is responsible each year for fifty billion dollars in purchasing power."

In the labor market the contrast is equally striking. West Germany, to alleviate labor shortages, encouraged mass worker immigration until East Germany, in an effort to avoid further international embarrassment, built the infamous wall sealing off West Berlin—the last escape hatch to the West. At the same time that West Germany was actively courting immigrant workers, the United States was figuratively wringing its hands, frightened by the prospects of an expanding labor force. Rather than seeing new hands as additional productive units, America was filled with ominous talk of the need for finding new jobs, that somehow room must be made for the young. The final irony in this contrast was to come, however, when West Germany offered to help the U.S. unemployment picture by employing some half-million American workers if the United States would assume the responsibility for their transportation.

The point should be clear. Germany, gutted by war, mustered every resource for the production of goods destroyed by war. In America it was different. The immediate objective was not all-out production of such things as cars, houses, and factories. Of these, had we been so inclined, we could have constructed untold numbers. More important than production itself was anxiety over maintaining unemployment at a tolerable level. But even this was secondary. Our primary concern was and is to preserve the basic nature of our values and our social structure. Theoretically these center on full production; in fact, they are uncompromisingly bound to the principle that profits must be the decisive economic driving force.

As a general proposition, I have no fundamental quarrel with the profit criterion. Without some kind of impersonal and largely automatic standard for organizing human conduct, a complex and interdependent society would quickly fly to pieces. Some kind of universal measuring device lending itself to easy interpretation and application is absolutely essential for motivating and disciplining human behavior. On all these counts the monetary unit scores well: it is understood by virtually everyone; it provides decisive guides for production decisions; it encourages efficiency and imposes order; and it distributes, in reasonably understandable and equitable fashion, the fruits of society. Even in government it has an important role to play. Although inadequate and frequently perverse, monetary measurements provide some check on governmental agencies and they permit quantitative evaluations of various alternatives open for consideration. Indeed as a general measuring device, the dollar, in this imperfect world of men, is probably as good as any other touchstone and most certainly better than most. Our difficulties arise not so much from profit measurements in themselves as they do from the idolatrous nature of man, which causes him to place them above himself and worship them as the conclusive arbiters of all personal and public conduct.

In everyday business affairs such idolatary does no grievous harm; only when it is permitted to assume a position of primacy in shaping high level national policy does it become satanic. However we may wish it otherwise, the people of a complex society have no alternative but to delegate responsibility for the provision of order, growth, prosperity, and protection from alien aggression. Making the economic measuring stick a jealous god before which we must blindly prostrate ourselves not only jeopardizes the attainment of these objectives, but invites disaster on a scale which threatens the very foundation of the social order we are so intent on preserving. Yet this is exactly what occurs when conventional profit theory is made the prime force in shaping national objectives.

Our eagerness to sanctify "dollar policy" is readily explainable. In ordinary life money is the common measuring device. We assess cars, houses, organizations, and even life itself in monetary terms. Anything that waxes financially is accorded approbation, and anything that carries a hint of financial impoverishment is looked at askance.

So it is with the government. Having learned to use the dollar as a swift and final measurement, we intuitively apply it to the most elevated governmental policy. That in so doing we work mischief, instinct tells us, we must not admit. To do so would not only be denial of the universality of our marvelous measuring device, but would, in effect, be an admission that top level governmental policy transcends the powers of even the best of quantitative measurements.

In short, faced with abandoning our traditional criterion for judgment, we are terrified by the prospect of being at sea without either anchor or instruments for determining position or course. We cling tenaciously to our ideal: a balanced budget. Unfortunately, circumstances, having little regard for man-made idols, forever demand that we violate this golden image. Perennially confronted with a sluggish economy, we are increasingly driven to rely on fiscal policy as a means of preventing the economy from floundering. In recent years, irrespective of who occupies the White House or controls the Congress, the debt mounts inexorably. This compromise with reality is, however, always a tortured one; and statements relating to an unbalanced budget inevitably are a bittersweet mixture of severe criticism and extravagant apologies suggestive of a profound yearning for the lost certainty extant when the dollar is imposed as the final measurement of truth. The exact influence of this yearning on even the loftiest of public policy decisions cannot be known, but surely it is substantial.

There is, of course, yet another, and in some ways more attractive, facet of our preoccupation with dollar measurements. Distrusting power and dreading tyranny, we have always employed budgetary restrictions to limit the scope of the state, and thereby preserve individual freedom. Recently Henry Wallich, in his book *The Cost of Freedom,* makes a reasoned plea along these lines. Observing that some loss of creature comforts may be a small price to pay for individual freedom, he declares, "We must be prepared to forego the extra gain that forced draft methods might yield because they would not be compatible with freedom in peacetime. The ultimate value of a free economy is not production, but freedom, and freedom comes not at a profit but at a cost." Essentially moderate in his approach, Wallich criticizes obvious governmental failures and abuses, but at the same time admits that forceful governmental action is necessary in such undertakings as road building and education. On the latter point, however, enthusiasm seems lacking; and his message might well be summarized by an article in *Harper's,* which was revealingly subtitled "Could Kenneth Galbraith Be Wrong?" Questioning those who argue that public needs are undernourished while private tastes are overindulged, he directed attention away from the popular private vs. public controversy. Whatever the merits of Wallich's position, it is this bewildering issue which divides us and to which we must now turn.

All arguments to the contrary, taxes restrict freedom of choice. At best the citizen's choice is limited; he may pay his tax bill, go to jail, or endure the pain of a guilty conscience. If he is the ordinary, reasonably honest citizen, each April he makes peace with the Internal Revenue Division and his conscience and then, with a sigh of resignation, ponders on what could have been done with funds forever lost. Occasionally a fortunate soul finds small solace in reflecting on the public services that his contribution helps to support. But vicarious satisfaction of this sort is rare. From hard experience the citizen knows that his wishes do not weigh heavily on public decisions and that some of his contributions will be squandered on projects to which he is bitterly opposed. This commonly shared experience has caused it to be said that, with rare exception, private spending is more productive than public action in providing personal and social welfare.

Superficially, the logic of this position appears as invincible as it is persuasive and attractive. And yet somehow it seems to have a hollow ring, a deceptive simplicity which suggests a theory largely irrelevant to this world of circumstances in which we are forever forced to live. Lest we be misled, we must look more closely at this private vs. public controversy.

That the market performs certain tasks with dispatch and excellence is irrefutable. Without equal as an instrument for recording consumer preferences, it reflects wants and directs the production and distribution of everything from automobiles to diapers, from cigarettes to fried grasshoppers. By doing so the market determines what and how much of any particular item should be produced. For a job well done, it deserves high regard both for its efficient operations and for the freedom of choice it accords the consuming public.

Unfortunately, the market is not without its limits; for even as it operates with grace and precision on some matters, it must be ranked as inadequate or impotent on others. Particularly is this true for the collective goods so indispensable to the operation of every organized society. That we as a nation must somehow provide schools, roads, and national defense is a matter on which there is virtual unanimity; and yet the market renders little if any assistance in providing the wherewithal for the realization of these goals. As an indifferent force, mechanistically operating to equate production with immediate consumer preferences (and vice versa), the market is automatically geared to frustrating the realization of these objectives.

The reason for this is to be found in our nature. Having learned that income is both valuable and hard to come by, we, as individuals, resent any suggestion of parting with some of it. For money is freedom, money is power, and with money we believe we can satisfy urgent wants or, if held in the form of savings, know a sense of virtue, accomplishment, and security. To sacrifice personal consumption or reduce "hard won" savings is, therefore, an immediate and painful experience which weighs heavily upon us. Nor does money paid in taxes conjure up inspiring thoughts on the value of collective goods. It is not in our nature to speculate on the advantages of an improved mental health program, or the merits of a better educational staff, or even a thing so close or immediate as the protection to be gained from a modernized fire department. At best, benefits from such undertakings are indirect and intangible; and in our subconscious we are prone to dismiss them as irrelevant, or, more precisely, generously financed, but wastefully administered.

The penchant to gratify our immediate impulses and enhance our total stock of personal wealth makes our society an easy mark for the built-in market mechanism which incessantly urges us to seek additional comforts and luxuries. Through aggressive selling efforts of all types, we are forever exhorted to indulge ourselves with everything from cigarettes to fascinating trips to remote and exotic lands. To deny that incessant exhortation has no impact seems nonsensical. Hitler's "Big Lie" and communist "educational programs" have made us aware that political indoctrination can be a powerful instrument for altering and shaping public opinion. That selling efforts can be an equally powerful force in economic affairs is often boasted by men of the marketing profession. Arno H. Johnson, Chairman of the Advertising Research Foundation, expressed this idea when, in talking of America's economic horizons, he warned against "general unemployment and under utilization of productive ability . . ." Bewailing the fact that consumer purchases were lagging behind national capacity, he declared, "We need now the courage and vision to expand selling efforts so that confidence can be restored and the level of consumer buying can be brought back into line with potential growth of productive ability and capacity . . . The importance of advertising, selling, packaging, merchandising, premium incentives, and consumer credit," he further noted, "as forces to bring these necessary changes over the next ten years can hardly be overemphasized."

There is no need for us to venture into that no man's land where the merits of superselling are so bitterly contested. Whether we as a people are happier, and better adjusted because of the abundance of goods promoted by aggressive salesmanship is one of those preposterous disputes that has no purpose but to obcure and confuse. None of this, of course, invalidates Mr. Johnson's eminently sensible proposition. Indeed, to disagree with the suggestion that vigorous and well-planned sales promotions stimulate consumer purchases would seem to fly in the face of all common sense. The door-to-door salesman who educates good parents to their children's urgent need for a set of encyclopedias, the advertisement that whets the appetite for the exotic luxury of a $2,000 fox-fur blanket, and the charity worker who convinces us of the merits of a worthy cause all have their role to play. Because of these and many other economic stratagems, the common man intuitively knows that the economic wheel rotates at a more rapid pace.

Despite this commonly accepted view, there prevails, particularly among the orthodox economists, a will to preserve the myth that although organized selling efforts of all types may change the composition of our national output, such efforts are in fact bereft of power to alter the total volume of goods sold. On the face of it such a denial of the obvious would seem to be inane, if not ludicrous. In fact, it is fundamental, for to accept the premise that the market contains an automatic and increasingly powerful mechanism which is forever unsettling consumer satisfaction through the manufacture of new wants is to subscribe to a blasphemy. According to conventional thought, it is the consuming public and not the market itself that is the source of energy driving the economy. In the context of this thinking, the market is nothing more than a passive servant which busily adjusts and enlarges the nation's productive capacity for the purpose of serving the unbounded reservoir of private wants. To confess that this is not wholly true is to admit that our whole value system has somehow been turned upside down.

In effect, such an admission says: the market has done its work remarkably well—indeed too well—and if we are to operate our economy at anything like full speed, we must resort to some artificial means for creating dissatisfaction within the individual. That is, we must in some way unbind his bounded wants; we must somehow convince him that his present state of economic welfare is not satisfactory, that he should have more and better things, that indeed he must never forget that the center of life remains, as it has always been, driving materialism.

Implicit in the notion of creeping stagnation is the prospect that time will compel increasing reliance on these artificial and self-defeating devices, and that, with each passing day, larger and larger doses of exhortation will be required to coax man to indulge himself in the rich fruits of materialism. One bad thing about this is that, like dope addiction, the process is as unending as it must ultimately be futile. For if the stimulant is successful, it provides the energy for a flood of new goods which presumably enhance consumer satisfaction and public benefit. Unfortunately, as even the Philistine must know, the gratification derived from added worldly possessions declines as the stock of personal property grows larger. Thus we face a paradox, for the greater the stimulant, the more the production of products and the smaller the satisfaction in additional goods. So we are compelled to resort to larger and larger doses of stimulant, all of which are skillfully designed to produce the distressing effect of unsettling the consumer by convincing him that life will have value only if he has a better car, a more luxurious home, and a heavier burden of debt. All of which seems embarrassingly analogous to the plight of the neurotic dog who exhausts himself in the frantic pursuit of his own tail.

At this juncture a caveat is in order, for although the point at issue is fundamental, it is often the subject of innocent misinterpretation. To suffer this is to fall victim of a misplaced emphasis which is at odds with the world about us. For our proposition is not that all or even that most men revel in a material splendor that fosters a jaded attitude toward wealth and the society which confers it. Such a proposition would be folly in a nation where the median family income still falls short of $6,000 per year and where deplorable numbers of Americans are condemned to live under the blight of poverty and ignorance. Nor does our proposition contradict the notion that virtually all men are profoundly committed to increasing their own individual stock of worldly possessions.

I suggest merely that a combination of factors conspires to obstruct the rapid solution to the economic problems that continue to plague our incredibly productive society. The source of this difficulty resides in two psychological facts. The first is that increments of material goods—such as washing machines, shoes, and mink-trimmed blotters—contribute less and less to individual satisfaction. The second is that we as a society are committed to the virtuousness of personal savings. From out of these two forces has emerged an unpleasant specter: the decline of private materialism as the singular source of social energy. While thrift and planning for a rainy day are admirable virtues, as a social practice in an affluent society, saving has consequences that are at best a mixed blessing. The savings process, however it may instill a sense of security and accomplishment within the individual, is an agent which, by tapping the income stream, saps the nation's economic vitality. In a rich society not only does it work to retard the total volume of economic output, but more seriously it precludes those in the low income groups from experiencing the self-respect that comes with the opportunity to earn by their labors a more abundant share of the fruits of the affluent society.

Nor should one seek comfort in the illusion that natural forces will somehow mysteriously alter the present state of affairs. The habits and traditions of private materialism run deep, fixed by inclination and training; it would be folly to expect us to discard them as if they were a worn-out shoe or an overripe piece of cheese. Indeed as our technical efficiency advances, we must learn to adjust our thinking to a new reality: that the independent market system, bereft of magical ingredients capable of generating the necessary added momentum, will require increasing amounts of human assistance and guidance.

Fortunately, there is much to be done in the realm of economics. Our only regret must be that we are ill prepared to do it; not because resources or technical know-how are wanting, or because the task at hand offers neither challenge nor reward. In such matters the job ranks high. Rather it is for lack of conviction that we hesitate. Before we can undertake this new assignment with vigor and enthusiasm, we must somehow construct a viable ideology which will elevate public materialism to the status of respectability, without violating deeply engrained conventional thought.

Historically our full trust in private materialism has not been without merit. Having blessed us with individual comforts and freedom, it made our nation a power second to none. But while the exclusive doctrine of private materialism once bloomed and bore rich fruit, in the world of today it is imperceptibly fading like cut blossoms transplanted from another age. In the modern affluent society the economic promise can be fulfilled, if it is to be realized at all, only if public materialism is permitted to assume a more important role in the economic drama. To fufill this promise, without infringing upon our precious individual freedoms, is a task worthy of our best efforts. To try to avoid it by extolling the virtues of a world gone by is not only pathetic, but comparable to glorifying the power of a cavalry charge on a planet threatened by missile warfare.

That anyone doubts the existence of public need is nothing short of astonishing. To the doubtful, I would suggest a trip on our highways, an honest look at the squalor of our industrial cities, some hard thinking on the economics of the South, an evaluation of our mental health program, and a close and painstaking study of our educational programs and facilities. But of these and many other inadequacies we hear little and think less, for on such matters we are without an instrument which educates us to community needs.

Occasionally, through the media of television or the printed word, we are provided with a brief survey of the problems and needs associated with juvenile delinquency, slum clearance, water pollution, or preventive medicine. But they are infrequent and weak substitutes for the unrelieved din that constantly urges us to gratify our every whim. At best these reminders of public need are educational projects often sponsored as a public service for the purpose of giving some small understanding of complexities of a difficult and perplexing problem. Little attempt is made to arouse action other than an occasional suggestion that a contribution would be welcome or that a postcard would bring additional information. Such attempts can hardly be ranked with the promotional campaigns mapped out by a battery of statisticians, psychologists, and copywriters who, in plying their trades, appeal to the prejudices, emotions, and predilections of the public. The aggressive pushing of private goods on one hand and our failure to develop an instrument to communicate the need for public goods on the other further reinforce our natural penchant to resist giving up income for the purpose of community development. All of this, of course, leaves its mark on society. The private sector of the economy flourishes, and the public realm is always on the verge of financial malnutrition. This contrast between private abundance and public poverty is colorfully depicted by Galbraith in *The Affluent Society* (Houghton Mifflin Company, 1958) when he observes:

The family which takes its mauve and cerise, air-conditioned, power-steered, and power-braked automobile out for a tour passes through cities that are badly paved, made hideous by litter, blighted buildings, billboards, and posts for wires that should long since have been underground. They pass on into a countryside that has been rendered largely invisible by commercial art . . . They picnic on exquisitely packaged food from a portable icebox by a polluted stream and go on to spend the night at a park which is a menace to public health and morals. Just before dozing off on an air mattress, beneath a nylon tent, amid the stench of decaying refuse, they may reflect vaguely on the curious unevenness of their blessings. Is this, indeed, the American genius?

To any thoughtful person these market failings are readily apparent. Even the most intransigent disciple of laissez faire would be hard pressed to demonstrate the capacity of the market to meet the need for police and fire protection, social work, national defense, anti-smog programs, and public education. But of all these and the many, many other needs which the market is powerless to cope with, it is education that must be ranked as our greatest social need. For ultimately the destiny of our nation and the hope of the world must rest on education. Today, more than in the past, the fate of civilization sits uneasy in the hands of man, and if man is to stop short of destroying himself with the science he has created, he must somehow find a solution to the "human problem." Education offers a twofold hope. First, through education the individual can gain the necessary qualifications to fill a productive role in society. The importance of this is almost impossible to overrate. With automation gradually taking over everything from assembly line jobs to bookkeeping, there is and will be a further dwindling of demand for unskilled and semiskilled workers. The need today is for medical men and political scientists rather than farm hands and punch press operators. Without the educational facilities to improve human resources, we can be certain of a pool of unemployed workers condemned to a fate of being unable to pull their own weight.

But education, as the shaper of the future, must be ranked first on another score. It provides us with new outlets for individual expression. In the past our chief goals have been material in nature. A home in the suburbs, a new car every other year, a chicken in every pot. Today many of us own homes in the suburbs, drive a new model car, and are giving serious thought to emulating our neighbor who has a second. What is true for many today will be a fact of life for more tomorrow. But once the immediate thirst of material desires is quenched, a simple truth emerges: mere worldly possessions do not make the good life. Out of this realization come new and disturbing thoughts. After two cars, what? After materialism, what then? What now will I strive for? How now shall I express my identity?

It is in answer to such age-old questions as these that education is to make its greatest contribution. Through education the individual must learn that external standards are at best fleeting and artificial and that real meaning and true satisfaction flow from within. Through study the individual is to understand the joy of workmanship and to seek contentment and self-expression in a job well done. Only in this way can the individual find genuine and lasting happiness. Without the inner peace of mind that comes from a heart-and-soul commitment to the job at hand, the prospects for the future are bleak, and we are confronted with the dreadful possibility of a society composed of individuals who wander through life without either direction or purpose. In *Our Age of Unreason* (J. B. Lippincott & Company, 1942) Franz Alexander, one of the pioneers of psychoanalytical work, sketches a glimpse of what the future may hold when he movingly observes:

> After long hours of daily work, spent listening to the suffering victims of these unsettled times and trying to extract sense from the . . . variety of sincere self-revelations, a . . . vision appears before the eyes of the pondering psychoanalyst. The analyst sees his patients—physicians, lawyers, engineers, bankers, advertising men, teachers, and laboratory research men of universities, students, and clerks—engaged in a marathon race, their eager faces distorted by strain, their eyes focused not upon their goal, but upon each other with a mixture of hate, envy, and admiration. Panting and perspiring, they run and never arrive. They would all like to stop but dare not as long as the others are running. What makes them run so frantically, as though they were driven by the threatening swish of an invisible whip wielded by an invisible slave driver? The driver and the whip they carry in their own minds. If one of them finally stops and begins leisurely to whistle a tune or watch a passing cloud or picks up a stone and with childish curiosity turns it around in his hand, they all look upon him at first with astonishment and then with contempt and disgust. They call him names, a dreamer or a parasite, a theoretician or a schizophrenic, and above all, an effeminate. They not only do not understand him—they not only despise him but "they hate him as their own sin." All of them would like to stop—ask each other questions, sit down to chat about futilities—they all would like to belong to each other because they all feel desperately alone—chasing on in a never-ending chase. They do not dare to stop until the rest stop lest they lose all their self-respect, because they know only one value—that of running—running for its own sake.

Such then is the affluent society. In many respects it is
something less than idyllic. America has an abundance of
resources, know-how, and productive capacity, but it is at
once opulent and impoverished. In private production it
stands incomparable, but its public needs seem forever condemned to struggle under the handicap of undernourishment. At once blessed and cursed by a technological revolution, the dirty, dreary, initiative-shattering jobs are becoming
mechanized at the same time that society is tortured by the
open sores made by a hard core of unemployed and a growing
number of unemployables who lack the qualifications necessary to compete in a world of automation and scientific management. As we draw closer to the realization of materialistic
dreams, we hear anguished cries bewailing our loss of national purpose, while everywhere the individual complains
of a gnawing sense of alienation—a feeling of powerlessness.
Indeed from one perspective the affluent society reminds us
of nothing so much as the college athlete who, in sacrificing
everything—social life, principles, academic achievement—
for All-American fame, suddenly finds he has no place to
go once he is awarded the prize. Without new fields to conquer, his world collapses and to escape acute anxiety he strives
to lose himself in sensual gratification.

To heal the wounds of the affluent society, the primary
recommendation is to turn now partially employed energies
and talents to satisfying our patent needs for collective goods,
through the advancement of human resources and by exalting the development of the individual. That there is much
to be done in the realm of public materialism is surely
irrefutable. We can and should dedicate ourselves to eradicat-
ing poverty and ignorance. But we would delude ourselves if
we expect too much from publicly sponsored endeavors, par-

ticularly education. Certainly formal instruction in schools
and universities can do much. It can train engineers, statisticians, and psychiatrists, and in this way elevate individual
worth and self-respect. But to assign education the heroic
task of preparing individuals to live by the tenets of existen-
tialism without falling victims to disillusioned nihilism is
to ask it to perform beyond its powers. In serious art the
flavor of human tragedy is already fashionable. Be it a painting, a literary effort, a Broadway play, or even a probing
movie, the creator's message seems to say, "Victimized by
alien forces beyond my control, I can do little more than
wander aimlessly through life, without either duty or destiny."

To undertake education of the common man, so that he
may rise above traditional external standards and draw meaning from day-to-day living—and this is the heart of existential
doctrine—not only threatens him with the dismal existence
of Camus' indifferent Stranger, but asks him singlehandedly
to defy all of Western tradition. From ancient Greece to the
present the mainstream of Western thought has taught the
individual to identify himself with and labor for some kind
of total good—be it Plato's *Republic,* the Christian Heaven,
or the perfectibility of man.

None of this, of course, negates Galbraith's imaginative
diagnosis of the affluent society, which, by compelling us to
face up to the divisive tensions within our social philosophy,
is a significant contribution. If Galbraith is to be faulted, it is
for failing to appreciate that our society, as the culmination
of Western culture, stands today in dire need of a new, unifying ideology. Until recently—some say 1914; others, 1933—
the social cement of the West was economic individualism.
Under this system of thought, the market, with all of its
many parts—money, prices, wages, profits, competition, personal riches, and the like—provided the common man with

a swift and sure divining rod for separating right from wrong and assessing the nation's progress toward the final goal of human perfection. However imperfect in fact, intellectually the market provided a simple unifying system of thought which could be understood by everyone, however lowly his status.

Today, as Galbraith so mercilessly and thoroughly makes clear, this conventional wisdom, in addition to losing much of its vitality, is often a mischievous and perverse force. Despite this, unless man abandons all hope of intellectualizing his society, he must cling to this philosophy, pathological though it may be. Lacking a substitute, he has, at the present moment in time, no choice. Only the existence of a rising intellectual force, which is at once simple and meaningful in the context of everyday living, can lead men to abandon the old and set a course by the light of a new-found star. Today a new philosophy is in the making. That it cannot center on simple private materialism is the final heresy.

To appreciate more fully why this is true, we must look at the forces which have elevated bureaucratic organizations to a commanding position in our contemporary world.

IX

Children of Technology

Egalitarian, LIBERAL THOUGHT IS FOREVER SUSPICIOUS OF power; by instinct both old and new liberals are hostile to it. Indeed, for the true 19th-century liberal, the perfect society is one populated by essentially equal and autonomous individuals, each of whom expresses his unique individuality in the free market and each of whom casts his enlightened vote to preserve the pure democratic process.

The position of the 20th-century liberal is not so pristine. Having rejected the notion that the laws of the market are innately benevolent, he admits that man must fashion forces which will exorcise unemployment and drive the economy forward at some satisfactory level of performance. Beyond this, however, he is in principle opposed to ordering things through planning or regulation except in those cases where he is clearly convinced that delegation of power will bring substantial individual benefit. Public schooling, social security, flood control and welfare payments are among many programs that the modern liberal will passionately defend on the grounds that their contribution to human dignity far exceeds any danger inherent in the creation of concomitant power centers.

However liberals may disagree on specifics, both groups are vigorously opposed to the use of authority simply for the purpose of preserving an established order. More anarchistic than monarchistic, more democratic than oligarchic, more Jacobin than aristocratic, liberals old and new are more the exponents of ordered change than they are champions of an unchanging order.

In practice neither group is without its blind spot. Seeing labor unions and big government as a wicked conspiracy to derail progress, the 19th-century liberal seems incurably oblivious to the power exercised by Goliath-sized business organizations. On the other hand, the modern liberal, obsessed with the evils of industrial monopoly, often appears constitutionally incapable of viewing burgeoning government as a threat to individual freedoms. Thus the interminable disagreements, the noisy charges and countercharges, the sharp ring of bitter rivalry. For the old liberal, all problems would be resolved if only union power was demolished, governmental authority was throttled, and business was liberated to develop naturally. The modern liberal, crusading against the injustice of inequality, cries for the discipline of industrial power, the redistribution of income, and the expansion of governmental services with the intent of elevating the social and economic position of the lower classes.

Both of these groups are at once correct and mistaken. Here is an element of pathos, for all liberals are led astray by their simplistic belief that most serious problems could be substantially resolved merely by curbing or eliminating certain power centers. By implication each group is saying, if only this or that selfish power group were eradicated or shackled, then the individual could once again reassert his independence. At its roots, whatever its vintage, liberalism is a philosophy applicable to and enchanted with a society of free moral souls, each of whom, in greater or lesser degree, is master of his own destiny. If in fact such a social order no longer exists, and if in fact society is inexorably moving toward the formation of power centers which weave individual destiny into organizational fabrics, then much of the controversy between the liberals is insignificant, if not irrelevant. If in fact the quarrels are really about the past, we must examine the organic forces which with growing momentum seem to be converting our social structure into a honeycomb of powerful, bureaucratic, hierarchic organizations.

There were times when a man working alone, unaided, often in solitude, asking little more than to be supplied with food and drink, could shape and alter the affairs of the world. Such a man was the Greek philosopher, Socrates; the Hebrew prophet, Jesus; the medieval astronomer, Copernicus. In ancient Greece, in the days of the Caesars, and even during the Middle Ages, the individual working independently could, without the help of large organizations, hope to accomplish great things.

Today the prospects for individual achievements are less favorable. There will, of course, always be men who leave their distinctive stamps on world events. If not a Henry Ford or a John L. Lewis, then a Lenin or a Mao Tse-tung. These men worked their accomplishments and gained their prominence by building and dominating vast and powerful organizations. As individuals they were powerless to effect their objectives; as directors of large and militant organizations, theirs was the strength that moves mountains. With exceptions—the writer and the artist may with a bit of luck and courage still exercise important individual initiative—modern man's main road to glory originates within the large organization.

Nowhere is this change more dramatically illustrated than in the field of science. Once scientists did their work as individuals, dependent hardly at all upon institutions for carrying out their work. Newton needed little more than his apple, Mendel his small garden plots; yet today, without expensive apparatus, large laboratories, and a battery of assistants, the modern scientist can accomplish little in the way of discovery. Thus the scientist, the most sought-after man in the contemporary world, is part and parcel of the large organization and so becomes a kind of high-class bureaucrat.

Nobody likes being called a bureaucrat; not when the label is largely used as an expression of contempt and scorn; not when the term brings to mind some ineffectual drudge who is bogged down in red tape, and who is everlastingly devising and perpetrating new and petty tyrannies which seemingly have no other purpose than to make life unpleasant for the nation's citizenry. However unfair, this is the popular image of the present-day bureaucrat—an image which is almost universally applied to lesser governmental officials.

But bureaucracies take many forms, of which the government is only the best known and most frequently disparaged. The large corporation, the political party, the formal religious organization, or, for that matter, any body of individuals bound together to promote a common purpose, almost surely is organized and operated along bureaucratic lines. To be sure, a General Motors, a Railroad Brotherhood, and a Federal Reserve System seek different ends. Each dominates a field of endeavor; each employs its own distinctive *modus operandi,* each differs from the other in organizational form and structure. But for all this, the variations these organizations display are overshadowed by their similarities. Each emphasizes efficiency, each is dedicated and authoritarian in its striving to bring about change and to reach goals. Were it not so, these organizations would surely have perished long ago.

In this world of competition—and there is always competition, whether between individuals, economic units, creeds, or states—there is a strong intuitive presupposition that the race goes to the efficient, or better yet, the strong. There is a further belief that might comes with bigness which is wrought only through the bureaucratic process. The process is an ancient one. Dynastic Egypt, the Roman Empire, and the Roman Catholic Church, especially since the Reformation, provide examples of bureaucracy. But the full bloom of bureaucracy had to await the coming of another development—the money economy.

Without the money economy, the greatest single artifact of the contemporary world, the modern organization, is impossible. It cannot be built on slavery, for the slave is reluctant and uninterested; at best he is capable of doing only routine work with the crudest of tools. Resenting his master and knowing that his position in society is irrevocably fixed, he is without loyalty, integrity, or the incentive to improve or promote himself or the organization of which he is a member.

Just as the Pharaohs and the Southern planters were powerless to fashion a modern bureaucracy, so the medieval prince lacked the tools and equipment to construct the towering institutions which are so much a part of present-day culture. Feudalism had its hierarchy and its rigid set of rules and obligations, but the feudal society was more than a mere set of rights and duties. It was an intimate society of human beings, a personal society which could and did make allowance for human frailties. The face-to-face contact made the uniform, machine-like precision of the modern organizations unattainable. Lacking impersonality, the feudal society lacked the will and the way to compel an unwavering commitment to a minutely detailed and fixed pattern, irrespective of individual variation and penchant. It was incapable of encouraging, training, and coordinating the vast numbers of technically skilled specialists, which are the raw materials from which modern organizations are made. Not until feudal ties were severed, not until the individual was forcefully evicted from his secure and personal society and driven into a free and dynamic world could the large organization emerge and take shape.

However, a free enterprise system is not necessary. That the system is, despite Marxian doctrine, largely irrelevant is made abundantly clear by the existence of powerful organizations in both Russia and the United States. Much more important than the system *per se* is the presence of a kind of cement capable of welding together large numbers of diverse, yet interdependent specialists into a smoothly functioning organization. Subjectively the members of such an organization need have no tangible common purpose; indeed, lacking direction and guidance, they, in serving their own interests, may operate at cross purposes. Only at the highest levels of administration is unity of purpose found. As one moves down the ladder of hierarchy, organization purpose becomes less and less significant; money, in the form of wages, more and more the disciplining force. Thus the money economy supplies, much more efficiently and effectively than either enslavement or a purely hierarchic structure, the cement necessary to the coordination of large numbers of individuals in pursuing a common goal. It is accomplished through some form of the wage and price system, as both communist Russia and Red China learned in many ill-fated experiments.

The rise of the modern organization is a familiar story. Customarily it begins by relating how from the efforts of such men as Day, Hargreaves, and Watt came the textile mills, the prototype of the modern industrial organization. How, as manufacturing shifted from the "putting out" system to the factory system, workers were transferred from the home to the factory, from the country to city, from the world of personal intimacy to the unpredictable and inhospitable world of impersonality. Later came metallurgical developments, which, when combined with steam-generated blowing, hammering, and rolling innovations, made the factory production of iron and then steel commercially feasible. When the metal lathe and metal boring machine were added, specialization of tasks had gone far beyond the simple separation of worker and owner. Inherent within these technological advances was the next stage, which would altogether and forever destroy the old order. Marked by political, economic, and social revolutions, this new stage is best symbolized by one momentous achievement, the railroad.

Men have always been more or less vaguely aware of the relationship between the speed of transport and the size of human institutions. On the political plane this is apparent throughout history. In earlier times, before the advent of modern technology, the holding together of vast empires all but escaped the reach of man. There were, of course, exceptions. The Nile unified Egypt, Alexander cut the Gordian knot, and the sea of barbarism surrounding Rome instilled, at least within the upper classes of society, a common sentiment, upon which the Greco-Roman civilization was founded. But control was at best always precarious. Without the means for rapidly moving troops to put down insurrections, and without the modern communication facilities and skill in propaganda, control exercised over vast geographical areas remained tenuous. Technology changed all this, if but slowly. As the travel time was reduced, as cost of moving goods and troops fell, as it became possible to communicate almost immediately over larger and larger areas, there arose inexorable forces causing the political unit—the community, the state, or the nation—to extend its jurisdiction and influence.

Sometimes the change was sharp and dramatic. On the eve of the 15th century, the Western world was organized around such city states as Venice, Florence, Nürnberg, and Ghent. Then the Portuguese gave to the world the ocean-going sailing vessel, and the center of Western culture shifted from middle Europe to the Atlantic seaboard of the Old World. City states blossomed into nations, and France, Spain, Britain and the Netherlands from the 16th until the beginning of the 20th century dominated the entire world with their shipping, their commerce, their manufactures, their emigrants and their empires. Equally dramatic changes were wrought by the railroads and air lines. Today, following the route of the old city states, the smaller nations are fading rapidly: Spain and the Netherlands have no voice in world affairs and France and Britain are given precious little. In a world made small by transport and communication technology, two great powers, the United States and Russia, have emerged, each attempting to outdo the other by extending the scope of its influence.

Nor is this phenomenon peculiar to the international scene. At home the authority of the federal government grows unabated at the expense of the prerogatives of the individual states, while in a lower political echelon we are all familiar with the officials who plead that city domination of the suburban communities provides the only hope for preserving the vitality and prosperity of the metropolitan district. Historically then, the forces unleashed by transport and communication innovations drive the political unit, whatever the level, toward increasing size and complexity.

As with political organizations, so with economic and social institutions. For without modern transport and communication technology, the opening and exploiting of national and even world markets could not be accomplished on anything like the grand scale of today. Without gigantic markets, the factory system, with its specialization and mass production technology, would have found meager application. Through the use of the railroad, "drummers" were able to cover and get to know vast territories at the same time that the manufacturing branch of the firm was, because of lower shipping costs, able to compete in markets farther and farther removed from the point of production. And as transportation was making strides, so communication, through the mass media, began to have its effect. Consumers throughout the nation were alerted to the joys of drinking beer brewed in Milwaukee, wearing suits manufactured in New York, drinking juice from oranges grown in California, eating cheese processed in Wisconsin, and driving cars assembled in Michigan.

The immediate extension of organizational limits is only the most obvious impact of modern technology. Innovations, particularly as related to communications, also shaped the internal dimensions and workings of the organization; and, in the final analysis, it is the capacity of the organization's communication system which determines its success, and therefore, its size. Indeed, without modern technology there could be no General Motors, no United Auto Workers, nor, for that matter, anything like our present income tax law which requires large numbers of expert civil servants to administer and police the boundless and all but unintelligible codes and regulations. Without the telephone, the telegraph, and high-speed mail service, not to mention the whole constellation of office equipment—typewriters, calculating and accounting machines, dictaphones, electronic computers—the power and glory of modern organizations would be impossible.

But it is not only of machines and equipment that organizations are made. However superb their efficiency and whatever wondrous feats they may perform, machines, lacking spirit and will, must somehow be integrated into the process which physiologists refer to as homeostasis. Often referred to as feedback or automatic control, this process is common to every organization, as indeed it is to every living organism. The subject of published volumes and the very essence of management "science," we are all more or less subconsciously aware of the operation of this process.

Beginning with the assumption that each organization has some general objective or objectives that it strives to attain, we, as a matter of habit, classify organizations according to objectives. In the real world, of course, organizations pursue a number of objectives, some of which are more readily realizable than others. In large measure, however, what the organization will or will not accomplish is determined by its communication system. And in general those goals which are amenable to quantitative measurement will be promoted, and those which resist or defy quantitative expression are likely to be honored only through lip service. As the organization grows and perforce becomes more impersonal, control becomes more and more mechanistic as quantitative measures, lending themselves to precise formulation and simple interpretation, are naïvely and erroneously praised as objective standards. A classic example of the operation of this process is to be seen at large universities. Because good teaching cannot be quantified, there is a tendency to measure a university professor's worth in terms of the number of pages he has published.

In practice, objectives such as profits, members, etc., can be approximated only through setting up "operational" goals and establishing centers of responsibility for the achievement of assigned standards. In the business firm, which is only exceeded by government in the delegation of authority and responsibility, operational goals take the form of quality,

cost, and output standards, which are further broken down
into quality controls, sales quotas, production-time standards,
cash flow programs, schedules of various types and budgets.
These standards permit policy makers to compare performance with objectives. If standards are met, the presumption
is that the organization is performing satisfactorily; if they
are not, corrective action is necessary which may take the
form of improving performance or modifying standards.

Thus information flows both ways through the communication system: from the policy maker to the policy implementer, and from the policy implementer back to the
policy maker. The greater the resistance or "noise" developed
in the communication system, the greater the difficulty in
extending the size of the organization. Conversely, new improvements in techniques, equipment, or procedure, which
improve the flow of information along the communication
system, extend the limits restricting the size of the organization.*

Many forces in our society are at work in pushing back
the barriers to organizational growth. Indeed, this is the very
essence of the science of management and administration.
The emphasis in this discipline is twofold: to increase technical efficiency (or to reduce costs), and to lead the organization to new heights by gaining a dominant position in the
field in which the organization traditionally operates, and by
invading and engulfing areas which previously lay outside the

---

* Classifying the multidimensional always presents problems. So it
is with the organization. If A reports sales of $1,000,000,000 and
a labor force of 200,000, and B enjoys sales of $2,000,000,000 while
employing 100,000 workers, it is meaningless to speak, except in a
well-defined context, of A being larger than B, or B than A. More
important to our discussion than the measurement of size *per se,* is the
direction of movement of the organization in expanding its scope of
influence.

organization's scope of operations. These objectives are facilitated by new communication techniques, which continue to appear on the scene. Not always communication mechanisms in the normal sense of the word, their contributions nevertheless enhance the flow and organization of information. Instead of such devices as the telegraph, the typewriter, and the balance sheet, these new procedures have such esoteric names as linear programming, queue analysis, game theory, probability analysis, and information theory. Essentially, they are control mechanisms. With them come more precise, more operational standards and through them a more penetrating analysis of performance is made possible.

Important as these developments are in themselves, when coupled with the present and forthcoming electronic computers, the nature and quantity of information which the organization's communication network will be able to process and produce astounds and bewilders. The ordinary computer can perform thousands of operations per second and, in addition to being faster than any living brain, is more accurate. Properly programed, these machines can formulate standards which precisely define action to be taken and levels of performance to be expected. At the same time performance can be measured, coded, and fed into the machines for the purpose of evaluating the appropriateness of the original set of control standards. If corrective action is necessary, using the feedback principle, the machine modifies standards to conform to reality or prescribes the changes in performance necessary to satisfy the desired objectives. Or as Norbert Wiener puts it, the over-all system corresponds to "a complete animal with sense organs, effectors, and proprioceptors."

This is not science fiction, nor does it come from *Brave New World!* The principles of control described above are now part of the everyday working apparatus of antiaircraft equipment which, in addition to sighting and aiming the missiles, measures the efficacy of the fire and automatically makes any necessary correction. Automatic machines are already extensively used in continuous-process industries like canneries, paper making, steel rolling mills, and especially wire and tin-plate factories. Soon routine clerical operations such as billing, filling, and, to a more limited degree, standard correspondence, will also fall under the regime of these machines. But however impressive the record of existing machines, by the standards of Ashby's *Design for a Brain,* present-day computers are crude instruments which in the last analysis are neither better nor worse than their "feeding." Future machines—self perceptron-based automata—may conceivably read print, drive a car in peak traffic, and respond to verbal commands; in short, interpret and respond to environmental factors without being dependent upon programming set up by mortals.

Less than a decade ago the United States could boast of perhaps two dozen computer installations, most of which were, in the eyes of many, employed by a small band of eccentric mathematicians and scientists who were tampering with things better left untouched by man. Now all this has changed. Indeed, it is the unfashionable organization which cannot claim at least one of the more than 10,000 computers which range in size from the $50,000 desk model to the Goliath, costing as much as $10 million.

What impact computers have had on our daily lives is largely unmeasurable, but we get glimpses which tell us that it has been monumental. We know, for example, that without computers our telephone system would collapse, that whole factories would be inoperative, that public utility services would, in many instances, be paralyzed; that our radar, antiaircraft, and missile systems would cease to function and that governmental and business organizations would be hopelessly incompetent to cope with the voluminous detail now so competently organized and administered by these remarkable and somewhat frightening creatures. Perhaps the extent to which computers and new procedures will enhance the power of the organization is best illustrated by the awesome plan of the Treasury Department. With the aid of a dozen or so immense computers, the Internal Revenue Service looks forward to the day when individual tax returns can be matched with savings and stock transaction reports made by banks and brokers. Everyone, at least in theory, would favor bringing tax evasion artists to justice. But not everyone, I would imagine, would be equally gratified by the invasion of personal privacy that this new communication device permits an organization, which is only one of many that is anxious and eager to extend its power and influence.

But the great impact is yet to come. Computer technology is still in its infancy; procedures remain clumsy, experts in short supply. All of this will change. Old techniques will be perfected; new ones discovered and adapted. The number of technicians capable of mastering these new creatures is already increasing, and large organizations are finding it profitable to rely more and more on new technology for the resolution of problems. Communication systems will be enlarged and the barriers limiting the size of organizations pushed back.

If not today, then tomorrow, it is difficult to see any internal restriction bounding the size of the organization. In such a world, where unassimilated and yet unborn technological advances will further exalt the might of already huge organizations, one may be permitted a moment of speculation on both the effectiveness and the relevance of a liberalism, the vitality of which depends upon the absence of power and supremacy of the individual.

X

Master and Slave

A ZINNIA SEED, CAREFULLY SELECTED, PROPERLY PLANTED IN fertile soil of the temperate zone, nourished by abundant moisture and sunshine, will, we can predict with reasonable certainty, gestate, grow, and eventually flower. But the reason *why* the seed, given these conditions, matures and blossoms still escapes the biologist.

As with the plant, so with the organization. Given certain conditions, such as technological advances, increases in population, and "new worlds to conquer," we can predict that organizations will continue to grow. But why will they grow; what is the life-giving substance that makes them grow? A partial answer to this question seems to lie in the nature of man, in his search for security, in his need for identification, which causes him to associate himself with some movement which is greater than himself, or as Erich Fromm calls it, his "Escape from Freedom." Without purpose man is lost and is little more than any other form of animal life.

Historically, religious and economic doctrines gave meaning to life. But with the spread of knowledge and the dissemination of scientific discoveries, the influence exerted by Christianity has declined. However unpalatable the truth may be, millions of Westerners are passionately anticlerical, violently positivist, or totally indifferent to Christian teach-

ings and beliefs. And even for many devoted church supporters, Catholic as well as liberal Protestant, the divine, the
miraculous, and the transcendental wonder of early Christianity has largely disappeared. With these went Christian
certitude. Having lost the certitude that goes with an omniscient God, man fashioned other faiths such as nationalism,
capitalism, and communism.

At best these are imperfect substitutes for Christianity because, unlike Christianity, they are creeds of this world. A
virtue of Christianity is that it differentiates clearly between
the ideal—the supernatural—and the real world of the flesh.
Built on the belief of original sin and the concept of the
imperfectibility of human nature, Christianity makes allowance for human mistakes, of which man can be cleansed
through repentance and belief in Jesus Christ. Unlike Christianity, which welcomes the return of the repentent prodigal,
nationalism demands unwavering fealty. The "Reign of
Terror," the communist purges, and our own treatment some
years back of alleged communists attest to the "inhuman"
demands of loyalty that these newer faiths impose on the
individual.

Worldly faiths suffer another handicap: impersonality.
Christianity provided an immortal soul and a personal God
one could look to for comfort and consolation, to whom one
could pray in times of crisis and of joy, for courage and in
thankfulness. Communism deifies Marx and enshrines Lenin;
but even the most dedicated party member would no more
consider praying to these national "saints" than would a
Texan to the hero of the Alamo. This illustrates one of the
great failings of most worldly creeds. Man looks for something more than a cold, abstract theory to cling to. He needs
something to which he can communicate his successes and
his failures, something that sees him as a distinctive, important, sovereign human being meriting the swift and un-

failing attention of the Almighty and whatever agents He
may employ.

If faith is to give meaning to life in addition to providing
an eschatology and a moral code, it must somehow make
allowances for the frailties of human nature and provide a
mechanism enabling the "sinner" to repent and gain forgiveness for his transgressions. If a faith is to be viable, it must
include some organizing force through which the individual
can find personal expression. On all these counts Christian
capitalism scored well. Promising eternal life through salvation, it also encouraged man to employ his unique talents in
achieving worldly success, the primary measure of which is
wealth and public esteem. As man taxed his strength in the
attainment of material goals, human perfection (measured in
money) gradually supplanted eternal salvation as the spiritual
force in the drama of life. But then this form of humanism
began to wane as the relationship between individual effort
and financial achievement grew tenuous and as complexity
undermined confidence in the simple perfectibility-of-man
doctrines.

Looking for a haven of refuge which provided a measure
of protection in a chaotic and tortured world, perplexed men
found shelter and security in the modern organization.
Whyte captures this thought when he writes of "the organization man" living by the code of the "social ethic." By identifying with the organization, by making the organization's
purpose his purpose, by believing that he is part of something that is powerful and good, the individual finds meaning and purpose in life.

The stormer of the Bastille, the singer of *Deutschland
ueber Alles* pledged to fight for the Third Reich, and the
member of the fraternity who solemnly promises to keep the
laws of the chapter, each identified with the aims of the group
to which he belonged. Such identification goes a long way in
relieving the individual of the responsibility of justifying his

action to either himself or his society. A meaningful life is achieved simply by working within the framework of the value system of the organization. He is relieved of the tensions that go with asking such questions as: Are my actions good or bad, productive or sterile, ridiculous or sublime? In short the organization eliminates the need for the individual to try to understand modern cosmology and the position he should assume in it. Given the surrogate of the organization creed, "What Makes Sammy Run?" need not be asked, much less answered.

Not only does the organization provide the individual with a *Weltanschauung*—or the absence thereof—it also meets the requirement that man must have a medium for self-expression. Within the organization, through status symbols, such as level of compensation, admittance into the inner circle, and special assignments, he gains recognition. Subject to organizational limits, he is permitted to achieve and to enjoy the satisfaction of "craftsmanship." In brief, he is encouraged to participate. In this role, while recognized as a separate individual who benefits from singular virtues and suffers from unique weaknesses, it is also understood that he possesses the qualities of universal man. He, like all men, is at once honest and deceitful, generous and selfish, courageous and cowardly, compassionate and villainous, glorious and wretched. As a member of an organization he is to exhibit only certain "strengths," not perfection. As long as he honors "thou shalt have no other organizations before me," a commandment common to all organization creeds, forgiveness of sins of the flesh—to err, to fear, to be expeditious, to offend—is freely granted with the imposition of a minimum of penalties.*

---

* Punishment, it would seem, comes by indirection. The greatest status in the group goes to those who best keep the organizational code of ethics. The "sinner" is therefore punished in that he does not attain the rank or position that his talents would otherwise merit.

Thus, through the organization, man finds two things: a creed to which he may cling and an outlet for self-expression. The first gives some explanation why men seek out organizations in which they may become immersed. The second provides at least a partial explanation of why organizations continue to grow unabated. The aggressive need is best fulfilled through achievement, not the least of which takes the form of leading one's subordinates to bigger and better things.

Indeed, what greater self-expression than pushing out organizational boundaries, making a small firm big, changing a listless governmental agency into a powerful public servant, and transforming an insipid labor union into a force to be reckoned with? These are achievements which stand at the very top of the success scale. The leader is to lead, to be imbued with "Protestant ethic," to be inner-directed. He may be barren of generosity, compassion, and principle, if only he possesses the spirit of progress which brings to his organization respect, acclaim, and power. By leading, not only does he satisfy his own need for self-expression, but he vindicates his followers who, by accident or design, threw in their lot with the organization which he heads. *Esprit de corps,* high morale, a spirit of purposiveness are characteristics of the vital, aggressive, rising organization from which the individual draws a sense of energy and dedication and even more significantly a feeling of superiority that comes from knowing that he is distinctly fortunate in having been chosen to participate in the promotion of something that is right, something that is vitally important.

Such then are some of the magnetic qualities of the organization. Technological progress, man's search for a meaningful life, and his desire for challenge and self-expression all have played their roles in organizational growth. Nor can we discern anything on the horizon which will halt or even slow this expansion. Technological advances beget technological advances, success begets success, and ambition begets ambition. The young look to organizations for a faith, and the powerful leaders look for new worlds to conquer. The inexorable result is a world of large organizations, a world of hierarchies, a world of bureaucracies.

The overt purpose of the bureaucratic organization is to get things done, and as cheaply as possible. Given a well-defined objective, the pure bureaucrat, like the pure scientist, is concerned only with "rounding up the horses," harnessing them, and directing them along the most expeditious route leading to the desired destination. The pure bureaucrat, then, like the lathe and the drill press, is in an amoral position in that he makes no ethical evaluation of the given objectives.* In an effort to abstract and present pure bureaucratic characteristics, Max Weber, one of the truly great social scientists, postulated an ideal type. In the Weberian system the ideal bureaucrat is an emotional robot. He feels neither love nor hate, enthusiasm nor discouragement, anger nor compassion, grief nor joy—or, if he does, he must subjugate these human emotions so that personal penchant or conviction will not interfere with the rational execution of his duties. Impartiality, the prime virtue of the pure bureaucrat, is possible only if he maintains an attitude of clinical disinterest.

It cannot be otherwise, for the bureaucrat who permits himself to become personally involved, whether in personal friendships or special interest in particular programs or proceedings, quickly loses his competence in clinical as-

---

* One cannot push this analogy too far. In theory at least, every individual has the power to disassociate himself from an undertaking which is repugnant to his sense of justice, if in no other way than through death. Thus even the lowest technician who helps to further an end must bear some responsibility for the results achieved.

sessment as his decisions become colored and then influenced by personal preferences and prejudices. Having lost impartiality, the personally involved bureaucrat may not only impair the efficiency of the organization but, and much more important, he may unwittingly corrupt and subvert the very purpose of the organization by granting favors and imposing penalties which are in direct contradiction to the *raison d'être* of the organization.

Not only is the ideal bureaucrat emotionless, but he must be disposed to unquestioning acceptance of authority. "His is not to question why, his is but to do or die," and the man who ponders, who questions, who shows initiative is indeed the antithesis of the pure bureaucrat. Herbert Simon in *Administrative Behavior* outlines the pure bureaucratic spirit when he declares, "Once the system of values which is to govern an administrative choice has been specified, there is one and only one 'best' decision, and this decision is determined by the organizational values and situation, and not by the personal motives of the member of the organization who makes the decision. Within the area of discretion, once an individual has decided, on the basis of his personal motives, to recognize the organizational objectives, his further behavior is determined not by personal motives, but by the demands of efficiency." So it must always be, for if the bureaucratic organization is to operate efficiently and impartially, it must be staffed with individuals who unquestioningly accept and who unerringly conform to the rules and directives which are the very quintessence of the bureaucratic organization. Thus, whether the organization's objective is selling cars, collecting taxes, spreading communism, or liquidating non-Aryans who threaten to weaken the master race, any breach of organizational directives, whether inspired by genuine need to serve humanity or by the thought of improving organizational efficiency, is a crime against the organization and hence cannot be tolerated. By these "ideal" standards, Adolf Eichmann was the model bureaucrat.

Such rigidity is not without purpose. Only through technical and detailed specifications can uniformity, and therefore impartiality, be realized when a large number of individuals are employed in performing the same task. A strict interpretation and conformance to directives is also necessary if various experts and technicians, many of whom do not fully appreciate the significance of their contribution to the total program, are to be coordinated as a functioning unit. What may appear to be irrational to the clerk in the lower echelon may indeed be rational as part of the total effort. The classic case of the uninformed man is the private in the army who, because he cannot possibly be instructed in the grand strategy of battle, must consistently follow orders which from his vantage point may appear to be totally irrational. Even where every worker is intelligent and skilled there remains a need for disciplined adherence to prescribed standards since, if some day each specialist decided to follow his own inclination, our modern world of organizations would suffer immediate and disastrous chaos. Suppose, for example, in the automobile industry that each engineer, designer, and production man decided to go his own separate way. Without the coordination of these specialists, not only would it be impossible to build an automobile, but even a transmission, an engine, and such a relatively simple thing as a spark plug would be beyond our reach.

The principle of hierarchy helps to provide a climate which is conducive to strict adherence to organizational directives. This principle provides that each level of operation is accountable to a superior level and that each official is responsible for the act of his subordinates. In order to assure control and at the same time assist in supervision, it is the prerogative and the duty of the superior officer to impose authority by issuing regulations which prescribe as well as confine the actions and decisions of subordinate officers. The official, however, possesses no personal authority; whatever he may have is ex cathedra. Since the office, rather than the individual, is the seat of power, dynamic personal leadership is unnecessary as well as undesirable, and the sole criterion for selecting the official becomes professional skill and technical ability rather than originality and creativity. And since the official is subservient to the office, even a rogue, a rascal or an incompetent may temporarily assume office without seriously disrupting the organization. Subordinates, long accustomed to responding to the impersonal authority of the office, can continue to perform their duties irrespective of the official on whom the authority is bestowed. Accordingly, the office can be transferred from one person to another with a continuity of action guaranteed.

Vesting the office rather than the official with authority places an effective check on the individual who might be tempted to use his seat of authority as a means of promoting personal interest. The knowledge that it is not his personal leadership qualities from which authority is derived and the knowledge that he can be easily replaced by someone else makes him more respectful of his superiors and provides him with additional incentive to adhere closely to the rules and regulations that prescribe the operation of his office and the role he is to play in the functioning of the organization. Primarily dependent upon the organization for income and identification, the only route leading to enhanced status, greater material welfare, and a higher sense of achievement is the promotion process. This dependence of the official upon the organization for material and psychological satisfaction, and the fact that his competence is judged by and equated with his fidelity in carrying out organization "law" makes for a stringency of discipline otherwise unattainable.

However fascinating the logic of pure bureaucracy, organizations are populated by mortals who rule and are ruled by the institutions they create. As such, organizations, rather than being soulless, possess personality; rather than achieving externally established goals, promote internally determined objectives; rather than being the machine so neatly depicted by bureaucratic theory, know the pain and benefits of men driven by the fears and aspirations common to mankind. It cannot be otherwise, for however man, in the sacred name of efficiency, may wish to mechanize and dehumanize his institutions, all his efforts in greater or lesser degree must be corrupted by that intangible yet undeniable factor referred to as the human element. Should efficiency alone be man's goal in life, human strength and human genius must still retain the rank of primacy in the organizational structure. For the rigid machine-like organization, although ideally suited to performing an unending standard assignment and uniquely adapted to maintaining an unchanging static society, cannot, without personal leadership, motivate, create, instill courage, or inspire men to attempt, and on occasion, achieve greatness. Slavish adherence to rules and regulations —red tape—plays havoc with efficiency by making "molehills into mountains," which can produce organization-shaking misunderstandings and which, for solution, require the time and energy of people operating at various levels within the organization.

It is the dull bureaucrat who does not know and condemn the curse of overorganization. Still the true bureaucrat who lives today with an eye for tomorrow, while enthusiastically advocating the need for exceptions to rules, knows deep in his heart that violating rules, in addition to being faulty and unsound administration, is wrong. Such a principle, if only by implication, makes allowances for individual idiosyncracies, a treacherous and pernicious doctrine contrary to all that is truth and justice in the world inhabited by honest, dedicated, and aspiring bureaucrats.

Nor is the bureaucrat to be blamed. Without rigid adherence to rules, modern organizations are beyond the reach of ordinary man. Absolutely essential on the production line, they are no less important at the "white collar" level; without central direction individuals in search of personal recognition and professional glory will inevitably, by sloth or zeal, ignore and pervert organizational goals. For man is a prisoner of the world which he perceives and is a part of. And from the saintly, singleminded idealist to the zealous fanatic is but a quick step which, if unchecked, would make for a bizarre and unbearable world.

Each group, division, and profession is confident that it has been endowed with special power for finding truth and promoting goodness. Each is parochial and each complains of restraints, crying of a deep, unsatisfied need that can only be met by according greater autonomy and discretion to those who understand and are capable of resolving grave and immediate problems. What such a step would do to the total organization, the subdivision cannot know; but if asked, it would surely demonstrate, certainly in its own eyes, that unless recommended actions are immediately implemented, the existence of the entire organization stands in jeopardy. Thus, to curb the personal ambition or honest "empire building" that inheres in human nature and especially in the heart of every eminent and dedicated expert, rules and restrictions must be imposed, without which the mightiest of organizations would surely flounder and then perish.

But, alas, although organizations cannot function and grow without strong central direction, centralization and the inevitable hardening of structure that goes with it maim and cripple the organization in its efforts to become efficient and to achieve greatness. For centralization is founded on rules, rules through which the ruled become the rulers. Precisely how the bureaucrat goes about achieving power cannot be foretold; only his achieving it is a certainty. Always a slave to rules, he also becomes the master, for just as he is directed by them, so also he molds and interprets them to serve his cause. He learns to hide behind them, to become secretive, to build them into a wall of exclusiveness which, while protecting him from hostile, prying eyes, also empowers him to release or suppress information depending upon whether it is favorable to his purpose.

When, with his highly developed sense of perception, he detects the slightest hint of danger in the atmosphere, he retreats to safe, familiar ground behind his façade of rules, avoiding all responsibilities or decisions that now or in the future may threaten or jeopardize him or the position of the subdivision to which he has pledged allegiance. At one time directives are quoted as eternal verities that preclude disturbing the *status quo;* at other times they are pointed to as unmistakable exhortations calling for vital dynamic action that should be effected before the day is through.

Thus while the system provides direction and imposes constraints on the bureaucrat, it also becomes a mechanism which the bureaucrat masters for personal glory and the enhancement of the subculture of which he is a member. If the letter of the law gives advantage, then he shall by all means live by the letter; but if it be the spirit, rather than the letter, that he finds attractive, then he will most surely live by the spirit.

The position of the subdivision or subculture to the large organization is not unlike that of the large organization to the whole of society. Being a small part of the organization and being far removed from completing any ultimate goal, the subdivision sees organizational goals as vague, undefined, abstract concepts having little meaning and falling far outside the scope of its power and influence. Not surprisingly the subculture concentrates its energies and attentions on immediate and concrete processes—processes for which it is responsible and for which there is real hope that they may one day be perfected and brought to fruition. Nor is it surprising that each of the subcultures strives to promote parochial aspects of the organization's total program; each subdivision, like individual organizations competing in society at large, is authoritarian, and each, in maneuvering to achieve particular objectives, is, in the last analysis, Machiavellian.

This then is the nature of large organizations. Presumably conceived and established to perform a specific task as they grow in size and complexity, they perforce become more and more impersonal. They are compelled to rely more and more on rules as the only available means of coordinating the multitude of specialists essential to the progress to which all large organizations are irrevocably committed. By its very success, the purity of the organizational purpose is destroyed. For as more and more specialists are employed and as lines of communication are necessarily lengthened, top management is less and less able to keep in touch with proliferated subdivisions—much less individual employees. Whatever unity the organization may have once known is slowly eroded, and separate and identifiable groups emerge. Each cares little for the espoused creed of the organization but fights hard for the cause or project which is near to its heart.

It cannot be otherwise, at least not in the Western world where, driven by a concept of progress and a better tomorrow, man is to find expression and meaning in life by using his talents for himself, his fellow man and for posterity. This is his goal and his purpose in life. We can see the naïveté of those who would depict the organization as a precise well-oiled machine, which, lacking both spirit and will, once set in motion remorselessly pursues its assigned task.

Such a portrayal is not without its attractions. It conveys exactness, spurious though it may be, as well as logical consistency, however irrelevant and perverse. To those minds terrorized by the infinite and pained by the untidiness of indeterminacy it provides absolute mooring posts, comforting and reassuring. Unfortunately, such a picture of the organization is a fundamental corruption of reality reflecting the misplaced faith of its creators—a faith that proclaims that ends and means are unique and separate phenomena, that it is meaningful to talk about one without the other, that a change in one will not effect a modification in the other. From such taxonomy springs only nonsense. Just as given ends dictate certain means, so means will influence, modify, and eventually determine ends.

The tender-minded may seek refuge and comfort in the thought that men's goals are timeless and universal, that man wants only peace and happiness. But this simply will not do, for if history teaches anything, it teaches that men of different ages and different men of the same age sharply disagree on what constitutes the good life. At one time it may be holiness, at another self-expression and creativity, and still another the unity of a classless society. Nor need one be an economic determinist in order to believe that changes in the state of the arts, or means, have and do influence man's thoughts, actions, and ends. To deny this is to deny that environment is an active factor in shaping men, and therefore the course of history. Who would seriously not agree that the development of accounting, the advent of the ocean-going sailing vessel, the invention of the railroad, the perfection of the factory system—all means—have not shifted man's attention, have not caused him to substitute one set of habits for another, have not caused him to evolve new value systems to displace those of an earlier age?

Even as I write I need only look out my window for illustration of how means transform ends. Across the campus lies a structure towering over the entire university complex. This great edifice, something no visitor could miss, rests atop the university football stadium and was constructed at no small cost for the convenience of the working press as well as representatives of mass media such as radio and T.V. But this impressive and comfortable press box is only incidental. Much more important than the structure itself is how it came to be there. To know this is to understand that the academic philosophy toward athletics has undergone a major change.

Once, in the distant past—or so it seems—there prevailed the belief that young college men, before they were sent out into the world, should be encouraged to realize the ancient ideal of the well-rounded man. To accomplish this, in addition to absorbing generous servings of academic fare, the undergraduate was expected to participate in some form of college athletics. As time went by and as enrollment increased and colleges became more affluent, specially trained staff members were employed to supervise and coordinate college athletics. Whatever the effect of this on spontaneity, there can be little doubt that this step added sophistication and discipline to campus sports.

From teaching physical education and supervising intramural sports to the scheduling of healthy intercollegiate competition is of course but a short way. Unfortunately, inherent in intercollegiate contests are certain hazards, not the least of which is an overwhelming desire to win, especially on the part of the expert who is responsible for training and fielding the team. Feeling that every contest is a test of his acumen and that on the outcome of every game rests the honor of his organization and the college, the specialist, who by this time has become a coach, thinks less and less about developing well-rounded young men and more and more about a victorious season.

Especially is this apparent in college football, where six to eight full-time men—not to mention the many behind-the-scene workers—are employed for the purpose of recruiting and training a winning team. Here, as in other sports, the initial idea that college sports were designed to add another dimension to the well-educated man now seems absurd, as scouting parties representing various universities crisscross the country foraging for young men who possess the athletic prowess necessary to bring success and fame to the college of their "choice." That these men are sought for their academic brilliance seems improbable; on the other hand, those people who are close to the athletes and who should know about such things vigorously denounce as malicious any charge implying that college sports have, in any way, been professionalized.

Whatever the status of college athletics, football is no longer a part of general undergraduate education and has become an immensely profitable undertaking. With the prospect of profits it was inevitable that great monuments would be erected: first, imposing football stadiums and more recently, luxurious press boxes, both of which dramatically illustrate how the means to an end can modify and then completely transform an end. For without specialists—means—to educate young men to the joys of physical education—the original end—big-time football and all that goes with it—new ends—could never have been realized, and I would have been deprived of the view that graces my window.

When on occasion an unkind word is directed toward the

new campus addition, I sometimes speculate on the response
of a classics or history department to similar circumstances
and affluence. Would universities be blessed with a grand
replica of Pericles delivering a funeral oration or perhaps an
extravagant reproduction of a stirring Triumph in the Forum
of Caesar Augustus? Such speculations, like the view from my
window, are amusing as well as interesting.

One can find instances of means influencing ends which are
anything but amusing. Indeed the calloused distortion of
ends by governmental agencies, particularly the branches of
the military, is disturbing, if not frightening. Originally set
up to protect the nation, military organizations have become
so powerful and demanding that today one cannot be sure it
is not the nation which is to serve the military. So vast, so
complex, and so powerful is the military empire that no mere
mortal, however elevated his position, is competent to comprehend it either in detail or in its entirety. In theory Congress and the President are to shape and direct the course of
this vast power complex, insuring always that the nation's
citizens do not become captives of a garrison state. In practice neither Congress nor the President has either the power
or the wisdom necessary to control or alter the objectives of
this immensely effective bureaucracy, which everlastingly
reminds us of the grave needs for military preparedness and
which, failing all else, takes refuge behind the esoterics of
modern arms technology.

Playing always on the nation's honest desire for peace and
its fear of war, the military is armed with a virtually unlimited budget for deploying a corps of professionals who
literally devote their lives to the cause of their service. As
students of the political and bureaucratic terrain of the nation and particularly of Washington, D. C., they are expert

strategists in mapping of campaigns, in conceiving and implementing tactics, and in the marshaling of favorably disposed political coalitions, but not with the intent of destroying some wicked foreign aggressor, but for the purpose of gaining greater freedom and autonomy from those who would constrain and direct the military. That such skilled professionals, armed with superior knowledge and painstakingly developed strategy, are more than a match for the most dedicated congressional committees is one of the harsh facts of contemporary America. Even when Congress, by sheer happenstance or as a result of "leaks" generated by interservice jealousies, can document gross mismanagement, congressional leaders are impotent to identify and isolate the guilty parties, and can do little more than lecture the military at large on the virtues of thrift, honesty, and efficiency.

So great is the perversion of this means—military defense —that General Eisenhower, in his final speech as President of the United States, warned against the grave threat of "unwarranted influence" by a "military-industrial complex." Along these same lines, a senior member of the House Defense Appropriations Subcommittee observed, "There is no question that the services and their contractors have an interest in maintaining a high degree of tension in the country." A member of the House Armed Services Committee saw national security as a popular cause permitting everyone with a vested interest to argue that he was acting in the public interest. "There is," he declared, "real danger that we may go the way of prewar Japan and Germany" if we continue to appoint industrial leaders to the post of Secretary of Defense.

However exaggerated these sinister warnings, there exist, beyond all doubt, certain forces that make for a coalition highly favorable to further enhancement of military power. Included within this coalition are the armed services, military contractors—such as aircraft builders and missile makers —and members of Congress representing constituencies, whose prosperity is closely tied to generous allocations of large defense expenditures. So persuasive is this coalition that its very existence must strike frustration and terror into the hearts of those dedicated to the easing of world tensions. For should the executive branch of the government, through some miracle of wisdom, imagination, and might, negotiate a workable international disarmament treaty, it is not inconceivable that this great and largely unmeasured political force would, under the guise of patriotism, mobilize with the intent of blocking Senate ratification.

Thus it is that the armed services provide at once the most classic and disturbing illustration of means modifying and eventually engulfing original ends.

It would seem that everyone is, intuitively at least, aware of the interdependence of ends and means. Yet there exists a strong compulsion to obscure and even deny this relationship, if for no other reason than because such an admission— especially for those obsessed with absolutes and terrified by indeterminacy—is at bottom a frightening confession that man is impotent to control or even predict the future dimensions or actions of his own creation, the modern organization. For if ends and means are really and irrevocably entwined, as they surely must be, then the organization, rather than being a stable, rational mechanism obeying its master's every wish, becomes a dynamic, living organism which, under its own momentum, fashions new dimensions and strikes out in directions alien and unknowable to those who conceived and created it.

Most Americans, if not all, like to think in sharp outlines of black and white. To see means and ends blended one into the other rather than as separate and distinct phenomena is likely to be an unpleasant experience which is to be avoided. Not only does such a perspective give an untidy and disorganized view of affairs, but it works at cross purposes with our passion for and our faith in efficiency. Whatever discomfort the thought of organizational discord may inflict upon us, it is not wholly without compensating advantages. Indeed its advantages are great, perhaps outweighing its costs. For it is the failure of organizations to achieve complete harmony that yet permits us some small measure of individual freedom. That this failure causes untold loss of efficiency can be and is argued; but, if so, it is the kind of loss that should be viewed in a very narrow context. In the last analysis central coordination, tight discipline, and rigid impersonality all lay a dead hand upon individual expression, be it spontaneity, ingenuity, creativity, or just plain hard work.

Nor is the disparity found within organizations without another and perhaps even more important benefit. Contradictory forces preclude and undermine unity and thus provide protection against those who would require that all men fit into a mold which they themselves have fashioned. Even the malignancy so apparent in the military is not without certain compensations. Certainly interservice rivalries and jealousies produce shocking wastes and a perversion of national purpose. Yet, despite our grim race with the USSR, this loss, however it may offend our sense of reason and justice, is one we should be willing to sustain. At bottom, even granting the unruly and irrational trappings they sire, interservice disputes impose healthy restraints upon those forces which, unchecked, would make America one great regimented military camp.

Surely one may be permitted the small hope that this nation will never see the military unity forged by a German General Staff. Out of diversity comes a conflict of opinions which compels each of the armed services to act as a check upon the other, forever forcing embarrassing exposures of otherwise undetected weaknesses, distortions and tyrannies. Certainly such disclosures uncover only a fraction of the authoritarian abuses extant in the military hierarchies, but given the complexities of military technology and the awesome state of international tensions, these limited insights are probably the best we can hope for. Without them the President and Congress, indeed the whole nation, would, to a much greater degree, become less the master and more the slave of the virtually unmanageable military bureaucracies, without which we could not survive as a separate political identity.

We have seen that the distinguishing characteristic of the industrial 20th-century world is the large, powerful organization. Through it men find identity, inspiration, and purpose. With the decline of transcendental Christianity and the recent crumbling of traditional economic philosophy, man more and more looks to authoritarian organizations for morality as well as a means of expressing his aggressive tendencies. Not only does the large organization give man a cause, but it permits him to feel superior, to draw gratification from belittling and persecuting those who question, deny, or fail to revere the righteousness of his work and the organization to which he has pledged allegiance. Thus men, like the organization to which they belong, model themselves, except in their personal relations with close friends and associates, after Machiavelli's *Prince*.

This spirit—the essence of man in an impersonal society—was succinctly captured when Reinhold Niebuhr entitled his famous work *Moral Man and Immoral Society* and when in the *Nature and Destiny of Man* (Charles Scribner's Sons,

1943) he observed, "Man is insecure and involved in natural contingency; he seeks to overcome his insecurity by a will-to-power which overreaches the limits of human creatureliness. Man is ignorant and involved in the limitations of a finite mind; but he pretends that he is not limited. He assumes that he can gradually transcend finite limitations until his mind becomes identical with universal mind . . . The ego which falsely makes itself the centre of existence in its pride and will-to-power inevitably subordinates other life to its will and thus does injustice to other life."

Unfortunately, for moral philosophers—such as Jacques Maritain, who would consecrate unity, and many social scientists, such as Herbert Simon, who would sanctify organizational rationality and efficiency—organizations are never so well integrated and disciplined as to bring about unified dedication for the promotion of a consistent and eternal set of objectives. Instead, as organizations grow in size and complexity, they must be divided into separate parts, each of which is primarily concerned with promoting its own self-interest, each of which views competing and restrictive forces as something evil, undeserving of life itself. This then is the position and composition of the modern organization.

If you find this an unattractive picture, you may wish for the days of a Thomas Jefferson or an Andrew Jackson or even a Theodore Roosevelt, when men were free, largely self-sufficient and optimistic about peace, prosperity, and progress. One may indeed argue that these were better days—carefree, secure, pious days when organizations were small and the nation lived under a happy spell cast by a simple and relevant capitalist theory. Unfortunately, such exhortations cannot restore the past, and the fact remains that even if each of us as separate individuals were anxious to turn back the clock to the simpler life, we would be helpless for want of a means to accomplish it. For better or for worse, our world by design and fact is committed to an industrial and hence impersonal society. As such, those who succeed know full well the words of Niccolò Machiavelli—though they have never read nor heard them—when he wrote, "A certain prince of the present time, whom it is well not to name, never does anything but preach peace and good faith; but he is really an enemy to both, and either of them, had he observed them, would have lost his state or reputation on many occasions."

Given our faith in progress, our passion for the mechanistic, our aggressive self-righteousness, and our uncompromising need to find individual security and purpose through organizational might and glory, it is inevitable that we will devote more and more of our originality and brilliance to furthering the invention and construction of new, more demanding organizations. In such a bureaucratic world, the diversity and conflict inherent in all contemporary institutions will still provide some small measure of opportunity for man to enjoy and express his individuality. Certainly this kind of pluralism, extant in even the most rigidly disciplined organizations, falls—except for those who crave moral absolutes—short of our ideal; but, given our nature and technology, it is probably the best we can ask or hope for. Failing this, for this world there is no hope—only tyranny. Fortunately, the picture is not so grim, for in democracy there are yet great forces of freedom. It is this liberal faith, democracy, that we will now **examine.**

XI

The Classical View

Men in general and scholars in particular are forever driven to pursue the eternal, the absolute. That such yearning has brought fruit, no one can deny. Without it there could be no science, no progress, no modern world. But our desperate need for answers also bears the curse of militant, unyielding orthodoxies. For it is in the nature of man, conservative or liberal, reactionary or reformer, to organize around and fight for some special brand of orthodoxy. There are, of course, many kinds of orthodoxy—religious, political, economic. But in recent years, we of America, and for good reason, have been most immediately concerned with the orthodoxy of economics.

It was not always so. In the not too distant past the great attraction of orthodox economics was its almost unanimous acceptance. As government has more and more become a factor in the economy, this has changed. There is a ceaseless cry that our fall from orthodoxy has been accompanied by the unpleasant prospect of the ominous welfare state that threatens to destroy everything that is fine and good, everything that made America the flower of Western civilization.

Signs of decadence, we are told, are all about us. We are continually warned that our very way of life is being undermined. Fortunately, we are told, there is still time, if only we change our ways, if only we return to the tried and true.

247

But we must give up our search for security; we must somehow overcome our compulsion to conform. For these, more
than anything, make for the syndrome which now afflicts us
—a profound national weakness. Should we fail to change
our ways, should we continue our immediate course, then
eventually our nation, and with it all of Western civilization,
must decay, must perish. To support such admonitions our
critics point to the inspired creativity of Periclean Athens,
Renaissance Italy, and Elizabethan England, emphasizing all
the while that these were periods not only of great men and
ideas, but also of deep and notorious instability.

No one can dispute the examples just as no one can dispute
that our immediate and dedicated quest for personal economic security is often inconsistent with transcendental
change. But to admit the historical event does not imply that
economic security and social change are, on all counts, mutually exclusive, or that America's social, material, or scientific
progress is slowly being strangled by a government-imposed
straitjacket. For the truth is that we of mid-20th century
America, in one decade, have initiated and completed more
radical, social, and technological change than did Egypt,
Rome, India, or the Byzantine Empire over the span of centuries. The cries of American detractors, like the cries against
all historic periods, are generated not because of our exaggerated loyalties to the past, but because in our excesses we,
like Renaissance Florence, are willing and sometimes anxious
to ignore and discard tradition.

Indeed those most fearful of the welfare state are the very
ones most opposed to change. At bottom they fear the prospects of replacing the workings of "natural law" with conscious and deliberate human decisions. Afraid of power, they
trust no power but their own, for the history of power is
also the history of abuse and tyranny. What escapes these
modern critics, especially those haunted by the specter of

the welfare state, is that in the contemporary world the logic of modern technology remorselessly compels the formation of power centers. The relevant question is no longer "Shall there be political power?", but "How shall power be organized and who shall control it?" On these matters men, especially those in power, have never seen fit to submit to the adjudication of natural law. For in the last analysis the distribution of political power rests in the hands of the state. And if the United States is, as its detractors allege, moving rapidly toward the welfare state, it presumably is to be accomplished in the public interest and through a political process—a process to which we are irrevocably committed, a process we are proud to call democracy.

There are almost as many interpretations of the word "democracy" as there are people who use it. Of one thing, however, we can be sure. Democracy is something good, something worth striving for, something that almost all men, whatever their plan or objective, are eager to invoke. We hear of democratic education, democratic economic systems, democratic labor unions. Mussolini, Hitler, and Khrushchev have all proclaimed the glory of their democratic governments. So used and misused is the term that one is tempted to agree with Carl Becker when he observed that it is, "a kind of conceptual Gladstone bag which, with a little manipulation, can be made to accommodate almost any collection of social facts we may wish to carry about in it. In it we can as easily pack a dictatorship as any other form of government."

Out of such a welter of confusion any attempt to simplify and clarify the meaning of democracy should surely be welcome. Nor is there any shortage of attempts, such as the one that classified as democratic all governments supported by the majority of a nation's citizens. Such a definition appears both simple and straightforward, but it is awkward and most surely has given its creators some very bad moments. For if support of the government by the majority of the people is the true criterion of democracy, then a Caesar, a Napoleon and a Khrushchev, all of whom have had the support of their people, could have rightfully claimed the title of democratic leader. Caesar's power was conferred by public mandate, but that made his government no less authoritarian. Napoleon referred to his democratic empire, but he had no illusion that his was a democratic rule. Khrushchev's government has been affirmed through a form of the elective process, yet the Russian political system bears no resemblance to a democratic republic. Clearly something more than support of the majority of the citizenry is necessary for the realization of the democratic process.

If majority rule is an unworkable description of democracy, then what is? Could it be that democracy is yet another illusion, another of those vague, meaningless words embraced by everyone who, in grinding his ax, flaunts it to curry public favor? Certainly the term is subject to frequent prostitution, but it can be meaningful, if it is employed to designate one and only one thing—a procedure for choosing government.

Such a use of the term is not as limited as it might seem at first glance. In this context, certain very definite bounds are imposed on both the source of governmental power and the means of attaining it. Perhaps of even greater importance is, as T. V. Smith points out, a democratic state of mind, which irrevocably commits the nation and those who control the power of the state to the unwavering belief that the ultimate means for determining who shall govern must always and finally rest in the hands of the people. According to the democratic creed, only free and frequent elections, safeguarded by the secret ballot, provide a practical and peaceable means of selecting major governmental policy makers. Thus under democracy the philosophically plaguing and morally insoluble problem of finding the all-wise ruler becomes largely irrelevant.

At this point a sharp distinction is needed; a distinction between who shall govern and the process of governing. Democracy is a way of choosing leadership, not a way of governing. Only in the broadest, virtually meaningless sense can the people actually participate in the actual governmental process. For under democracy, as indeed under all systems, duly chosen officials and their subordinates, as agents of the people, must make and administer law and public policy. How these men govern and what instruments they employ are in the last analysis no real test of democracy. The United States system of government, for example, is founded upon the separation of powers, federalism, written constitutions, and judicial review. But these, contrary to opinion inspired by national pride, are by no means prerequisites to democracy. The English system has virtually none of these features, while the Soviet Union boasts both a form of federalism and a written constitution. Yet England rests secure in its long democratic tradition, while Russia has never known anything but totalitarianism.

Above majority rule and above a unique set of institutions stands law; just as government rules by law, so government must itself submit to law; and just as restrictions are imposed upon the governed, so limitations are imposed upon those who govern. For more than majority rule itself, the essence of democracy is the right to form a majority.

To preserve this right, and therefore assure that democracy "shall not perish from the earth," certain fundamental liberties must, at all costs, be guaranteed. Under no circumstances may the government, in the sacred name of the majority, strip from the minority its freedom of political discourse, its right of assembly, or its privilege to organize for the purpose of nominating and electing a candidate. Government power then, under the rule of law, has its limits. Although no law can be passed, no measure taken and no policy formulated against the will of the majority, the minority, more than the majority, needs protection and is provided safety and shelter under the shield of democratic law.

Democratic government must do more than merely tolerate criticism; at least in theory, it should do everything in its power to promote a climate favorable to a viable opposition. For if the demands imposed upon the majority are great, so also are the responsibilities of the loyal opposition. Although loyal, in the sense that the minority accepts the right of the majority to rule, it is the burden of the minority not only to block the measures of the majority, but to work, within the "rules of the game," at overthrowing the majority and placing itself in the position of law maker. Although it is the task of the majority to formulate policy, it is the prime duty of the minority to dissect, interpret, and criticize it. To do this and do it well the minority must be a self-respecting group or party which is confident that its purpose is legitimate, its end fruitful. Only then can the minority fulfill its sense of *noblesse oblige* by pointing out the dangers inherent in majority measures, by criticizing the majority action, by posing alternatives, and generally by emphasizing the weaknesses and deficiencies of the majority and the policies formulated by it.

The only really effective check on public power resides with a vigorous minority which highlights, in a manner understood by the public, aspects of majority policy otherwise undisclosed. If the public in this complex world is ill informed on public matters, without a dedicated minority the people would have even less knowledge of what the government is actually doing or planning to do. Without debate and disclosures forced by the minority, the public would be hopelessly incompetent to interpret and understand the real meaning of the issues which face the nation.

Although democracy must unconditionally guarantee certain civil rights, there is one line of action it must not tolerate. Democratic government cannot resort to or countenance the use of force, "the last argument of kings," to perpetuate a position that runs contrary to prevailing opinion as expressed through the election procedure or the lawmaking and administrating bodies. "If men are not," McIver declares, "content to win their ends by making enough converts to turn their cause into the cause of the majority so they can legitimately triumph at the polls, they are rejecting the only ground which, in democracy, they are entitled to ask for."

The use of force by either the majority or the minority can be catastrophic as was so dramatically illustrated when the South fired on Fort Sumter. Still, the employment of force by those out of power does not pose the grave threat that arises when those in power resort to the use of raw force. Ordinarily the use of violence by the "outs" is easy to combat because the majority has at its disposal the full resources and military might of the state. But should those in power, having been recalled by the people, refuse to turn over the government to the newly elected majority, then the democratic process has ceased to exist.

The gravest threat to democratic government comes not from those who would forcefully challenge governmental leadership, but from those who, once in the seat of power, would use the virtually unlimited strength of modern government to negate the public will as expressed through the elective process. To be more specific, the great peril to American democracy is not the Communist party, pledged as it is to overthrow our system of government; rather, it lies in the possibility that government one day may fall into the

hands of some who, in the name of 100 per cent Americanism, free enterprise, and Christianity, would destroy the very
bricks and stuff from which democratic government derives
its authority.

Americans often talk of the tyranny and injustice of totali-
tarian systems—of the monarch, the emperor, the lord, and
the dictator. But tyranny is not peculiar to authoritarian systems; democracy, however pure, provides no absolute guarantee against it. For the majority can be as despotic as any
prince or dictator. "If the law is to be made by majority,"
proclaimed De Tocqueville, "the minority is always subject
to a degre of tyranny."

A common situation, a simple case of disagreement over
the desirability of constructing sidewalks in an expanding
residential area, will illustrate this thesis. We may assume that
100 families live in the area, some living in a well-established
section, others in a newly developed division. Of these 100,
51 go on record favoring the construction, and 49 vote against
it. We may assume further that the distribution of construction costs between the opposing camps would be 10 per cent
and 90 per cent, with the group militantly opposing construction being compelled to contribute the larger amount.
To dramatize the conflict we may also assume that the 51 who
favor walks will find them both useful and beneficial to their
property, but those against, because of the loss of trees, lawn,
and shrubs, see the walks as a nuisance which can only make
their property decline in value.

Clearly, undertaking the project will do a disservice to the
minority. Yet if pure democracy is to prevail, the walks must
be built, and the 51 who favor the walks can, if necessary, call
upon the full powers of the government to impose forcefully
the will of the majority on the recalcitrant 49. In this case

the minority may well speak of the tyranny of the majority.

Nor does the democratic majority suffer from excessive restraints. It could through legislative enactments abolish the system of private property, dispense with public school education, order the destruction of every other female child under the age of two, enslave religious and racial minorities, or outlaw all but the "true" faith. In the United States, as in all democracies, the citizens of a nation are protected from such governmental madness by a Constitution—written and unwritten; but in theory at least, all of the citizens' rights (except certain political liberties which themselves may be eroded away by the pressure of popular opinion) could be eliminated through majority action without doing violence to the concept of democratic process: the right to form a majority for the purpose of taking over the government. In practice, of course, one would be permitted to speculate as to whether such monstrous inhumanities could take place without bringing with them the complete and total collapse of the democratic process.

In reality, those out of power accept—with a certain amount of healthy dissent and grumbling—the policy of the majority; but in a considerable number of instances the majority rule is simply not accepted either by the minority or the people in general. Legislation making the consumption of alcohol illegal is honored more in the breach than the observance; high income tax rates are circumvented through depletion allowances, expense accounts, and capital gains; business restrictions are often meaningless simply because business units neglect to observe them. Examples of the latter phenomenon are legion, running the gamut from the failure of the proprietor to observe archaic blue laws to the corporate executive's "oversight" causing him to forget the statute which makes illegal any contract or combination in restraint of trade. The Civil War, of course, is the classic case of a large minority reacting violently to the "tyranny of the majority," the upshot of which was four tragic years of human suffering.

Yet one should not asume that the arsenal of the minority includes only a stubborn disregard for the law of the majority and the use of force, which is the antithesis of democracy. These are weapons of last resort, which most democrats do not employ under any circumstances. There are a multitude of more appealing gambits which, while not endangering the game itself, give promise of greater benefit. To those of us on the sidelines this can be disconcerting, for it makes it all but impossible to predict which of the boundless stratagems and tactics the players will deploy. Uncertainty, however, is part of the democratic process, for the spirit and the workings of democracy are a wondrously subtle and intangible business which, however thorough and painstaking the efforts of the systemizer, can never quite be captured, never fully described.

In these few pages I have tried to examine the theory of democracy in classical form. But theory, like football rules, is studied more with the intent of circumvention than for the purpose of living by the letter of the law. It is time that we see how the game is really played.

XII

Harsh Realities

In a democratic society the citizens determine who of the active contestants for leadership shall govern them. More they cannot do, for, lacking the information, the temperament, and the power needed to rule, they are impotent to participate actively in the governing process. Whatever the form of government, its actual workings in an impersonal society must be conducted by a select few.

The ordinary citizen, rather than waste his time worrying about the finer points of governing, does better to invest his personal resources in gaining excellence in the performance of his assigned duties. Some men are accountants, others are engineers, still others, telephone technicians; all, however, are specialists and all are expected to demonstrate proficiency, assume responsibility, and exercise authority commensurate with their respective positions. For the typical specialist, the "race" within his chosen trade or profession monopolizes his thoughts and attention. Political activities or ruminatings must compete for leisure hours with woodworking, socializing, or playing tennis.

To the typical contemporary American most political questions are remote, intangible, even unimportant; warnings of impending dangers are exaggerated, and somehow, even in the shadowy world of politics, things will work themselves out to a tolerable conclusion. For his optimism or lack

of interest in world events he is criticized by would-be reformers and intellectuals. But the citizen is faced with a complex society whose issues are not easily definable.

In the past, women's suffrage, slavery, and prohibition were
problems which the citizen understood and on which he could
take a stand. Not that the citizen lacks information. So great is
the surfeit of daily and conflicting news that he is overwhelmed
by the crises that beset the world. The newspapers carry
stories telling of the hardships of unemployment or the
dangers of inflation; editorialists rail at the abuses of leaders
in government, business, and labor; books on the best-seller
list explore the shadowy world of psychology and psychiatry;
and even man's means of escaping the troubles of the immediate world, television, turns on him with an hour long
documentary detailing the shattered position of the United
States in Africa.

In this world made small but infinitely more complex by
science and technology, the typical citizen, however learned
he may become in world events, knows that he can have no
real voice in the forging of public policy. "He is," wrote
Schumpeter, "a member of an unworkable committee, the
committee of the whole nation, and this is why he expends
less disciplined effort on mastering a political problem than
he expends on a game of bridge." Thus ordinary men are
prone to retreat from the dour world of politics. And in so
doing, being ignorant of and uninterested in most political
issues, the people have no alternative but to give *carte
blanche* to the elected official in representing them. Such
delegation makes the dictates of the politician's conscience,
rather than the will of the people, the prime determinant in
policy making.

To the booster of 18th-century classical democratic theory,
this can be a disconcerting thought. In making policy, the
public official is, in theory, supposed to reflect the will of the

people. He is to be a sort of passive agent who attends legislative assemblies for the purpose of protecting and furthering the interests of the group he represents. He is, in short, a kind of elevated errand boy, an important one to be sure, but nevertheless, at bottom, always a hireling, "the servant of the people."

At this point certain tensions would seem to appear in this system, for surely anyone who is worthy of being elected to a high public office must be a man of principle. And the purist faces the dilemma of representation vs. principle. Should the public official take for his guide the will of his constituents, ignorant and selfish as it may be, or should he listen to his conscience and live by his principles, even though they may be in direct conflict with the values of those he represents? Such questions can inspire exhilarating, fascinating debate, but fortunately they are largely irrelevant to the discussion of the democratic process.

One can cite instances of conflict between principle and representation, but in general the elective process minimizes such polarization. On issues of direct and immediate public interest, it is the exception when principles and values are deeply at odds. In matters where the consensus is unmistakable, it is contrary to logic to assume that the principles of the leader collide with the desires of his constituents. For the leader, a product of the environment from which these values spring, probably not only subscribes to, but actually may have contributed to the attitudes which go into the making of the public will. Thus the congressman who is a product of an area dominated by militant union members will find great satisfaction in killing a "right-to-work" proposition, just as a Southern congressman will consider himself a true patriot as he gallantly carries the fight against integration.

To deny this would be to fly in the face of years of diligent and painstaking research conducted by social psychologists and cultural anthropologists. The findings of such research point overwhelmingly to group contact as the primary factor in determining individual behavior. Of particular importance in the formation of the individual personality are group contacts experienced in the early years of life. Through group association the child, and later the man, learns to interpret, understand, and finally to react to an immediate situation. The family, the neighborhood, the school, the church—all primary groups—play important parts in shaping values, developing personal skills, and teaching the individual to adjust to an inhospitable physical, and often cruel social, world. Participation in the same groups and activities is the great leveler pushing for uniformity of attitudes and behavior.

The modern American can hardly escape group membership. If he is a father, a Methodist, a Mason, a Republican, a midwesterner, and a corporation executive, many groups will claim his loyalty. But although many organizations are anxious to claim the loyalties of the individual, the individual can be loyal to only a few. It is these few reference groups that play a significant role in shaping his behavior. For it is from the reference groups—those to which the individual looks for guidance and purpose—that values, norms, and frames of references are taken.

Just as values differ from time to time and place to place, so norms may vary from group to group. Midwestern rural asceticism, the excesses of the Hollywood set, the violence of East Harlem and the aloof gentility of the Lawrenceville-Princeton tradition, all reflect group values. Hard physical labor, education, church activities, and conspicuous consumption will be seen from one perspective by a midwestern farm boy, from another by a product of the Hollywood *nouveau riche,* from a third by a youth of the New York slums, and from still another by a lad reared in the New England subculture portrayed so effectively by John P. Marquand. When the individual is confronted with an unfamiliar situation, he attempts to structure it—to put it in some form that reflects the context of values and norms subscribed to by the group with which he identifies himself. To do this he may very well seek out the advice and counsel of his friends. He describes his problem and asks how they would respond to these new and enigmatic circumstances that puzzle him. Thus when a problem requiring decision or action arises, the ultimate resolution comes not from an isolated, lonely individual, but from someone who is a member of a reference group.

What is true for the follower is equally true for the leader. If the leader is to preserve his position of leadership, he must, above all else, honor group norms. "The leader," declares Homans, "must live up to the norms of the group—all the norms—better than any follower." Only when he has demonstrated that he is truly fired by the spirit of group virtues will the followers willingly bestow upon him the prestige and authority necessary for effective leadership. No man, whether a politician, corporate executive, clergyman, or union leader, can escape this reality. He who leads must, by word and deed, honor the ethical and moral values of his followers. It is this unyielding reality that makes largely academic the purist's debate as to whether the politician shall be an errand boy or a man of principles. On issues that touch the voter's heart the politician, like any other leader, is impotent to escape the role of the errand boy. To attempt to do so would require him to violate his basic credo, which was fashioned from the norms and values of the subculture which he now represents in democratic process. This he cannot do, for without a credo, a set of beliefs, a philosophy—call it what you will—there is only madness.

As political scientists, particularly those of British and French extraction, have pointed out, American democracy cannot escape certain other realities. Particularly disturbing to many students of American democracy is the public's apathy toward political candidates and elections. The failure of millions to exercise their voting privileges and the voter's abject ignorance of such matters as political platforms and candidates' ideologies are cited as prime evidence of the typical American's almost total lack of interest in government and political issues.

Perhaps voters should be encouraged to take advantage of their right to vote; perhaps additional efforts should be made to stimulate voter interest in the operations and prob-lems of local, state, and federal government. Yet to judge and condemn the public for lack of interest and participation in politics must be founded on the rather childlike faith that the public is not only politically informed, but competent to comprehend and evaluate the course of political events. Rather than expressing contempt for the ignorance of the masses, one may be tempted to ask whether apathy cannot be interpreted to mean that all of the candidates are more or less satisfactory. One often hears such expressions as, "They are both good men," "One is just as crooked as another," or "I see little or no difference between the candidates and their respective positions." Implicit in such statements is the con-viction that neither or both of the candidates subscribe to the important beliefs held by the voter. Accordingly, the result of the election may be of no moment to the individual. Finally, for elective offices of sizable responsibility and sta-ture, the voter finds comfort and security in the knowledge that only those committed to the basic cultural values of the time are, through the nominating process, given an oppor-tunity to become a serious candidate. This aspect of voter behavior explains why the percentage difference separating the winner from the loser—although the absolute gap in the ballots cast for contending candidates may be wide—is, in hard fought elections, customarily small.

Inherent in voter behavior is another reality eloquently and sometimes embarrassingly expressed by voter response to questions calling for an assessment of the candidates' qualification for the office contested. Made uneasy by searching inquiries, voters seek to evade the issue and respond by citing the virtues—he is a dependable, honest, sincere, God-fearing man—and the favorable surface features—he is a handsome, fatherly, common man—of the candidates of their choice. When pressed further to voice their opinions on platforms and specific issues or proposals, many voters reply that they are incompetent to discuss intelligently such matters of state.

On the basis of such voter performances, it has for some time now been fashionable to cry out against public apathy as the prime threat to freedom under the democratic process. Perhaps the dangers are real; perhaps for want of dedication, or lack of public scrutiny, we Americans are in jeopardy of losing our individual freedom and rights only to serve the purpose of a small band of malevolent men.

Such an explanation is facile and wicked. At bottom it implies that ballots are cast without thought, almost at random. Is the American public so extraordinarily stupid and so easily misled that almost any demagogue can capture high elective office? To deny this is not to deny that voter standards are crude, for indeed they are. But if crudeness is their curse, simplicity is their virtue. And in this modern world of complexity and organization, where not even the most elevated has the background or scope of understanding necessary to comprehend world problems in their entirety, the voter, if actions are to be at all rational, must act on the belief that simple, forthright standards are indeed valid. Thus the voter, rather than squandering his energies on studying com-

plex and baffling issues, rather than evaluating the merits of
ambiguously worded platforms, rather than painstakingly
detailing and contrasting the minute differences between opposing policies, concentrates directly on the competing candidates or, especially if the office involved is a minor one, on
the party affiliations of the candidates.

Some voters do listen to speeches and read campaign literature; but even these public-spirited citizens are more often
than not seeking to comprehend the values and ideals of
the candidates. In the candidates' specific policy recommendations—unless it is a matter near the voter's heart or pocket-
book—for such things as agricultural surpluses, labor abuses,
or foreign aid, voters are remarkably uninterested except as
discussion of these specific issues provides insights into the
true beliefs of the candidates. It is the successful campaigner
who can convince his listeners, however bizarre his specific
policy recommendations, that his beliefs, values, and behavior coincide with theirs. But the office seeker who gives
the impression that he, better than his listeners, knows what
is best, is doomed to defeat.

All of this is part of the game. The politicians, knowing
the voters are sly and crafty, would fool them by drawing up
long, ambiguously worded credos and platforms. The voters,
knowing the politicians' strategy and their facility with words
and phrases, disregard their studied obscurantism and look
directly at more concrete, sometimes inconsequential and
misleading facts to help them with their evaluations. Is the
candidate married? Is he wealthy? Is there any scandal attached to him? Where was he reared? What church does he
attend? Most important of all, what is his party affiliation?

For the majority of citizens, these are more meaningful
questions than the incredibly difficult inquiries relating
to proposed policy recommendations. For at best, political
proposals are only immediately relevant. Issues have a

remarkable capacity for changing, submerging, vanishing; office holders do not. At the time of an election the economy may be tortured by the brooding shadow of unemployment and depression; a year later it may be burdened by rampant inflation. Who possesed the wisdom to forecast all the miseries and disturbances associated with the partition of India and the Korean War, the ferment in Asia and the awakening in Africa, or unremitting inflation coupled with endemic unemployment? In this intricate and therefore confusing modern world clairvoyance is a quality few possess.

Not surprisingly, it is the sharing of beliefs between the candidate and the voter which determines the casting of ballots. If only subconsciously, the voters ask, "How will this candidate and the party he represents respond to the problems that will inevitably arise during the coming term of office?" When the time for decision arrives, the ballot will be cast for that contestant who most closely approximates the voter's image as he sees it himself. This is one of the harsh realities of contemporary life and modern democracy. For some this must always be an unhappy, disquieting, but curable and therefore temporary sore on the body politic. But these eternal hopes are ill founded, for in our confusing, chaotic world, there is no doubt that this is the very best we can hope for.

At this point an unmanageable and unpredictable element must be introduced: the function and role of leadership. As has already been noted, broad group attitudes and class interests, rather than campaign events, bear close watching if one is to follow the course of the contest; but it would be a mistake to assume that the candidates themselves—the leaders—are impotent to alter attitudes and therefore change the direction of play.

Not that all victorious candidates are active, vital, imaginative leaders. Warren Harding and Calvin Coolidge, whatever else may be said about them, were not liable to the charge of domineering leadership; and Herbert Hoover, for all his good intentions and engineering genius, was overwhelmingly defeated by Franklin D. Roosevelt, who, in speaking of the destiny of man, promised a kind of willingness to experiment that was antithetical to the philosophy of a Hoover.

Nor is the case of Roosevelt unique; history is replete with deeds of men who gained stature by appealing to some latent, unfulfilled desire which, when brought to the surface and used as a rallying point, not only made great leaders, but indeed altered the whole sweep of history. Jesus and St. Paul, Charlemagne and Bernard of Clairvaux, Elizabeth I and Washington, Joseph Smith and Gandhi, Hitler and Churchill were all great emotional, charismatic leaders. Each of these persons, in his own fashion, polarized and popularized a body of doctrine which inspired men to participate, even to the laying down of their lives, in activities the leader had persuaded them were just and worthy. More recently, Walter Reuther champions a shorter work week, and Barry Goldwater preaches the virtues of a free society. Both seek to rally the rank and file around some hope for social improvement and thereby strengthen their own positions. But these are only two examples of a general approach used to bring organization and group solidarity to men who experience shared needs. The pronounced proliferation of new organizations, bent on correcting abuses and eliminating injustices, bears eloquent testimony to the brilliant success of leadership in activating and formalizing previously dormant wants.

The influence of leaders has caused critics of democracy to speak of a synthetic "public will" created by the cunning and unprincipled propaganda artist who, in combining psychology and advertising tricks, manufactures a consensus favorable to those in power. Joseph Goebbels, the master of Nazi propaganda, is frequently cited as a prime illustration of an intellectual who prostituted his talents and genius for the purpose of fashioning a kind of national lunacy. Certainly political leaders, particularly the heads of government, possess power which, if unchecked, may produce a pathological society. The spectacle of Germany, the Russian experience, and the fate of the People's Democracies such as Hungary, must make it altogether clear that planned terror, lies, thought control, systematic manipulation of rewards and punishments, and remorseless appeal to fears and emotions, can all subvert individual principles and beliefs as well as group attitudes.

Fortunately, violence at home is repugnant to what we cherish and hold to be true. No political leader, whatever his oratorical skill or personal charm, is unbounded in his capacity to persuade by logic or emotion. It is foolish to dispute the axiom that great crises make great leaders, but it is also true that in a stable, prosperous, democratic society, the political leader is essentially impotent to change deeply ingrained beliefs and attitudes. Indeed the leader's primary function, rather than altering values, is to translate them into action. And inevitably this assignment involves conflict. Each group endeavors to promote its general values and specific objectives. These can be inconsistent, for citizens may demand less governmental intervention, more farm support, more effective foreign policy, less aid to underdeveloped countries, etc. The men responsible for converting these values into reality appreciate the impossibility of realizing all these demands much better than any of the voters. Desperate indeed is the young, inexperienced politician who is caught between an unyielding reality and an unrelenting pressure from the home folk to accomplish hopelessly visionary tasks.

Picture a spirited freshman congressman, representing a predominantly pro-labor district, dead set on modifying the "union-busting" provision of the nation's "slave labor" law. His campaign on this issue, he believes, led to his victory, and as he bids farewell to his friends and backers and leaves for Washington, he sees the elimination of onerous labor legislation as his sole mission in life. Once he is officially seated and becomes a working member of the House, he begins to learn that the nation's labor laws are neither as irresponsible nor as wicked as he had depicted them in his campaign. Yet because of his deep loyalties to his friends and promoters and because he genuinely believes that improved labor legislation is essential, he joins forces with other congressmen committed to the enactment of legislation more favorable to labor. But as he begins to understand some of the congressional realities, he finds that although he may be able to influence other noncommitted members of Congress, he also learns that their support will not be secured without paying a price—his vote, or the votes of those aligned with him—which takes the form of endorsing some measure that may well be in conflict with the values of the group to which he looks for identification. Finally he discovers that under the very best of conditions the pro-labor group is probably impotent to muster anywhere near the strength necessary to overturn existing labor law.

Thus our freshman congressman finds himself facing a dilemma. If he fails to drive for the repeal of the "slave labor" law, which only a few months earlier he sincerely and vigorously denounced, he has reneged on his promise. But if he bargains for a lost cause, and in so doing casts his votes for measures contrary to his principles and the convictions of his followers, he not only sacrifices the best interest of those to whom he owes his loyalties, but endangers his own position by going on record as favoring legislation opposed by those to whom he looks for acceptance and authority. Caught between the real and the ideal, his only hope seems to be an honest, forthright description of the forces aligned for the purpose of blocking his efforts.

If our freshman congressman weathers the storm, he will learn that the elected politician must be always a transmitter as well as a receiver of information. While never neglecting his constituency, he must also educate it to the political problems of converting values into action. As he gains experience he will strike a fine balance, satisfying his constituents on issues which fall within his power and educating them directly or indirectly to the fact that certain goals are unattainable—at least, so he will tell them, temporarily.

Today, more than at any time in our history, there exist growing forces which make contact between the politician and his constituents more difficult, more infrequent and more tenuous. In the not so distant past direct persuasion and personal leadership were vital forces in voter-politician relationships. Such intimate contact, in a nation marked by a burgeoning population and modern technology, has virtually vanished today. The politician is no longer the servant of a small isolated group sharing common attitudes. Confronted with a multiplying, heterogeneous populace of conflicting ideals and objectives, instead of relying on close personal contacts he must resort to the use of mass communication media, running the gamut from handbills and posters to radio and television. Even the once powerful ward boss who, knowing the pulse of every event and citizen, ruled his "manor" with a rare combination of legerdemain, ruthlessness, wisdom, and kindness has been dethroned by education, rising living standards, full employment, and the welfare programs sponsored by local, state, and federal governments.

With the passing of the ward boss have come new tactics, new strategies. No longer does the politician speak directly to his constituents, no longer does he hammer hard on concrete, specific issues, no longer does he appeal to narrow self-interest. Now he must speak in glittering—and not so glittering—generalities lest he offend one of the many diverse and powerful groups which populate this land. He becomes not a defender of principle, but a master of platitude.

Another change in the politician occurs as he moves up the ladder of political society. Slowly he is wrenched from his roots as his contacts more and more are confined to what C. Wright Mills calls "the power elite"—his fellow politicians, appointed governmental officials, lobbyists and his close political supporters and advisors. He may retain a few ties with lifelong friends in a place he once thought of as home. But with each victorious campaign, these personal ties grow weaker, more strained until his contact with the group he represents is almost completely broken and he can no longer be thought of as a personal leader. It becomes necessary for someone to replace and represent him in the direction and education of his constituents. To this end the official builds or turns more and more to an already established organization—the political party, which employs every available technique to convince the voters that the politician is deeply loyal and that he is marshaling every resource at his command to translate into practice the ideologies of those he so "ably" represents.

And this too is one of the harsh realities of modern democracy.

XIII

The Threat from Within

THE PERFECT SYSTEM, THE SUBLIME INSTITUTION, SEEMS JUST beyond the reach of man. Even the modern faith, democracy, is not wholly free of tensions or strictures. Of all the evils and deficiencies invented or discovered by democratic foes, one is admitted and condemned by virtually all democrats. The essence of this blemish, which (we are told) is fast becoming an incurable malignancy, is captured in such common expressions as "selfish interest group," "vested interest group," or, more simply, "pressure group." Almost without exception these terms carry a stigma implying that the group under discussion is seeking to promote some particular cause beneficial to a limited number of individuals, specifically those promoting the scheme at the expense of the majority.

We live in a nation of interest groups. And of those we can identify, perhaps the most outstanding and effective are the National Association of Manufacturers, the AFL-CIO Confederation, and the various farm organizations. Each of these has deliberately and successfully nurtured influence and cultivated power with the prime motive of shaping and directing governmental policy in such a way as to benefit its membership. That these are dedicated, imaginative, and selfish interest groups, few dispassionate observers will dispute. But what of other groups that proclaim that they are objective, that they are solely concerned with advancing the

271

public welfare? The American Medical Association, it would seem, is quite certain that its primary function is to insure the best possible medical care for the people of this nation. Yet only the very naïve or the most intransigent would subscribe to the proposition that the immense power of the AMA is concentrated exclusively on the advancement of medical knowledge and service. Its defenders are hard pressed to deny the unflagging vigilance with which the AMA protects and enhances the economic and social pre-eminence of medical practitioners, particularly general practitioners.

Thousands, perhaps tens of thousands of organizations follow much the same pattern as the AMA's. The American Legion, while waving the flag of patriotism, works diligently and much less ostentatiously for a minority group—the veterans; the U.S. Corps of Engineers speaks of its public mission, while concentrating on channeling increased federal funds into waterway development, many of which violate every economic standard; the life insurance industry, ostensibly protecting the hard-earned savings of the common man, wages an unrelenting, though ineffective, war against inflation, knowing full well that further declines in the purchasing power of the dollar will cause its wares—contracts calling for a payment of a fixed number of dollars at some future date—to be less appealing.

All of these groups press for some objective. Frequently objectives call for some kind of change. More security for workers, lower corporate income taxes, and increased federal expenditures for farm supports, all are goals requiring some measure of change. Other groups favor the preservation of the *status quo*. A manufacturer, dreading foreign competition, fights tariff reductions; a union threatens to paralyze the railroad industry if firemen are not employed on a job which the diesel locomotive eliminated; the Army battles fiercely to maintain its position despite the fact that hydrogen bombs and guided missiles compel a complete revamping of military strategy.

One may readily understand why men of a common profession or economic activity band together with the intent of promoting a common interest. But what of those seemly altruistic organizations which derive no immediate tangible gain from their efforts to influence governmental policy? Are these also nothing more than selfish interest groups? Do they also have "axes to grind," or are they, as they would have us believe, solely concerned with the welfare of the nation? What of the Daughters of the American Revolution, the Red Cross, the Americans for Democratic Action, and the Women's Christian Temperance Union, to mention only a few of the seemingly infinite number of organizations that are purportedly and singlemindedly devoted to the goal of making ours a better world?

Customarily pressure groups or interest groups are thought of as seeking pecuniary advantage. No one can deny the driving force of material gain, but it is only one, and often not the most significant, of many motivating forces. Organizations are formed for many reasons—to promote political and moral philosophies, to proselytize members for religious denominations, to wipe out poliomyelitis, to increase the appreciation of classical music, to provide food and shelter for disaster victims, to encourage physical fitness through exercise, and to recruit winning football teams for Alma Mater. Clearly many of these groups are not inspired solely, or even partially, by immediate pecuniary gains. Often the group objective is one of education or persuasion. Members of a religious organization that finances and trains missionaries dedicated to converting heathens to Christianity expect no tangible, worldly benefits from their efforts. Likewise, representatives of the American Cancer Society anticipate no direct personal advantage from funds distributed to support its research.

However, these organizations cannot escape the stigma that in greater or lesser degree falls upon all interest groups. They, like all organizations, are pledged to a cause which can only be fulfilled by imposing claims and demands on the remainder of society. As such they are interest groups, good interest groups if you prefer, but interest groups nevertheless. But painting all organizations with the same brush creates more problems than it solves. Humane, public-spirited organizations such as the American Cancer Society and the Girl Scouts, must be distinguished from such narrow pressure groups as the oil, the labor, and farm lobby. The latter groups work at changing policy so as to enhance their own immediate financial positions, while many other groups give unstintingly to high-minded causes, bringing benefit to all mankind. Thus there are two distinct and separate kinds of interest groups: those promoting private advantage at public expense; and those of an altruistic persuasion that strive to promote the public good.

What is the eternal measuring stick for separating the good from the sinful? Certainly most, but unfortunately not all, men would agree that the demise of the Mafia could bring only good to this tortured world. But what of the White Citizens Council, The League for the Single Tax, or the Veterans of Foreign Wars? In what category would these organizations fall? No doubt some individuals would praise them all with enthusiasm; others would denounce them with vigor; and still others, perhaps most, would be largely indifferent to one or all of them. Public opinion, therefore, helps us not at all in differentiating between those groups. And if some are right and proper and others are selfish and heartless, we must look elsewhere for means of distinguishing the sheep from the goats. But clearly where are we to find such a standard?

In the year 1095, fired by the glory and the love of God, led by saintly kings and knighted warriors and carrying the blessings of Pope Urban II, Western Christendom set out to conquer the infidels and free the Holy City from Moslem tyranny. This, the First Crusade, was an idealistic, high-spirited, and successful undertaking. Under the leadership of Walter the Penniless, the Crusaders began their campaign by massacring Jews in the Rhineland, and as they proceeded on their 2,000-mile march of hardship and peril, they slaughtered and plundered all the way to the Jordan. When the victories of the organized host were crowned by the conquest of Jerusalem in 1099, they celebrated their achievements by massacring both Moslems and Jews until, as cleric Raimundas de Agiles described it, "one rode in blood up to the knees and even to the horse's bridle, by the just and marvelous Judgment of God."

Men before and since the crusaders have fought for things they believe. The purpose of the First Crusade was to fight and, if necessary, to die for the glory of the one true God and to exorcise the infidels from the Holy City. Men have pillaged, killed, and been killed for lesser causes, but each society, each organization, and each individual must have a cluster of ideals, a set of beliefs worth fighting for and, if necessary, worth dying for. Without purpose, without morality, a nation lacks the cohesive cement necessary for its survival as a political unit; without a *raison d'être* for which its members can strive, an organization will quickly disintegrate; without a personal philosophy the individual must wander aimlessly, always seeking, but never realizing the satisfaction of achievement.

Nor, search as we may, can we hope to find a common set of beliefs, an eternal ethos, a universal culture. For centuries the mysticism of India made its people largely indifferent to political unity and independence, and Confucianism stamped upon the Chinese a kind of fixed mentality which for more than a thousand years caused an unchanging set of basic social and political institutions. Only recently has the ethos of the West—one founded on a belief in material and social progress—been adopted by the leaders of these great peoples. But cultures, like the people who share them, are resistant to change, and the forced assimilation of Western values into Eastern cultures must be assigned a prime responsibility for the domestic strife and international conflict that tortures our modern world.

As with cultures and nations within cultures, so with organizations and groups within nations. Idealism becomes bigotry; virtue, vice; the magnificent, ludicrous; and a high-minded cause, a silly absurdity by the mere shifting of a mental perspective. Diversity is so prevalent and inherent a part of the American scene that we are largely oblivious to all but the most abrasive disagreements which abound and flourish all about us. And we are often more amused than incensed by the demands of pressure groups.

Thus a few years back most people, particularly those looking forward with favor and enthusiasm to the age of interplanetary travel, could not quite believe that the Humane Society was dead serious in its pledge to obstruct the use of mice in experiments designed to measure the effects of space travel on animal life. Yet the Humane Society, committed to the principle of "preventing cruelty to animals," was quite serious in its demands. That being so, the Society, much to the embarrassment and discomfort of certain defense officials and congressmen, acted very much the part of a passionate interest group, a good—or foolish—interest group, but an interest group all the same. Determined to teach the public both truth and justice, it not only condemned the immorality and heartlessness of our national policy, but, and more important, would have imposed its will on all of society.

Each organization is quite sure that its creed and its purpose are uniquely blessed. Active and inspired members would, whenever and wherever possible, convert others, hoping that they too would become apostles, or at least accept and live by their newly embraced beliefs. Thus the Humane Society, like all other groups, is forever on the lookout for anyone who might be enlisted in the cause of spreading truth, thinking always that one day the entire human race will appreciate the wisdom of its doctrines. In so behaving, the Society is entirely selfish, as is the National Association of Manufacturers, the Farm Bureau, or the Teamsters Union, when these great powers engage in the process of forming public opinion.

The more members become involved in group activity and the more highly structured organizations become, the greater becomes the individual's willingness to accept unquestioningly the goal of the group. The "nerve of failure," as David Riesman calls a determination to go it alone when individual values fly in the face of the dominant social ethics, requires extraordinary courage. Most men, lacking both the courage and imagination to go it alone, associate themselves with socially approved movements. But it is never quite enough to be simply a member of a movement or a crusader working for a cause. Man wants to believe that he is part of a movement which is highly significant, if not all-important.* Man takes pride in backing the winning horse, in being an

---

* It is this characteristic of man that Hitler, despite his apparent lunacy, grasped and exploited so effectively in his use of the "big lie" technique. "We," Hitler wrote in his manual on rhetoric, "must burn into the little man's soul the proud conviction that though a little worm he is nevertheless part of a great dragon."

alumnus of a college with the winning football team, of living in the town with the highest water tower, or even of being in the town with the coldest temperature. Through such relationships man gains a feeling of superiority, and although he may be opposed to sharing these relationships with all but a few of his fellow men, he nevertheless wants his brethren, all of his brethren, to believe that his particular cause is superior to any competitive movement. In this respect most men and all organizations are willing to follow the example set by Jesus when he said to his followers, "He who loveth mother and father more than me is not worthy of me . . ."

Frequently organizations are formed primarily to provide their members with entertainment or a congenial, friendly atmosphere where members can relax and bring their friends. The Wednesday night poker game, the local gun and shooting association, and perhaps the small country club would fall into this class. Often, however, organizations which began with only a simple purpose find, under the leadership of a public-spirited member, that some particular cause needs championing. Once this occurs, sacrificing some of the comfortable atmosphere in exchange for some heretofore unrecognized and needed reform appears to be a natural step. Moreover, formalizing lines of authority within an organization is tantamount to converting it into an interest group. Once a group is committed to a full-time leader—a president, a director, a chairman—the wheels are set in motion for the creation of another interest group, if indeed one does not already exist. The desire for recognition, particularly the recognition gained through socially approved activities, provides the driving force which quickly can convert a social organization into an interest group.

In a young, unknown, and unproven organization, aggressive leadership sometimes becomes imbued with a messianic spirit which, if infectious, stimulates organizational pride and

loyalty which makes for increased membership and the realization of previously impossible achievements. As the organization gains in size and public stature, the leader may be accorded by its members the status of a savior or patron saint.
Thus to the leadership, the protection and expansion of the
organization becomes a prime objective in itself. Whatever
the overt function of the organization, whether it be to
manufacture and sell automobiles, promote organic gardening, or campaign for the return of *laissez faire,* the first re-
sponsiblity of its leader is an intense, spirited, organizational
loyalty that will guarantee the formation of policies designed
to protect and elevate the position of his followers and his
empire. It is this innate, yet intangible, quality of organizations which, in compelling leaders to dignify and glorify the
status of the agency, automatically causes all organizations
to take on the characteristics of an interest group.

An eloquent and somewhat disillusioning illustration of
the drive for organizational self-preservation was provided
some years back when, by decisive action, the National Foundation for Infantile Paralysis shattered the uneasy peace
which prevailed in the world of charitable institutions. Confronted with the perfection of Salk vaccine, a development
the Foundation had enthusiastically and generously helped
to finance and publicize, the Foundation foresaw the distinct
possibility that the need for its services would sharply decline, if not disappear. Fully appreciative that it could not,
as a charitable institution, exist or grow without some dramatic cause, the Foundation set out on a determined search
for other crippling ailments and maladies against which its
ambitious and enterprising talents for money raising and
public education could be marshaled.

Much to its dismay, upon discovering that all the highly
publicized illnesses and dramatic afflictions were already
"staked out" and sponsored by well-established eleemosynary

institutions, the Foundation had no alternative but to anticipate its day of extinction or to broaden its scope of coverage
by including diseases already sponsored by other alms-giving
agencies. To no one's surprise the Foundation chose the latter
alternative and expanded its mission to include congenital
defects, arthritis, and other assorted ills. And although rival
agencies, such as the Rheumatism and Arthritis Foundations,
were deeply annoyed by the Polio Foundation's forceful invasion of their private domains, none have wasted any time
seriously deliberating the merits of abandoning the field to
the new entrant.

Our society is honeycombed with interest groups, each
with its own ideology, its own creed, its own evaluation of
the immediate unsatisfactory state of affairs, and its own
prescription for making the world a better place to live in
the future. Such a picture bears little resemblance to idyllic
18th-century democracy which dignified the enlightened,
independent voter and glorified the "man of principles" elevated to the position of leadership. Not, to be sure, that the
Founding Fathers were ignorant of the proclivity of men for
joining together to form special interest groups. James Madison observed that society is everywhere tainted by a "factious
spirit," causing numbers of citizens to unite in common cause
and set themselves against "the rights of other citizens, or the
permanent and aggregate interests of the community." "Liberty," he proclaimed, "is to factions what air is to fire."
Yet Madison was optimistic, for while he saw the factious
spirit "sown in the nature of man," he also believed that a
vast, sprawling republic would reduce the damage wrought
by unavoidable factions, because, although a common motive
may exist, "it will be," he declared, "difficult for all who
feel it to discover their own strength, and to act in unison
with each other."

Not even Madison possessed the clairvoyance necessary to perceive that startling advances in communication technology and the findings of the social sciences would one day make possible the extension of common sentiments and unified actions to literally all corners of the earth. Thus power, the mainspring of politics, and organizations, the ultimate seat of power, were at best hostile forces to be exorcised from the ideal world of the 18th-century democrat. That the single, isolated, unorganized individual is both politically and economically helpless is something about which classical democratic theory has little to say. How, one might ask, is the legislator, even if he feels a deep sense of responsibility to the unorganized individual voter, to serve him? For individual citizens, like disparate groups, do not agree on all matters, and even when they do, they are without the means to communicate their wants, their needs, their beliefs, to those responsible for conducting the governing process. The individualist who would refuse to align himself ideologically or economically with some group of influence and power must dwell in an inhospitable world ruled by unfriendly forces.

Once an organization has proven itself, there exists a certain inherent vitality and momentum which enable it to adjust to, shape, and in some measure, even control its environment. But what of the unborn or the struggling unknown infant organizations? How are these fostered? How do they gain recognition, success, power? As with all human activity, the conception, formation, and elevation of an interest group inevitably involves certain cost.

If a fledgling organization is to have any real chance for survival, much less achieve its overtly established purpose, there must be reasonable hope that personal gains—economic or ideological—from solidarity will more than offset personal sacrifices. Cost, of course, takes many forms: rent for office space, salaries paid to officers and employees, expenditures for the publication and distribution of literature. But other costs, no less important, do not submit to such easy and precise measurement. How, for example, does one calculate the individual's cost of becoming involved in, or giving his attention to, some particular movement, when literally thousands of separate groups are eager to enlist his enterprise and imagination as a supporter and champion of countless and conflicting causes?

The individual, living in a world bounded by time and energy, learns that a cursory, much less exhaustive examination of all the competing creeds and activities is not only prohibitively costly but beyond his scope and powers. Understandably, therefore, he ignores all but a few select groups. Intimately involved in some, he will also support and exalt those which he, rightly or wrongly, believes will protect and advance his best interests.

Cost as a determinant of group structuring is no doubt most eloquently articulated in the field of economics. Invariably, when citizens associate and combine to influence economic policy, they do it not as consumers, but as producers, exerting pressure, as is exemplified by business, labor, and farm organization, on the selling rather than on the buying side of the market. The reason for this is readily apparent. As producers, prospective gains from organizing far outweigh anticipated costs. But quite the contrary would be true for consumer groups. Obtaining information and translating it into action require expenditures of time and energy. For the consumer these costs, not to mention the monetary costs inevitably associated with organized activities, exceed any anticipated gains that he might hope to realize.

It cannot be otherwise in a highly industrial society, where intense and detailed specialization of labor compels the individual to concentrate his productive activity on a minute segment of the vast interdependent economy. In contrast, the individual consumer has an almost infinite number of brief and light contacts with the economic spectrum. Thus delicate, almost unnoticed changes in governmental policy may materially enrich producers but have a negligible impact on individual consumer welfare. Governmental action, leading to increased sugar, oil, or gold prices, may bring millions of additional dollars to the producers of these commodities. For the typical consumer, unaware that his weekly budget has gone up several cents, such action escapes his interest and attention.

So it goes with all groups fired by a need to influence national economic policy. Each group, fully aware that the loss its members suffer as consumers is only a fraction of what they will gain as producers, urges programs that will aid its members in their productive capacities while imposing burdens upon them in their consuming roles. Thus the steel worker, contrary to the pious incantations of management, knows full well that by demanding and receiving higher wages and better working conditions his economic lot will improve. That rising labor costs may increase the price of the steel and some of the goods he purchases bothers him not at all. However bankers may denounce the evils of inflation, however politicians may accuse him of sacrificing national interest for personal gain, however management may instruct him that his efforts are hopelessly and innately self-defeating, the steel worker—confident that his union's militant demands will bring him greater take-home pay and a higher standard of living—will, like farm, business, and other labor groups, not be deterred.

Without exception economic pressure groups advocate and sponsor governmental measures which work at cross purposes with capitalistic ideology. As we saw earlier, under classical capitalistic theory, the producer has but one purpose: to serve the consumer by diligently and unhesitatingly responding to the consumer's every wish registered in the market place. Anything that places the producer above the consumer, anything that would impair the free workings of the market, anything that would impede or make unnecessary quick and determined producer reactions to consumer wants, whims, and passions not only destroys efficiency, but is *per se* socially perverse and morally wrong. Unfortunately, interest groups are little concerned with the will of the consuming public, unless to thwart it.

Nor can one look forward to the day when there will be fewer, rather than more interest groups. As the unending advances in communications and transportation are further exploited, with the intent of increasing organizational size and solidarity, national policy must inexorably move further and further from any purely capitalist prescription. For those of an orthodox persuasion, particularly doctrinaire neoclassical economists who would force life and society to conform to their urgent personal needs for a neat and determinate economic system, governmental policy must always fall far short of any acceptable ideal. Indeed, for those who rely on traditional economics as their guides, the politician, who lives in and comes to grips with the world of reality, must always appear either as a well-meaning but ignorant pawn or a "Prince" who, in heeding Machiavelli's advice, substituted fraud and villainy for his principles.

The politician's growing disregard for principle and the increasing number of enterprising and ambitious interest groups has been the despair of many American social theorists. Although social critics have largely given up the politician as incorrigible, economic pressure groups are frequently depicted as the ultimate specter which, if not successfully curbed, will make a mockery of democracy and capitalism— the systems that guarantee the greatest personal freedom and at the same time provide a standard of living unequaled anywhere and at any time in history. But although these anguished cries are loud and unmistakable, the prescription for resolving the pressure group problem is not.

These cries sound hollow and hypocritical. The politician who with relish belittled and attacked his opponent's integrity and patriotism, proclaims that we must always place national interest and brotherly love above private aggrandizement and self-love. Simultaneously the high-minded business executive, through one of his eager and loyal assistants, dispatches from his spacious New York office a gentle but firm admonition warning the people of the everlasting need for self-discipline against fits of unreasoned and emotional outbursts stimulated by greed and bigotry. At the same time, he commends one of his assistants for developing a new, hard-hitting advertising campaign which, to all the world, makes clear that his competitors' goods are, at best, counterfeit and faulty duplicates of the products pioneered and sold by his firm.

But need we despair? Are these merely weak, sinful men who lack strength and character to resist temptation? Are they sincere and honest when they counsel us to restrain our personal enterprise and ambitions, to subjugate our own interests to those of the nation and society? What do they think of our systems of capitalism, which at bottom are founded on the creed of "buy low and sell high," and democracy, which instructs each that he strive to impel government to carry out his will? One must believe that these cries are forced, synthetic, unreal, that these men are proud of and would fight for these systems which, in exalting the individual, are built on self-development, self-reliance, and above all self-love.

This being so, to decry our world as morally wrong is to no avail, just as admonishing, cajoling, or pleading alters neither the objectives nor the effectiveness of the many powerfully organized groups. In a society where organized groups are the rule rather than the exception and where each group is free, and indeed expected to promote its own interest in the market, every weapon and strategy will be deployed to stave off the humiliation of defeat and bring forth the victory of material success and ideological supremacy. To deplore or be ambivalent toward the present state of affairs is one thing; to deny it is to ignore, even contradict, the Judeo-Christian image of man, the very foundation upon which rest our systems of capitalism and democracy.

Still, one must ask, can American democracy, torn by a disparate, powerful, insatiable, and expanding number of pressure groups, survive? This is the question that faces not only the nation but the world as we move further into the second half of the 20th century.

XIV

Unprincipled Salvation

"THE DEMOCRATIC AND REPUBLICAN PARTIES," A WAG ONCE said, "are like identical empty bottles, each affecting a different label." To doctrinaire idealists who view American political parties and their leaders as outrageous frauds, this metaphor must seem delightfully appropriate. For American politicians and the parties they represent are committed to mastering the art of ambiguity. Lacking precise doctrines and uncommitted to fixed programs, American parties appear willing to make "deals" with any group capable of delivering a sizable block of votes. They are, much more than European parties, overwhelmingly inspired by a pragramtic desire to gain the power and personal advantage that go with winning elections and assuming control of the government. To many an American social theorist, this apparent absence of political principles remains a source of frustration and embarrassment.

Such was not always the case. There was a time when statesmen talked not of the virtues of selflessness, but of the realities of self-love. But this was before the Civil War, when John C. Calhoun—one of the last of a distinguished line of brilliant American statesmen–political theorists—saw the public as anything but a homogeneous, benign people, united in common beliefs, and striving for common objectives. To him American society was dominated and shaped by bound-

less and conflicting interests emanating from North and
South, capitalists and laborers, merchants and planters. Nor
did he see this as a wholly unsatisfactory state of affairs. For
widespread diversity, Calhoun felt, was inimical to any alliance which would use its power to exploit minority interest. But although he placed value on diversity, he was not
blind to the abrasive, frightening tensions wrought by a
people of disparate climates, mores, religious faiths, economic
outlooks, and ethnic origins. From this inevitable disunity,
the ultimate task of the statesman was, as he saw it, to forge
a principle which would bring national unity from sectional
disunity. To this end Calhoun exposed his doctrine of the
concurrent majority. As a devout Southerner, committed to
the impossible task of justifying and expounding the righteousness of slavery, Calhoun was pressed to elaborate his
theory in an extreme, unworkable form.

To preserve the fast-declining power of the South, which
he accurately foresaw would be greatly overshadowed by the
burgeoning North, he proposed that the United States submit to the rule of two presidents—one chosen by the North,
the other by the South. Not unlike the elaborately impractical systems of checks and balances of the early Roman Republic, which had two Consuls, each of whom could veto the
other, and ten Tribunes, each of whom could veto the Consuls and the other Tribunes, Calhoun's proposal for revamping the executive powers of the government had little doctrinal or practical appeal. Nor were his proposed revisions of
Congress workable. Suggesting that various power blocks be
empowered with a veto to thwart the actions of other groups,
he meant to ensure that no decision having a bearing on the
welfare of the Republic could be adopted without unanimous
approval of all the interested parties. If Calhoun had had his
way, substituting a "tyranny of minorities" for the "tyranny

of the majority," the nation would have been burdened with a kind of political and economic paralysis not unlike that imposed by the veto power of the members on the United Nations Security Council. Instead of a dynamic, vital, and exuberant America, the nation would have taken on the characteristics, as each interest group vetoed real or imagined threats, of a society forced into a fixed, emasculating mold.

Calhoun's doctrine of the concurrent majority is not as alien to American politics as it may appear at first glance. In many respects, particularly when one group or coalition lacks strength of domination, Calhoun's theory still provides the most incisive and accurate insights into the workings of American democracy. Unfortunately, Calhoun, like other theorists, erred in making his system too formal, too stiff, too mechanistic. Where the explicit delegation of sanctions of his doctrine would have made for a rigid, fragile system subject to the shattering force of violence, the American process was, after 1865, to take on the subtle informality and apparent plasticity so essential to the survival and vitality of a nation operating within the framework of our Constitution. Fundamental to this entire process is not implacable hatred, but tolerance and indifference, coupled with a profound respect for and a genuine acceptance of the belief that each group is expected vigorously to pursue its own self-interest.

Compromise is the very essence of American politics, and the fanatic, "the man of principle," the doctrinaire are the very antithesis of democracy. Thus in a real sense, each group is empowered to exercise a veto—a veto that must, if the system is to remain viable, be employed with discretion and wisdom. A ruthless and callous exploitation of the veto power would call forth hostile coalitions bent on punishing anyone who would irresponsibly violate the rules of the game. The loss of influence by business interests in the 1930's and the decline of the labor star in 1947 and again in 1959 provide examples of the discipline that may be imposed on those who would misuse the veto power.

But although punishment awaits those who break the rules, the rules themselves call for hard, rough, and demanding play. The political process resembles nothing so much as the economist's concept of the economy's ceaseless and automatic movement toward a delicate but constantly shifting market equilibrium. Just as economic pressures in the world of markets push toward a balance reflecting the diverse and manifold interests of consumers and producers, so in the political arena a moving equilibrium approximately reflects the incessant pulling and hauling of the growing number of interest groups.

Nor does this imply that all participants possess equal power or exert equal influence in determining the state of balance. Obviously, in the market the millionaire carries more weight than the pauper, the giant corporation more authority than the small, single, proprietor. And so it is in the political sphere. The Farm bloc, the NAM, and the Labor lobby exert more influence in the making of national policy than the League of Women Voters, the American Association of University Professors, and the Association for the Advancement of Scientific Management. At any given time the pressures generated by various groups will determine the political equilibrium and national policy, striking an orderly and legal balance without the need to resort to violence.

Although such a process is peaceable and is intended to foster a higher level of justice, it cannot and does not look upon all men with equal favor. Some groups are more effective in making known the urgency of their needs or in gaining the ear of the policy maker. These groups are rewarded; others, for lack of followers or resources, less successful in pressing their cases, are not. Thus democratic equality implies not a benign or indifferent government, but only the right of every individual to join and participate in group action for the purpose of influencing and, if possible, shaping national policy.

Such a picture of democracy is sharply at odds with the more attractive Jeffersonian ideal of pluralism, which sprang from and was deeply rooted in a society overwhelmingly populated by free, independent proprietors of one kind or another. But the world of the Founding Fathers is not ours; nor can it ever be. Just as the individual or the small entrepreneur is no longer the basic political or economic power unit, so the concept of 18th-century democracy and the theory of the competitive market is not an adequate or satisfactory intellectualization of our social system. Organizations—political, social, and economic—are the primary sources of power. To lament these hierarchic structures, to decry the gradual feudalization of our society or to deplore the gradual decline of the individual seem neither to have lessened organizational growth nor in any way changed the path of history. In the contemporary world, if one is to appreciate the workings of democracy, one must observe these power groups in action.

"The nation" John Adams observed, "which will not adopt equilibrium of power must adopt a despotism. There is no other alternative." In this brief statement is captured the essence of the age-old political dilemma. On the one hand lies relativism with all the pitfalls of change, restlessness, and uncertainty; on the other hand, a forced unity, in danger always of becoming rigid, inhuman and authoritarian. No human society can be either totally relativistic or completely authoritarian. Every society has its absolutes and every government must, if only because the power of the state is inevitably finite, tolerate a certain diversity of public action and beliefs. But, as with all great philosophical questions, the matter of degree is of supreme importance.

In principle the predominantly relativistic society is committed to the belief that no final, eternal, universal rule exists for evaluating all human behavior. This absence of fixity springs from a faith that denies the existence of an overriding, consistent set of immediate objectives toward which a society must direct itself. In the United States, where the final brokers of power, the political parties, are pragmatically oriented, certain ideas are taboo, and others may be advocated or expressed only at a considerable personal risk; but there is only one political doctrine that is altogether unacceptable—destruction of the democratic process through coercion and violence. In the Soviet Union, with its standard of the classless society, the Kremlin explicitly, through social disgrace, physical force, and even punishment by death, opposes any doctrine contrary to the "party line" or those in control of the government.

From the standpoint of individual emotional security and inculcating a belief in national destiny, the absolutes of authoritarianism have their attractions. Given determinate, unchanging objectives, the individual and the society can distinguish right from wrong, good from evil, justice from injustice. The free, relativistic society can, on the other hand, never know the satisfaction or the security that go with such certainty. Committed, if only tacitly, to the doctrine that ultimate truth lies always beyond the horizon and to the belief that social improvement and the good life are dependent upon the dynamics wrought by uninhibited human thought and vitality, the free society is never quite able to set forth a glorious, pristinely integrated system applicable to men of all places and all times. To the idealist, the dedicated planner, and the self-appointed expert, the free society must always seem a tangled web of inefficiency, inconsistency, and hypocrisy. Not that these critics of American politics want for lack of ammunition. Farm supports, silver policy, public utility regulation, labor law, subsidies to the merchant marine, and watershed developments are only a few of the examples they cite to illustrate the prevalence of inefficiency and the common democratic practice of penalizing the many to appease and anesthetize momentarily the insatiable demands of the favored few.

That democratic government often imposes burdens on the many to grant generous favors to a few is an unpleasant fact of life. But to attempt to evaluate or provide insights into the democratic process by examining selected and separate programs is tantamount to admitting a lack of understanding of the democratic process. Individual programs, such as farm supports, are no more fashioned in a legislative vacuum than silver policy, for example, was enacted into law on the basis of its own distinctive merits. To isolate one program or policy from the whole is to ignore the reality that every program is conceived, shaped, and made viable though a process which the political scientists refer to as "accommodation," and which the laymen, being less enchanted by euphemisms, are prone to call "horse trading," "log rolling," or "pork barreling." Whatever the process is called, it is the very essence of the workings of democracy. For it is through this dramatic process that disparate interest groups forge the compromise from which comes mutually beneficial legislation.

Blinded as we are by immediate involvements and chauvinistic persuasions, we frequently fail to appreciate the fine art and the vital contributions of compromise. Only by looking backward in time are we accorded that degree of detachment which provides breadth of perspective. The whole history of legislations is a story of hard, often bitterly fought, compromises.

A case in point is the economic legislation enacted during the muckraking year of 1890. Congress, reflecting an almost universal hostility toward malevolent monopolists, was pressed hard to do something about the abuse of industrial power. But Congress, to no small degree, was composed of "principled" men who owed both their philosophical perspective and their personal loyalties to the business community, which at the time was committed to increasing tariff rates. Farm representatives, voicing the sentiment, "the tariff is the mother of trusts," bitterly fought the proposed tariff changes. To induce a softer agrarian attitude toward higher taxes on imports, the business interests offered to back anti-trust legislation and, as a further means of appeasing inflation-minded farmers, to support legislation requiring the Treasury to step up the purchase of silver.

Ultimately, the year 1890 saw the enactment of three major pieces of economic legislation: the McKinley Tariff, the highest tariff the nation had ever known; the highly inflationary Sherman Silver Purchase Act, supported to a man by the "sound money group"; and the Sherman Anti-Trust Act. By this means a bargain was struck which appeared to confer benefits upon both business and agrarian interests. The fact that, although business influence in Congres was at or near its apex, the Sherman Anti-Trust Act passed both houses without debate and with only a single dissenting vote should, it would seem, dispel any doubts that the three measures came as a single package.

Liberal critics, although disillusioned over the years by the implementation and judicial interpretation of the Anti-Trust Act, have traditionally shown a marked sympathy for antimonopoly philosophy expressed by the law. At the same time, particularly if of an economic turn of mind, they are unfavorably disposed toward the 1890 tariff and silver policy. Rarely is there the recognition that this was an "all or nothing" proposition; that anti-trust legislation was not to be obtained without paying the price of a higher tariff and an uneconomic national silver policy. This glorification of anti-trust on the one hand, while condemning the madness of high tariffs and silver policy on the other, is tantamount to confessing an ignorance of the basic workings of the democratic process. To be meaningful, any historical assessment of virtues and faults must encompass the legislative program in its entirety. In short, the relevant question becomes, "How, on balance, do the various programs and policies enacted in 1890 measure up?" On this score, the consensus of expert judgment would quickly disintegrate into a tangled web of diverse and conflicting opinions.

Even this perspective grossly oversimplifies, if for no other reason than because of the implied notion that individual policy determinants can be isolated and examined. Except in a very general and often misleading way, this is not, of course, the case. For the democratic process is a dynamic one, reflecting not only the experiences of the past and the anticipations of the future, but a multitude of minute and often unmeasurable factors such as the rules under which the legislative body operates, the ideology and background of key members, the immediate tally of political debts, and the balance of broad sectional compromises operative at various levels and on heterogeneous policies. As these dynamic forces change, the maneuvering and negotiating, the deals and the barters, the reasoned persuasion and the emotional power plays are also transmuted so that it is altogether impossible to determine fully, much less to measure accurately, the true forces which go into fashioning national policy. Thus one can never fully appreciate the price—what must be given in return—of any particular piece of legislation or policy or, from a broader perspective, how the whole legislative and national policy pattern would have been modified had the law under discussion not been enacted.

Thus we see that the citizen of democracy and the partisan football fan have much in common. Both know the disappointment and frustration that come with an unhappy turn of events; both, for all their intense concentration and observation, are never quite sure of the last play's heroics and action; both are largely ignorant of the general forces shaping the direction of the games; and, more significant, both, except through emotional but forceless vocal expressions of elation or distress, are altogether powerless to alter the outcome of the contest being watched.

This then is the present state of our secular hope and our liberal faith. Never pure, always short of perfection, it is, like the mortals who fashioned and manipulate it, both slightly soiled and noticeably marred by innumerable blemishes and scars. For all its inadequacies and defects, it is the best we have to offer. For those who, needing unity, cannot live without political and moral absolutes, this is not enough. Yet hopefully, democracy, more than any other social system, tenders and compels acceptance of the most precious and demanding of all the gifts conferred on man. What is this treasure? It is intellectual and spiritual freedom.

Other systems, like democracy, can provide order, security, efficiency, even justice. But only a pluralistic society can ensure and encourage the searching, restless, questioning mind. Thus the distinguishing characteristic of democracy is the opportunity if offers the individual to develop himself in following his own beliefs, habits, interests, and prejudices. Since man is neither a vegetable nor a robot, he refuses to be standardized as production engineers have standardized desks or washing machines. Leaders of the state, the church, and a variety of other institutions have been impotent to convince men of the wisdom of renouncing the individualism and the multitude of causes which have brought to the human race both the benefits and the intellectual discomfort that flows from a diversity of opinions and objectives. In a free society the pursuit of different ends by individuals and a multitude of organizations produces endless disagreements and vigorous conflicts of a type which dictators cannot countenance. It is not too strong to state that a society which is not characterized by a clash of interest is not democratic, for democracy without opposition is inconceivable.

Somehow this natural and beneficial conflict of interests must be resolved without resort to violence. No modern industrial society can survive if force is the primary means of resolving disputes. If conflict cannot be settled peacefully within a framework of freedom, then suppression must be the lot of mankind. The achievement of a working harmony is, under any political system, no mean accomplishment; and it is especially challenging to democracy. The process that preserves the freedom, that permits the individual to follow his own conscience and pursue his own interests, and at the same time precludes the development of group or class warfare, is commonly known as compromise. In this sense the idealist is the antithesis of the true democrat; for he, like the doctrinaire, the crusader, the uncompromising ideologist, all of whom are contemptuous of expediency and glib in belittling the unprincipled compromiser, is a handmaiden of a political absolutism that strongly resembles the political doctrine upon which the concepts of the master race and the supremacy of the proletariat were founded. As Judge Learned Hand so aptly put it, "The spirit of liberty is the spirit which is not too sure that it is right."

But man is a most complex animal. While he yearns for freedom, he actively seeks absolutes. Nor is his search without value. The whole scientific process is essentially a search for general laws which are useful for purposes of explanation, prediction, and control. Once man embraces an idea, however, he is extremely reluctant to discard it, and he neither encourages nor welcomes competition, be it ideological, religious or political. Either by accident, as when he becomes a member of a labor union, or by design, as when he actively promotes one of the political parties, a man becomes a member of a group and accepts, almost as a secular religion, the ends of the organization to which he looks for identification. In developing and pledging loyalty to a group or discipline, he tends to feel he is superior to the poor mortals who work for competing organizations; that he and his associates hold a monopoly on truth; that opponents are not only wrong, but often wicked. In short, man's need for absolutes causes him to associate himself with some movement that provides him with a relatively simple doctrine for evaluating human activity. Historically the family, the tribe, the nation, and the church satisfied this need. More recently man has turned to other social and economic organizations such as the corporation and the labor union.

As the individual has faded more and more into the background and the size and power of the organization has continued to expand, our society has been faced with new problems while old ones have either disappeared or taken on a new perspective. Although democracy is remarkably efficient in providing an atmosphere in which freedom has thrived and grown, it is inefficient in many other respects. Often characterized as a government of inaction, democracy often suffers from procedural paralysis during the seemingly interminable debate and compromise which is so much a part of the democratic process. Moreover, if the doctrine of the concurrent majority is operative, a small well-entrenched minority may veto new developments which may in any way threaten or impinge upon the interest it represents. The delay in correcting business abuses late in the 19th century, the tardiness of social legislation in the 1930's, the difficulty of enacting corrective labor legislation during the late 1950's, and the impossible tangle of private and public interests which have for decades posed an effective barrier to harnessing much of the Western river system are only a few of the many examples that show how minority groups may use their veto power to thwart policies inimical to their position. One may expect, as groups become more numerous and more powerful, that it will be even more difficult to push through Congress legislation that on one count or another is not subject to a veto under the doctrine of the concurrent majority.

Nor can one be optimistic about forthcoming legislation as a growing number of ethnic, economic, religious, and so-called social groups continue to press for advantage with scarcely a thought being given to the impact of their recommendations on the general public. In practice the equilibrium that compromise produces is a crystallization of relative sectional and group forces. The general public, lacking organization and means of communication, is incapable of focusing force on most issues and therefore, except in some vague and shadowy way, cannot be expected to be a factor in the making of public policy.

The fact that the public is little more than an uneasy and discomforted spectator viewing the frequent and bitter power struggle between labor and management illustrates well the helplessness of the people in affecting policy. The pattern of compromise between labor and management is a familiar one. Accompanying a strike in a basic industry is a creeping paralysis which pervades the entire economy as one industry after another is compelled, for lack of supply or market, to contract its operations. In the end both groups are appeased: labor through higher wages and larger fringe benefits; management via price increases. The consumer, already the victim of the economic paroxysm induced by the strike, now stoically accepts new inflationary pressures which were foreordained the moment labor and management leaders decided to exercise monopoly powers. Nor is this a unique situation. Countless other cases, running the gamut from fraudulent advertising to road policy, may be cited to show the tendency of democracy to neglect matters that affect the whole while taking action that favors a few.

That ours is a society of group rather than individual politics is no longer subject to dispute. One may lament the concentration of power within the group and one may bewail the passing of the equalitarian philosophy. At the same time one should recognize that the society of the small entrepreneur and the wonderful world of the 18th-century philosopher met their demise, if indeed they ever really existed, at the hands of the Industrial Revolution. Admittedly, our system appears defective when evaluated in terms of some idealized version of democracy, but it remains unequaled in providing material comforts while at the same time protecting basic civil rights.

These two factors—the preservation of basic freedoms and the advancement of material welfare—have made a civilization that raised the dignity of man to new heights. This progress is substantially attributable to the completely "unprincipled" pragmatic approach of the American politician, who continues to demonstrate a remarkable facility for educating his conscience to deal with any group that is capable of delivering a sizable group of votes. Along with the "unprincipled" politician the great diversity of groups, which continue to compete for position and favors, must be ranked as a protector of the democratic system. As long as myriad groups representing different geographical, professional, social, and economic interests continue to vie for stature and influence, one can rest assured that the moderate rather than the extremist will carry the day. To those who have diagnosed and would prescribe for the world illness this must always remain a pity, but to those who believe that man's destiny will be realized only through a continuing search for ideas, ours remains a truly glorious system, resting on a profound and unshakable unity dedicated to revering and protecting the intellectual and spiritual sovereignty of the individual.

To close on such an optimistic note would be comforting. To say that our combination of national splendor and individual rights represents the highest achievement of mankind would be to conclude with a traditional American happy ending. Regrettably, this I cannot do; for in the contemporary world the liberal faith—democracy—alone is not enough. In the world of yesterday it was; in the 19th century and even for the better part of the first five decades of the 20th, democracy was enough.

But not today; not in a world tortured by a communist Russia, a rising China, and stirring underdeveloped peoples. In the world of unrelieved international crisis, it is simply not enough to have a mechanism for peaceably settling domestic quarrels, however important they may be. Something more is needed; something that will at once energize the nation while preserving individual freedom, and something that will empower us to marshal our untapped might to convince ourselves and the rest of the world that the liberal faith in the dignity of the individual and the democratic process is something to be treasured and sought after. To understand what is required, it is necessary to turn again to history for one further insight into the relationship of man and his society.

XV

Diverging Realms

In 480 B.C., Xerxes set out to conquer Greece. Through treachery and overwhelming numbers, he annihilated the Spartan force at Thermopylae and then advanced and fired Athens, only to see the tide of victory change as the Athenian fleet destroyed his ships in the Bay of Salamis. With his lines of communication cut and the defeat he subsequently suffered at Plataea, Xerxes had no choice but to retreat, leaving Greece unmolested, free to develop its own culture. So began the Golden Age of Greece, a period of approximately 50 years, the close of which came with the Peloponnesian War in 431 B.C. One of the most creative periods in history, the heart of this classic age was Athens, a city which, until the Persian defeat, had lagged behind in producing both ideas and great men. Under the stimulus of victory and the need for reconstruction, Athens blossomed forth, producing a culture that was destined to influence profoundly all Western history.

The excellence of this period was not—as is sometimes thought—so much intellectual as it was commercial, cultural, and artistic. Little troubled by war, Athens prospered and grew rich and powerful under a democratic constitution administered by aristocrats. The great temples, whose ruins remain the glory of Greece, were built to replace those destroyed by Xerxes. Under the wise leadership of Pericles, which lasted for about thirty years, Athenian wealth and culture were enriched by foreign trade and travel, and provincial morality and customs were supplemented by knowledge gained from the entire Ancient World. In this brief span of time from a population that never exceeded an estimated 230,000 (including slaves) came men of extraordinary genius: dramatists, architects, and sculptors, whose work remains unsurpassed to the present day.

Important as these contributions are in themselves, it is the spirit of Athens rather than her tangible accomplishments that we sanctify. Her emphasis was the worth and dignity of the individual; her goal, a free, intelligent, self-reliant, fully developed citizenry. The Athenian was to be the master of his own fate, a rational animal who could order and direct his own personal affairs, a creature who through reason and knowledge was to find his own means of developing and expressing his unique personality. Above all he possessed a soul, which in the quest for justice and wisdom acquired an incentive for developing moral and intellectual integrity. If these contributions are further distilled, the essence of the celebrated Age of Pericles is best captured in the high ideals of a free, humanistic society. Our enduring fascination and our devout consecration are therefore right and proper, for it is to humanism—Christian humanism, if you prefer— and a free and open society that America and the rest of the Western democracies are committed.

But the legacy of Greece is more than the exaltation of man's creative powers and the Athenian love of freedom. In every society there are always men anxious to undermine material achievements and discard precious freedoms for the opportunity to feed their ambitions and impose their wills. Even as Athens grew into a splendid city of stately architecture, high drama, and personal freedom, some men were jealous and envious. Pericles, these men declared, out of aggressive arrogance and a will to demonstrate his own strength, had defied Sparta and sacrificed the best interest of the beloved city. Unable to discredit Pericles directly, these men turned their wrath on Phidias, whom Pericles had commissioned to supervise the rebuilding of Athens. As magnificent structures of ageless grace and beauty rose and as the fame of Phidias spread, these men conspired to convict him falsely of embezzling the gold to be used in producing the great statue of Athena. Although the charge was proven to be false, Phidias was censured for pride and sent to prison where he fell sick and died.

Soon the troubles of Pericles were compounded as the cold-war truce between Athens and Sparta was broken by the latter's invasion of Athenian territory. Believing that Athenian pride and anger would compel Pericles to come out and do battle, 60,000 Peloponnesian and Boeotian hoplites pitched their camp near Athens. Within the city Pericles was pressed by his friends to take aggressive action, while his enemies taunted him for cowardice in abandoning everything to the enemy. All of this abuse he endured while he dispatched 100 ships to the Peloponnesus. As he watched over the city, reassuring his friends and placating his enemies, the Athenian fleet scored victories, sacking villages and towns and ravaging large territories. But just as victory was at hand, heaven seemed to intervene, causing the city to be beset by a plague that cut down the flower of Athenian manhood.

In a further effort to snatch victory from the hands of the Spartans and the gods, Pericles again dispatched the Athenian fleet, this time with himself in command. But the gods would not relent; the plague continued, frustrating Pericles, and destroying his men and everyone that came in contact with them. On returning to Athens, he tried to console its citizens. Crowded by people who sought refuge from the attack of the Spartans and ravaged by diseases that afflicted both body and spirit, Athens, however, turned on Pericles, stripped him of his station and command and, before a court of 1501 judges, fined him for misappropriation of public monies. Shortly thereafter, he fell victim to the plague, and dark days descended upon Athens as the Peloponnesian War consumed the energies of Greece until, in 404 B.C., Athens was totally defeated.

So ended the Golden Age of Greece—a time of peace, material splendor, and finally disillusionment—an age in which the free human spirit was raised to an apogee, only to fall victim to personal ambition, militant nationalism, and cruel nature. Greece became the living embodiment of the spirit of great tragedy that pervaded both her drama and literature. It was as if the people as one cried out against a heartless world. They labored, they built, they exhausted themselves trying to create a hospitable and meaningful realm where the human spirit could dwell with freedom and dignity. But it was all for naught; the world was incorrigible, and typical of the history of mankind was the fate of King Sisyphus, who, condemned to Hades, was eternally doomed to roll a large boulder up a hill, only to see it come careening down just one turn short of the summit.

Even as Athens lay mangled and bleeding from the disillusionment and tragedy of the Peloponnesian War, new forces were gathering that were destined to leave an equally deep impression on the world of the West.

The origin of these new forces was intellectual. Through the philosophy of Plato and Aristotle, Athens was to find new purpose and once again touch the Western mind. But unlike Periclean Athens, which, in its cultural, commercial, and artistic pursuits, dignified man's creative powers in this world, Plato's Athens was enchanted with the sheer beauty of a kind of "other-worldly" contemplation. In the thinking of Plato, Pericles' world of the senses was by its very nature deficient. In Platonic thought, perfection, an unchanging ideal of fixed absolutes, could be found only through the process of pure contemplation. Men could discover truth, beauty, and justice, not through the process of searching experiment and scientific inquiry in the world of the senses, but by way of esthetic contemplation of a fixed and flawless universe.

At best, said Plato, the physical world was deceptive and would betray those who placed their confidence in it. Eternally imperfect, the physical world's fall from grace was marked by a changing nature pronouncing that something was wrong, something was incomplete. Thus the high-spirited and graceful realm of Pericles and Phidias, as well as the world in which ordinary men were forever condemned to live and die, was denounced by Plato as a place tormented by opposition, diversity, and conflict—all marks of imperfection.

Out of this dualistic view of the apparent and the ideal, Plato derived inspiration for conceiving and drawing up the blueprint for society. His *Republic* called for three classes of men: those of Gold, of Silver, and of Brass and Iron. Philosopher Kings—men of Gold—through the process of dialectic and Plato's theory of forms, were to discover the eternal ideal and with the help of men of Silver—the warrior class—impose the good life upon society. Plato's ideal order was a rigidly prescribed society. Children were to be assigned to classes according to their abilities and the government was to exercise justice, punishing *hubris*—man's inclination to transcend the natural order—and ensuring that each was accorded the rights and fulfilled the duties of his assigned position.

Rather than Periclean Athens, it was Sparta, which had long lived without freedom, that Plato used as a model. As with Sparta, the pure spirit of Plato's ideal state was implacably authoritarian. Sparta, of course, did excel; not in

creativity, not in honor, not in morality, not in respect for
the human spirit, but in organizing a stable society of unimaginative citizens pledged to absolute obedience. From the
modern viewpoint the political entity which most nearly approximates Plato's ideal would be an impractical and dreadful place to live. At best Plato's blueprint called for a hum-
drum world capable of feeding a warlike, stable population
under such rigid conditions as to preclude the spontaneity
and freedom necessary to either artistic or scientific achievements. In looking for a comparable state in the contemporary
world, the stability, order, and discipline of the Platonic ideal
reminds one of nothing so much as Hitler's Germany or
Stalin's Russia.

Perhaps we should not expect more from Plato. Living
through a period when Athens suffered the wounds of famine,
plagues, and total defeat, Plato's preoccupation with sufficient
food, a stable order, and a well trained army seems natural
today. But if these were his only contributions, his name
would long ago have been lost to the ages. What gave him
immortality was not his specific recommendations or even his
general thoughts on statecraft, but his dualistic view of the
universe which separates the world of appearance from the
world of the ideal. From Plato on, this dualistic view runs
through and dominates virtually all Western thought. From
St. Augustine's *City of God* to the present day, this dualism is
unmistakable in both religious and economic thought. Christianity differentiates between the transitory body and the
eternal soul; the vale of tears of the physical world and the
sublime harmony of the spiritual world; the fallible historic
Church and the infallible True Church; and, in Roman
Catholic doctrines, a Virgin Mary who dispenses unequal
justice to sinners and a God who created all men equal. This
dualism is no less apparent in economic thought. In a world
of eternal waste and repair, a John Stuart Mill is enchanted

by the stationary state; the capitalist mind idealizes the perfection of man in a consummation of the free market forces, while the devout communist, although less and less frequently, proclaims the flawless splendor of the Marxian classless society.

To Christianity and capitalism the West is greatly indebted. Within these systems men found inspiration and ideals upon which they constructed logical edifices. In Christian thought the God of the Old Testament is the God of power; in the New Testament, the God of love; but the theologian's God is a God that does no violence to human logic. In economic thought the 19th-century liberal enshrines individual self-sufficiency, the 20th-century liberal deifies general material welfare; but the high priests of economics worship only at the altar of intellectual consistency and determinacy. Yet ideals, however they may lend themselves to elegant intellectual elaboration, are not enough.

If ideals are to be truly great social energizers, they must contain an organizing force that somehow is meaningful to the commonest of men in everyday existence. The organizing force of Christianity was the sacraments. As long as the "Age of Faith" prevailed and men believed that the Church held a monopoly upon and could with discretion give or withhold the sacraments—the only key to eternal salvation—the "Philosopher Kings" of the Church could command the obedience and loyalty of prince and peasant alike. For centuries this organizing force was to fashion a spirit of unity out of a vulgar, defiant, wanton population of a Europe split into thousands of essentially autonomous political units. In the personal manorial society, the Christian doctrine, in addition to promising in the next world something better than a hard life of poverty and fear, justified in this world a static order in which each individual was assigned a specific, fixed role. However doleful such a life may now appear, in the integrated manorial society, "Each man," to use Professor Tannenbaum's words, "each act was a part of total life drama, the plot of which was known and in which the part to each was prescribed. No one was isolated or abandoned." In these intimate societies the admonitions of "Love thy neighbor as thyself" and "Do unto others as you would have them do unto you" were pregnant with both meaning and force and tempered man's innate aggressiveness with compassion and human kindness.

But the high energy and full radiance of the "Age of Faith" were not to come until the 12th and 13th centuries when, through the impetus of an expanding population and growing commerce, long-dormant town life stirred, flourished, and then burst into the vitality of the city. In describing the love of the Virgin Mary as the "greatest force the Western world ever felt" and the "highest energy known to man," Henry Adams, in *Mont-Saint-Michel and Chartres* (Houghton Mifflin Company, 1936), observed, "The 12th and 13th centuries were a period when men were at their strongest; never before or since have they shown equal energy in such varied directions, or such intelligence in the direction of their energy; yet these marvels of history—these Plantagenents; these scholastic philosophers; these architects of Rheims and Amiens; these Innocents, and Robin Hoods and Marco Polos; these crusaders, who planted their enormous fortresses all over the Levant; these monks who made the wastes and barrens yield harvests—all, without apparent exception, bowed down before the woman." In depicting the completeness of Western man's commitment to glorifying a perfect God and sanctifying a very human Virgin Mary, Adams further declared:

> According to statistics, in the single century between 1170 and 1270, the French built 80 cathedrals and nearly

500 churches of the cathedral class, which would have cost, according to an estimate made in 1840, more than five thousand million to replace. Five thousand million francs is a thousand million dollars, and this covered only the great churches of a single century. The same scale of expenditure had been going on since the year 1000, and almost every parish in France had rebuilt its church in stone; to this day France is strewn with the ruins of this architecture, and yet the still preserved churches of the eleventh and twelfth centuries, among the churches that belong to the Romanesque and Transition period, are numbered by hundreds until they reach well into the thousands. The share of this capital which was —if one may use a commercial figure—invested . . . cannot be fixed, any more than the total sum given to religious objects between 1000 and 1300; but in a spiritual and artistic sense, it was almost the whole, and expressed an intensity of conviction never again reached by any passion, whether of religion, of loyalty, of patriotism, or of wealth; perhaps never even paralleled by any single economic effort except in war.

Thus the Christian ethos, through the doctrines of love of fellow man and just price, dampened the innate selfishness of man's sinful nature at the same time that it provided the creative energy for the flying buttress, the symbolic rose window, the sculptured façade, the finite arch, and the soaring spire pointing into infinite space and beyond in search of unity.

But Christianity was more than this; it was, in fact, a fighting faith for which men killed and were killed. It was a faith that inspired the infamous and materialistically oriented Fourth Crusade, the culmination of which was the pillaging and firing of centuries of accumulated priceless treasures, and the orgiastic slaughtering of infidels and Christians alike. It was a faith that energized the appalling and pathetic Children's Crusade, the climax of which was the death or the selling into slavery of thousands of innocent Christian youngsters. It was a faith that gave the Abbé Arnaud Amalric, in his Crusade against 200 Cathri heretics hidden in a Christian city of 20,000, the courage to command: "Kill them all, God will recognize his own." It was a faith that caused monks to cry, "No hospice for the rebel," and motivated the Church to embark upon the Inquisition to combat a flourishing and spreading body of heresy. It was a faith that for a century fed Christian hatred and fired the religious wars that made Europe a battleground of brutality and horror.

The fact is that as an energizing and unifying force, despite its humane admonitions, Christian idealism has, like most idealistic creeds, demonstrated more success in inflaming than in restraining man's aggressive passions. It is as a personal religion rather than an energizing force that Christianity has made its greatest contribution to humanity. Teaching that each man, however unworthy, has an immortal soul which, through grace, may find eternal salvation, Christian doctrine admonishes man to rise above his simple, selfish nature and encourages him to understand, forgive, and love his fellow men. By idealizing individual virtue in this life and promising immortality in the next, it has made ours a more civilized world. In our personal relationships, in the family, in the corporation, the Church, or the neighborhood, the Christian ethos continues to have a marked influence on our daily experiences, making them richer and more meaningful.

Unfortunately, in shaping the conduct of large organizations—the centers of power which are the primary energizers of the contemporary world—Christian doctrines have too little to contribute. What meaningful instructions does Christian doctrine provide for the large organization, each of which—like the Crusader inspired by an ideal—comes to do battle in an impersonal arena? How is Christianity operative when the power blocs of labor and management become involved in a bitter dispute over automation and the displacement of workers? What decisive words, if any, does Christianity have for two giant business firms fiercely engaged in a market struggle? What instrument, if any, can Christianity provide for resolving the desperate fight between California and Arizona for the waters of the Colorado River? And how can Christianity arm us to meet the challenge of a thoroughly evil but zealously idealistic Soviet Union which, like us, also comes out of the Christian tradition?

When in recent years the electrical industry was found guilty of scandalous price fixing, the Church had little to say. Torn between the need to give aid and comfort to good Christian men and the desire to condemn the violation of social morality, the Church stood mute, spiritually and morally helpless. To say that without our Christian heritage things would be worse is doubtless true, but this misses the mark. However Christianity may imbue the individual with virtue while promising him eternal life, it has not demonstrated the capacity to provide in the contemporary world an energy which at once exalts the individual and raises society to the level of its potential brilliance.

Where orthodox Christianity failed, liberalism succeeded. Rising out of the humanism of Renaissance Florence, energized by the Protestant ethic, inspired by the perfectibility-of-man doctrine, liberalism produced a radiant and free society unequaled and unapproached in all of human history. Under its power the United States, in less than two centuries, converted a wilderness into the richest, most powerful nation the world has ever witnessed.

To accomplish this, it was necessary for liberalism to turn

traditional values upside down and inside out. Rather than shackling and punishing individual pride and initiative as was customary in older orders, it provided an atmosphere that encouraged and rewarded these characteristics. Founded on the belief that a benevolent system of natural laws resolved the diversity-unity dilemma by blending individual effort into a sublime whole, liberalism provided a youthful continent with political and economic freedom—the distinguishing mark of the age of individualism. As the American social order was gradually transformed from a personal to an impersonal, from a simple to a complex society, the organizing force inherent in liberalism played a greater role in determining the shape and course of the nation. In the contemporary world the essence of this organizing force, in its most formal and sterotyped dress, appears in the form of the profit and loss statement. With this measuring device success and failure are guaged, courses of action to be pursued and abandoned are determined. Still a guiding light for most individuals and virtually all organizations until 1929, this balancing of cost and revenue provided the United States with an inexhaustable supply of social energy.

When this energizing force faltered and staggered, the nation was left confused and prostrate, impotent to organize idle resources capable of conferring plenty. For ten years, America suffered a sense of listless bewilderment until the terrible specter of Hitler and the agony of Pearl Harbor shocked and activated the nation. After victory, a war-engendered momentum and a boom in population growth carried the nation to a new and higher life; but it fell prey to recurring recessions and a general state of doldrums as simple economic materialism was powerless to provide an adequate challenge for the incredible capacity of a mighty nation.

Since the Great Crash, nothing has preoccupied us more

than the will to repair and patch this vital organizing force which in the past served us so well and so faithfully. Those most active in leading this movement have been contemptuously branded by the conservatives as Keynesians. Admitting that man and not the economic machine must in the last analysis be the master, these "Keynesians" have placed their trust and hopes in governmental monetary and fiscal policy, seeing it as an instrument capable of injecting renewed vigor into a seemingly tired, run-down society. A swelling chorus, particularly in recent years, has called for the unleashing of a great burst of energy through the improvement of currently inadequate public facilities and services. But in the thinking of this group, public materialism is only a halfway house on the road to a better society.

Ultimately, these men envision a fundamental change in the basic order with the result that the individual will derive satisfaction by transcending the traditional values tacitly accepted by virtually all liberals, orthodox or Keynesian. Believing that man, through technological progress, has in good part conquered the economic problem, the modern liberal looks forward to an increase in what John Galbraith calls the New Class: the expanding group of people who are motivated not by the "urgency of Goods" or by a sacrosanct attitude toward work, but rather by the desire to "find an occupation from which they will derive satisfaction—one which will involve not toil but enjoyment." "There is," he observed, "every reason to conclude that the further and rapid expansion of the class should be a major, and perhaps next to peaceful survival itself, the major social goal of society."

Along these same lines, Riesman, commenting on "the vacuum created by high productivity," declared, "People's real 'work'—the field into which, on the basis of their character and their gifts, they would like to throw their emotional and creative energies—cannot now conceivably coincide, perhaps in the majority of cases, with what they get paid for doing." Riesman does not despair; and observes, "As we come to understand our society better, and the alternatives it holds available to us, I think we shall be able to create many more alternatives, hence still more room for individual autonomy." Discussing the concept of play in the broad sense of leisure, he goes on, "Play, far from having to be the residual sphere left over from work-time and work-feeling, can increasingly become the sphere for the development of skill and competence in the art of living."

Very recently W. H. Ferry, Vice President of The Fund for the Republic, warned, "The United States is advancing rapidly into a national economy in which there will not be enough jobs of the conventional kind to go around. . . . Substitutes for presently accepted goals as full employment will have to be found. Fresh definitions of the conception of work, leisure, abundance, and scarcity are needed." In prescribing new goals for the Age of Abundance, he sees the removal of the economic machine from the middle of the social scene as "ever more efficient automata will provide the goods and services required by the general welfare" and as "humanity, with its politics and pastimes and poetry and conversation, will . . . occupy the central place in the landscape."

The recommendations these writers make and the social picture they paint are not without a certain amount of appeal. Their philosophy is humanistic; their central tenet, the worth and dignity of the individual; their ultimate goal, the full development of individual powers. In essence they advocate a society that permits, encourages, and compels the calling into play of all personal resources. Only in this way, they seem to imply, can the individual generate the inner strength and self-discipline that are so essential if he is to experience the freedom, the spontaneity, and the self-expression that make for a distinct and sovereign personality capable of

finding the meaning of life and knowing the supreme satisfaction of existence. To achieve this state of worldly grace,
personal virtues must be developed and practiced. Among
these are courage, endurance, initiative, self-reliance, and
economic and intellectual independence. In sum, this new
tide of liberalism rests on a philosophy that calls for transformation of society at the same time it exhorts the individual
to strive for and achieve personal excellence.

For all the virtue, joy, and tranquillity promised by this
new liberalism, as a workable social theory it, regrettably,
does not succeed. Not because we lack the economic wherewithal to support a society of free, intellectually independent,
men, but because in its very essence this oversimplified humanistic philosophy is contrary to the nature of man. First,
it provides no grand ideal from which men can draw strength
and meaning. Both Christianity and capitalism have their
heavens; Christianity in the next world, capitalism in the
perfectibility of man in this. Both of these closed systems of
thought provide internally consistent answers to virtually
every conceivable question, and by so doing, instill within the
individual the belief that his life is committed to something
worthy, indeed something of singular importance.

Nor does this new liberalism possess the organizing force
of either Christianity or capitalism. Capitalism, whatever its
deficiencies, provided a clear and unmistakable basis for
assessing individual conduct. The wealthy are good; the well-
to-do, respectable; and each man could determine not only
where he stood, but where his efforts were taking him. Thus
capitalism not only gave man a goal—an energizing force—
but it provided him with a yardstick for measuring success
in achieving it—an organizing force. The new liberalism
fails on both these counts. If anything, this new philosophy
seems to deny the existence of any universal goal and asks
man to become the Kierkegaardian Knight of Infinite Resig-

nation who—understanding the absurdity of the traditional trappings of an organized society—renounces and transcends conventional values in order to become sufficient unto himself. Essentially skeptical in nature, it is a philosophy that says, "Nobody knows and nobody can know," or, to use the words of Jean-Paul Sartre, "Life has no meaning but the meaning that you choose." In short Sartre, like Nietzsche before him, believes that "God is dead" and that each man must invent his own values. Like Sartre, the rising forces of liberalism, implicitly if not explicitly, seem to deny the existence of any great unifying ideal. Unfortunately, the whole of Western history, since Plato and Pythagoras before him, is one grand testimonial to man's need and quest for such an ideal.

Civilization, writes Toynbee, is "an audacious attempt to ascend from the level of Primitive Humanity, living the life of a social animal, to the height of some superhuman kind of being in the Communion of Saints. . ." In his study of 21 civilizations Toynbee concluded that civilized cultures are a product of a successful response to challenge and that they continue to flourish and rise only so long as there is adversity which is satisfactorily met and conquered. In the beginning, according to Toynbee, it is the "creative minority" that responds to challenge, and with the aid of enthusiasm and magnetic charm carries with it the great bulk of the unimaginative and imitative populace. "There is," writes Toynbee, "an overwhelming majority of ordinary people in the membership of even the most advanced and progressive civilization; and the humanity of all these people is virtually primitive humanity." In following the creative minority, these common men can only copy, never invent. Lacking fire and vision, these men, rather than conceiving and implementing unique responses to conquer new adversity, ritualize in a stereotyped pattern that which was created to cope with a challenge lost in history. What previously had been fresh and directly applicable, these men, in their compulsive conformity, converted into hard standards which structure the society, draining its vitality and making it less and less able to meet new and rising challenges. Thus, according to Toynbee, there is an inexorable rhythm of disintegration against which all civilizations have vainly struggled, as every favorably creative act is imitated, dogmatized, and frozen into a fixed structure which thwarts subsequent, creative minorities in their attempt to breath vibrancy into floundering civilizations.

In our society of organization men, Toynbee's comments on destructive conformity seem particularly appropriate. Subconsciously aware that he is a pitiful cog in a monstrously complex machine, the 20th-century individual must fight with all his resources if he is not to suffer the fate of an alienated, passive personality. Having had his self-confidence shaken by the complexity of things, he is tempted to degrade himself by submerging his identity, by abandoning his individuality, and by looking outside himself for standards of conduct and life goals. Without fixed standards that distinguish good from evil, morality from immorality, justice from injustice, the habits and goals of his fellow man dominate his thought and cause him to exaggerate the importance of prestige symbols. In doing so he thinks of himself as a vice president, a chief surgeon, a professor, a part of something bigger and more important than himself. Whatever his position, he never experiences gratification or contentment simply from a job well done. The exercise of his talents, the performance of his duties, the completion of an assignment can never be ends in themselves; at best they are means to an end —one that quickly turns out to be an illusion once it is realized. Always there is another step to climb, a greater height to be scaled, another level that carries greater recognition, which, he naïvely believes will eliminate anxiety, guarantee happiness, and make life truly profitable and worthwhile. Terrorized always by the nagging doubt that he may err, that he may be guilty of the unpardonable sin of offending his organization, he craves conformity, suppresses his distinctiveness, and struggles all the more intensely, fearing always that he will be left behind in the race which determines his status, his success, his very identity.

The new voices of liberalism oppose this conformity which haunts our society. But unlike Toynbee, these men express genuine optimism about eliminating this social affliction. Through education they evidence hope of spreading a kind of elevated frontier individualism whereby the individual learns to find satisfaction, if not in busting sod, building fences, or reaping corn, then in repairing autos, healing the sick, or writing a poem. On this score the record is somewhat less than encouraging. If anything, the drive for conformity appears to grow as the formal level of education is increased. Certainly this seems to be true at America's institutions of higher learning where, staffed by the country's most educated and learned men, the cult of conformity is plainly seen in one of its most crushing forms.

For the modern large university is a composite of essentially autonomous intellectual islands, the heart of each a fighting faith—a discipline—to which each member is expected to pledge undying allegiance. Within the discipline, as within any priesthood, members are expected to live by a rigidly defined set of norms. Those who are diligent and devout are rewarded; those who are not lose respect and are punished. The most esteemed conduct of all is the writing of scholarly papers which, to assure favorable reception, must be bewilderingly esoteric and not deviate in either subject or manner from the ritualized code of the discipline. In theory such writing is to further individual development and advance the state of human knowledge; in practice the primary motivating force is the desire of the author to exalt his position within the tight discipline to which he is bound. All of which was crystallized by Professor Paul A. Samuelson in an address before members of the American Economic Association. Speaking from the Association's presidential platform, he charged his profession with these words, "Not for us is the limelight and the applause. But that doesn't mean the game is not worth the candle or that we do not in the end win the game. In the long run, the economic scholar works for the only coin worth having—our own applause."

Within the very large universities such chauvinism is the source of a perpetually undeclared war in which the population of each of the intellectual islands proclaims the superiority of its doctrines over competing creeds. Ranking himself above the sociologist, the political scientist is looked down on by the historian, who in turn suffers the contempt of the mathematician; while the philosopher, suspended in sublime Platonic contemplation, is amused at the fevered efforts of these poor mortals everlastingly condemned to live in the grubby world of physical existence.

What is true in the academic realm is no less true in government, labor unions, large corporations, or any large organization. None of which is at odds with Toynbee's idea that ordinary men—however long they may study and learn—require a rallying creed which, in providing simple stereotyped standards, permits them in their strivings to prove to themselves and their fellow men that they are capable of performing and achieving. To hope that men of common clay will find fulfillment in the sheer joy of individual creativity—painting, gardening, writing—is to embrace a soothing dream; but if the lessons of history are to be taken seriously, nothing more than a dream. In a world of militant communism, one is tempted to speculate on the virtues of such a dream.

The point has been made that the great energizing force which we loosely call capitalism is slowly burning out. This is not to say, barring all-out war, that our current social system is in any serious danger of general collapse or that it will be impotent to confer a still higher standard of living. On this score the system will continue to function quite satisfactorily. But this is not enough.

We are forever engaged in a kind of self-flagellation, excoriating ourselves for individual softness and national loss of purpose. Living in a constant state of contradiction, we are proud of our immense material achievements which bestow comfort and luxury at the same time that we censure ourselves for *La Dolce Vita*. Contrary to our glorification of individual leisure, rest, and development, we seem to cry out for a new energizing force that will produce the radiance of Chartres, or the robust vitality that was so characteristic in America until very recently.

We still look to pure capitalist theory as the best expression of our ideal. From it we draw inspiration for explaining why our society is superior to others, why ours, more than Russia's, is better equipped to move man along the road of human perfection. However we may continue to draw intellectual power from this ideal, everything must hang on the thrust provided by the profit and loss concept which is the organizing force at the level of everyday existence. In the past this simple, ritualized measuring stick has unleased tremendous individual energy at the same time that it related daily experience to capitalistic ideals. Thus both the energizing and the organizing force centered on simple economic materialism. Unfortunately, as we have become more affluent and more powerful the challenge inherent in private materialism has not been equal to the immense capacity of the system.

Accordingly, our nation is not only maimed by depression and then recession, but even during prosperous times the energy released is never more than a fraction of total capacity. Finding it more difficult to relate their efforts to the traditional organizing force—the profit race—men fashioned new, albeit parochial "yardsticks" for gauging and guiding their conduct. Inevitably, out of these new standards have come conformity and an exaggerated emphasis on status symbols. Despite the fact that we in our personal lives pay declining heed to our traditional organizing force, at the social level it continues to be the prime shaper of destiny. All the large organizations, public as well as private, live within the constraints imposed by the profit and loss statement. In so doing, rather than channeling and exploiting our boundless energy, the centers of power are compelled to erect dams that frustrate national power, causing it to be lost forever.

If it is true that our society is crippled for lack of challenge, where shall we find new purpose? The Russians have looked to the German tradition and have taken from Kant and Hegel the notion that pleasure is despicable, that joy is ignoble, that heroics are admirable, and that discomfort is desirable. We could doubtless find purpose by subscribing to the belief that the individual, rather than striving for mundane happiness, should commit himself to worship the god of war. But this is contrary to our whole tradition which, although not always making for a perfect state of bliss, did, in following the utilitarian philosophy of a Locke and a Smith, spare us the gross brutality and bloodshed of the authoritarian German idealism.

Fortunately, however, we need not turn to the German way; within our traditional commitment to simple happiness there still remains untapped challenge. At home we need roads, schools, hospitals, and many other things. Even if domestically there were no unsatisfied want, no untended sickness, no incurable ignorance, no lack of individual opportunity, there would yet remain the greatest challenge ever known to mankind. In Asia, Africa, and South America the great majority of the people have never read a book, know nothing of modern medicine, and live under the constant threat of famine or controllable disease. The Kremlin has served notice to all the world that, in the name of mankind rather than man, it is pledged to communize these rising peoples.

Here then is our ultimate challenge: to teach and implement our belief in the worth and dignity of the individual in these lands, where only recently the doctrine of life, liberty, and the pursuit of happiness has barely pierced the curtain of centuries of poverty and ignorance. Our problem then is not lack of challenge, but rather how we can arrange society and its institutions to respond successfully to this new challenge without losing the precious values we prize so highly.

In his 1961 Inaugural Address John F. Kennedy recognized this challenge when he eloquently proclaimed, "To those peoples in the huts and villages of half the globe struggling to break the bonds of mass misery, we pledge our best efforts to help them help themselves, for whatever period is required—not because the communists may be doing it, not because we seek their votes, but because it is right."

A similar expression of dedication of purpose is to be found in the Charter of the Alliance for Progress. The moving spirit of this organization, the United States, along with most of its Latin American neighbors, pledged:

> We, the American Republics, hereby proclaim our decision to unite in a common effort to bring our people accelerated economic progress and broader social justice within the framework of personal dignity and political liberty . . . The men and women of our hemisphere are reaching for the better life which today's skills have placed within their grasp. They are determined for

themselves and their children to have decent and ever
more abundant lives, to gain access to knowledge and
equal opportunity for all, to end those conditions which
benefit the few at the expense of the needs and dignity
of the many. It is our inescapable task to fulfill these
just desires—to demonstrate to the poor and forsaken
of our countries, and of all lands, that the creative
powers of free men hold the key to their progress and
to the progress of future generations. And our certainty
of ultimate success rests not alone on our faith in ourselves and in our nations but on the indomitable spirit
of free man which has been the heritage of American
civilization.

To the promotion of these ends the United States Congress
initially appropriated several hundred million dollars and
the Secretary of the Treasury talked of a 20-billion-dollar
assistance program for Latin America during the 1960's. Such
an expression of national sympathy was not without precedent. The Marshall Plan speeded the reconstruction of postwar Europe and as European nations regained economic
health we shifted our attention to the underdeveloped world.
Never in all of history has any nation shared its abundance
so unselfishly. In the 15-year period following the end of
World War II, American aid in its many forms totaled more
than 70 billion dollars.

This is an impressive sum; yet it is not enough. Averaging
in recent years slightly more than four billion dollars a year,
it is inadequate to provide an outlet for our immense national energy, which, because it cannot find expression, is
frustrated and a source of general social discontent. Nor can
our present efforts do much in the way of achieving the lofty
objectives of freeing the world from political tyranny. Inadequate in magnitude, foreign aid is too often narrowly
conceived as an instrument for winning an immediate battle

in the cold war. In the past, more than half the aid going to underdeveloped nations has been for military assistance and defense support. Although recently our efforts have been divided more equally between economic and military aid, even our economic assistance is more often the product of a desire to counter communist strategy than of a will to elevate the poor of the world to a state of dignity and freedom.

Our aid to the Far East illustrated this only too well. Aimed primarily at "buying time"—preventing such nations as South Korea, South Vietnam, and Laos from falling prey to communism—billions in aid has done little to provide either economic development or political stability. Largely compelled by circumstances to exhaust aid allotments on such consumer goods as food and clothing, the nations of the Far East are no more independent today than when the focus of our aid program shifted to the underdeveloped world in 1951. Without our consumer goods, these weak and impoverished nations would no doubt have quickly been victimized by communism. But this type of aid can only do so much. It cannot instill a sense of purpose and it is impotent to provide the economic development that is essential if these peoples are to construct healthy, viable nations in the Western tradition.

The fruits of an inadequate aid program are to be seen in Laos, where, after years of giving hundreds of millions of dollars to a floundering nation, we find it necessary to abandon the country to a neutrality that may someday turn to communism. Even as Laos is being deserted by the West, we may be witnessing a replay of the same drama in South Vietnam. Nor can we claim great success in other parts of the world. Indeed the further removed from the threat of communism, the smaller appears our interest in helping an underdeveloped area. Not until Castro did we evidence more than passing concern about Latin America and not until very recently have we given serious thought to the peoples of Africa.

The inadequacies of the past and present need not presage failure for the future. Gradually the American view is being broadened; the isolationism so long dominant in foreign policy was laid to rest years ago. Our dollar-and-cents commitment to the world and our urgent search for new vehicles of assistance stand as honest tributes to this changing perspective. Only recently our determination to spread the spirit of the West found dramatic expression in the infant Peace Corps. The objectives of this new organization are many; above all others, however, its mission is to teach or at least give insights into the spirit and beliefs of the West. To accomplish this purpose we have asked our finest youths to renounce virtually everything that high civilization can bestow —fame, fortune, comforts, convenience, entertainment—to undertake a pilgrimage into foreign lands where, by submitting to physical hardship and disease and by sharing the same food and shelter as their native co-workers, they may become the living, practicing symbols of the democratic habit.

There can be no simple Washington-conceived formula that guides the volunteer in his will to render assistance. In East Pakistan he may stress the curbing of livestock disease; in the island of Saint Lucia, the enhancement of agricultural output through rock terracing; in Ghana, the prevention of typhoid; in Tanganyika, the wonders of reading and writing; and in any one of a score of countries, the need for drilling wells, for laying water and sewage pipes, for creating neighborhood gardens, for building access roads, for constructing local schools, or for organizing youth clubs.

Despite concentration on immediate problems, these apostles of human dignity are expected to do much more than alleviate poverty and lessen sickness. By working elbow to

elbow with inhabitants of underdeveloped lands the corps-
man is to instill a feeling of confidence, a belief that through
conscious effort and democratic practices man can alter his environment for the better. Whether it be through digging a
ditch or operating the tractor, the volunteer, by initiating
tangible improvements, is to convert emptiness into purpose
and provide enduring symbols that will help combat the
hopeless sense of impotency prevalent in impoverished lands.

So far the performance of the Peace Corps has been encouraging. Staffed by alert young people who possess a remarkable range of diverse talents and who know a deep
sense of personal commitment, the Corps has been blessed
by an uncommon mixture of intelligence and practicality.
Initially small and serving a limited number of overseas
areas, plans are now underway to enlarge the number of
volunteers and to extend the scope of operations to 38
countries. One can only look with favor on this development, hoping that early success will be repeated throughout
the world on a larger scale. Such a mission is worthy of our
best efforts.

The accomplishments of the Peace Corps must, of course,
finally depend upon the personnel and the resources it can
enlist. On this score prospects may not measure up to achievements and early experiences may be misleading. The Corps
was born under and inspired by the most favorable of circumstances. The center of public attention, it was launched
into an atmosphere charged with excitement and vitality.
Radiating a rare combination of romance and purpose, it
convinced many a clear-headed young American that the
giving of two years of his life to the helping of unfortunate
people in alien lands represented the most elevated form of
social behavior. To sustain such a high sense of social mission and personal commitment is difficult, if not impossible,
in the context of present-day America. Even under ideal re-

cruiting conditions the Corps has been confronted with serious opposition. Interpreting its demands as a denial of simple materialism—money, prestige, career—and traditional American values, parents and employers are prone to counsel caution, describing the life of the volunteer as a socially worthy, but individually foolish venture.

As long as the Corps remains in the national spotlight and as long as the need for volunteers is quickly met, staffing the organization with sincere, helpful members presents no great problem. But when the glamor fades, as surely it must, and as the search for additional volunteers is extended, it will become ever more difficult to attract the superior personnel that has been responsible for the Corps' splendid record. Recently this fledgling organization boasted 1,000 volunteers; plans are to increase this number to 5,000. Already, however, there are signs that the initial momentum is being exhausted; that fresh college graduates are having some hard second thoughts about the virtues of heroic sacrifice without promise of either personal riches or glory. This is crucial, for if the Peace Corps is to realize its bright potential it requires the services of not 1,000 or even 5,000 volunteers, but of hundreds of thousands of vigorous, understanding Americans who feel strongly about and are willing to take their turn at being "missionaries" spreading the "faith" of the West.

Even if by some miracle such talent could somehow be recruited in the present context, there remains the very real task of convincing Congress of the advantages of appropriating the necessary funds for the financing of an undertaking of this magnitude. Today, U.S. support is less than $100 million per year. In the absence of any major change in public sentiment, there is nothing to motivate Congress to increase this figure to many times this amount. Thus the Peace Corps, like virtually all other aid programs, stands in danger of being seriously crippled—not for want of a way, but for lack of a will.

That the world needs our assistance there can be no doubt. Nor can there be any doubt that we have the power and the resources to provide it. But if we are to have any hope of achieving the goal of raising the well-being of the population of the world, and if we are to undertake the challenge necessary to release our national energy, the aid program must be closer to 50 than to four billion dollars per year.

To attempt this overnight would be not only impossible, but unwise. Yet it need not exceed our reach in the near future, should we be so inclined. We have the power and we have the know-how; the underdeveloped world has the need. All that is lacking is a state of mind. From our present mentality emerges a will to believe that the ultimate test of life must be material success and that any act of giving things away, even to help the poverty-stricken in far-off lands, not only violates certain absolute rules, but threatens the very foundations upon which society rests. If any real gain is to be made in elevating the dignity of the individual in the underdeveloped lands, if any significant long-term progress is to be achieved in fighting communism, and if any marked advancement is to be made in releasing now-frustrated domestic energy, there must be a major change in our nation's "state of mind."

The task should not be underestimated. It requires a complete transformation, not of our technology or social institutions, but of our traditional energizing and organizing forces. To accomplish this we must develop a full intellectual system which, like Christianity, capitalism, and communism, provides answers to virtually every conceivable question. Not only must these answers prove the justness of our position, but they should show that our methods can move man along the road of human perfectability. To go along with this new energizing force we must also search for and discover an organizing force to operate at the prosaic level of everyday existence.

Our current organizing force will not permit us to respond successfully to the new challenge. Indeed, rather than unleashing energy, this stereotyped standard has now reached the point of perversity as, instead of assisting us to respond to the world's need for our help, it releases only that energy that does not violate the profit and loss concept. It thereby works at cross purposes with any effort to contribute aid to underdeveloped peoples. In a world where men are dying of hunger, suffering from sickness, begging for technical aid and education, in a world where a rising Russia is making a calculated effort to conquer the uncommitted lands, in a world where the United States has the resources and the men anxious to test their strength and contribute their powers to the making of a better life, we are currently constrained by a ritualized standard which sets the balanced budget as the minimum goal of life for the individual, the organization, and the government.

But what shall these new forces be? I do not know. What I believe is that on the answer to the question hangs the trial of liberalism. Today America lives with two liberalisms: 19th-century liberalism which can be idealized but not realized, and 20th-century liberalism which, to some extent, can be realized but not idealized. 19th-century liberalism in its most radical form is represented by the extreme right which, in yearning for the intellectual certainty of pure capitalism, is opposed to government spending, relief payments, federal aid to education, medical care for the aged, urban renewel, Social Security, and, on the grounds that they are wasteful and helpful to communism, foreign aid, and the United Nations. Because of technology, growing affluence, unemployment, large organizations, and a militant Russia, the nation has with each passing day found it necessary to follow a policy deviating further and further from this philosophy. This constant movement away from the simple capitalist ideal has perforce caused it to be a waning, unifying spirit.

The 20th-century liberal, by focusing his attention on the raw world of physical existence, sees how things can be improved by human effort and organizaiton. Unfortunately, the modern liberal has not developed or articulated any grand ideal from which common men and society can draw inspiration and a sense of purpose. In essence the 20th-century liberal says: "This is a world filled with problems; let us make the best of it with what we have." And the best he can offer is a kind of muddling through, which for most men is not good enough.

Men since Plato and before have inhabited the two realms of the real and the ideal. Neither alone is satisfactory and just as *Pax Romana* was shattered because, with all its bread and circuses, it could not be idealized, so the medieval spirit faded because it could not be realized. Today nothing is to be gained by either of the liberal groups attacking or defending one or the other of the two realms. If, instead of exhausting our rich powers in such futile pursuits, we were to turn our intellectual resources to deriving a new ideal with a vital organizing force, we would pass through this ordeal and provide a new, successful response to the challenge which now confronts us. It would be folly to expect most men who, like priests, are preservers rather than makers of doctrine, to engage in this quest. But let us hope that somewhere there is another Locke, another Adam Smith, or another Keynes who, like Copernicus, has the imagination and courage to ask a question that will make intelligible a whole new universe.

Until this new prophet appears our society must, however,

continue to function in the context of the contemporary climate of opinion. On this score the record is encouraging, the outlook hopeful. In the face of fearful danger and intellectual uncertainty we have demonstrated increasing resolution in recognizing and meeting our problems head on. Escaping less and less into the idealism of a simpler age, we exhibit a growing spirit to use our mortal powers in search of solutions—however temporary or inadequate—that will contribute to the dignity of the individual and elevate the human race. As long as man has the courage to believe that through his finite will he can improve himself and enhance the direction and course of mankind, one can find comfort in the knowledge that the West will endure.

INDEX

333